Studies of Urban Society

Blue Collar Community

William Kornblum

With a Foreword by
Morris Janowitz

University of Chicago Press   Chicago and London

The University of Chicago Press,
Chicago 60637
The University of Chicago Press, Ltd.,
London

© 1974 by The University of Chicago
All rights reserved. Published 1974
Printed in the United States of
America

International Standard Book Number:
0-226-45037-6
Library of Congress Catalog Card
Number: 74-5733

William Kornblum is assistant professor of sociology at the Graduate
School of the City University of New
York. He is also a research sociologist
studying the ecology of urban leisure
areas for the National Park Service.
[1974]

Contents

Foreword

Sociological research on social stratification and politics has been dominated by the enormous wealth of statistical analysis of census and especially survey research materials. Nevertheless, it is striking that a handful of key community studies have commanded extensive attention and have served as powerful correctives to the tendency to over-generalize about mass political behavior. This is the case because community studies carry with them a strong historical dimension and a richness of detail. They are particularly rewarding because they have highlighted the complex yet fragile institutional arrangements by which leaders of socioeconomic groupings seek to aggregate their political power. Community studies of this variety have a remarkably enduring quality. William Kornblum's study of the steelworkers of South Chicago builds on this research tradition. This piece of one-man scholarship also calls into question and helps to explicate important themes which have been offered by the statistical and survey research approach to political sociology.

Of course, over the last half-century there has been a gradual but profound transformation in intensive community studies. When Robert and Helen Lynd selected Muncie, Indiana, as "Middletown," they believed that the study of a "representative" community was the appropriate locus for the study of the political process. No doubt Lloyd Warner thought his contention that Yankee City and Jonesville were "America" was more than an aphorism; for him, it was the essence of a research strategy.

The elaboration of the community study has been more than an extension of analysis from small communities to highly urbanized settings and segments of the metropolis. The research sociologist today views community research as an approach for exploring the mechanisms by which the parts of the social structure are linked—or fail to be linked—to the larger whole. *Blue Collar Community* is both a historical and a participant-observation study of working-class politics—trade union and ward—which epitomizes this more trenchant and more analytical perspective.

On the basis of almost three years of observation and research, Kornblum presents a concise overview of the elaborate social organization of a locality dominated by heavy manufacturing for nearly a century. His underlying question is a version of the classic one in political sociology: Why was there and is there no powerful working-class political movement which could be called socialist in the United States? As he traces the development of the trade union movement and local ward politics, he is dealing with the linkage between South Chicago and the macrosociology of the United States. The vital issue he seeks to explain is the inability of trade union–based power to translate itself into effective domination of at least a segment of the political party apparatus.

Kornblum, as an enthusiastic adherent of the "Chicago urban school," was attracted to South Chicago by its dramatic labor struggle and by the sheer fascination of its intricate ethnic and communal life. He had the advantage of being able to draw on an extensive body of earlier historical research and documentation. South Chicago offered him the opportunity to explore working-class politics not in a small detached community but within the political boundaries of a massive central city.

Analytically, he proceeds on the basis of one of the critical elements in the classic definition of industrial society—from Auguste Comte to Karl Marx to contemporary empirical research—namely, that machine technology created the factory system which in turn separated the organization of family and residence from that of work and industry. For Kornblum's purposes, South Chicago is especially useful in this regard; it is, in fact, a kind of experimental setting in the dimension of the separation of work and residence. The industrial core—the plants for making steel—are within the local community. This means that, for some of the longer established ethnic groups, particularly the South Slavs, there is a close overlap between work and residence. For new groups, especially for the blacks, there is a longer journey to work and a strong discontinuity between work and residential community.

The separation of work and family is at the root of the notion of alienation which is so widespread in the sociological literature. The reader of this study, however, will be struck at once by the complete absence of the idea of alienation as a key concept in it. Kornblum neither acccepts nor rejects the centrality of alienation. He is deeply and persistently aware of the terrible impact of decades of heroic efforts to organize a labor movement in South Chicago in the face of ruthless opposition, culminating in the Memorial Day Massacre of 1937. He is painfully sensitive about the incomplete participation in union and local elections and the sense of frustration among local activists who are unable to achieve the political power which they believe their group deserves.

But Kornblum proceeds from a set of observations and frame of reference different from that inherent in the idea of alienation. His direct observations impress him with the existence of potent and variegated sets of interpersonal networks and social solidarities. The term "division of labor" is not sufficient to describe the complexity of the social structure, since it encompasses only occupational stratification. Kornblum observes the impacts of residential segregation, of ethnic identification, of age groupings, and of the subtle patterns of leisure styles that produce a system of "ordered segmentation." The ordered segmentation has created fragmented groupings and delimited social worlds—rather than a pattern of alienated individuals. His frame of reference juxtaposes the social processes which produce ordered segmentation and those which he sees as seeking political segregation.

Working-class solidarity is in part a political category which rests on building group loyalties in the factory and translating them into coalitions of ethnic leaders. In a style reminiscent of W. I. Thomas's study of the Polish community in Chicago, Kornblum traces, in a comprehensive and holistic fashion, the impact of local institutions, including the family and the neighborhood taverns, which create primary groups and ethnic social cohesion while simultaneously implying social cleavages.

Kornblum is here studying a multiethnic community which has incorporated elements of each wave of immigration, from the North Europeans to the Slavs to the Mexicans and the black migrants. Although, in the past, employers were able to pit one group against the other in the factory, it would be mistaken to conclude that ethnicity persists as the main barrier to working-class solidarity. Of course, deep cultural antagonisms operate; nevertheless, working-class solidarity, as it is reflected in trade union activity and political loyalties, rests on a sense of ethnic loyalty and the political aggregation of these sentiments into partisan formations.

Kornblum's analysis, however, is not based on the rediscovery of ethnicity that has come into vogue in sociology, nor is there any evidence that the decade of the 1960s produced a resurgence of ethnicity in South Chicago. This is a working-class community, and ethnicity here does not have an "intellectual" character such as that found among upper-middle-class elements searching for "personal" identity. In South Chicago, the content of ethnic solidarity undergoes change and the boundaries of ethnic identification are fluid—but they reflect the cultural response and adaptation of Old World traits transplanted to a United States social setting. The absence of a national set of cultural norms (such as there is in Great Britain) as well as the reluctance of government bodies to press the importance of assimilation (as in France or pre-Nazi Germany) have supplied a much more sympathetic context for ethnic groups.

If, over the decades, there has been a strong persistence of ethnic sentiment, it has been by no means unanticipated. The continued arrival of immigrants since 1945 from eastern Europe has served to reinforce these feelings; and the influx of the new ethnic groups, the Mexicans and the blacks, has maintained traditional notions of the validity and legitimacy of ethnic sentiments. However, let there be no misunderstanding. Kornblum observes that the long-term trend has been toward an attenuation of these attachments, especially in the third- and fourth-generation offspring who mix their communal social contacts with new interests, including new types of leisure and travel.

The conscious efforts of voluntary associations—the new ethnic mass media, the foreign-language press transformed to ethnic FM radio, and especially the deliberate efforts of factions seeking political power— serve to accentuate and maintain these ethnic attachments. If ethnic solidarities reflect group efforts at collective problem solving, the persistence of ethnic appeals by political leaders is more than a basis for exercising political power. Ethnic solidarity also reflects defects in the political system, the fragmentation of social groupings, and the frustration of social and political goals.

The result of Kornblum's fieldwork is a penetrating analysis of the institutional mechanisms in the different ethnic groups for aggregating and exercising political power. Trade union politics is built on the ethnic solidarities of the workplace. The brilliant description of the knitting of work groups within the internal ecology of the steel mill is one of the high points of this study. But the ecological pattern of residence serves either to assist or to retard the building of a political base and the formation of a coalition. The older Serbian trade unionists, although they are faced with generational cleavages in their own group, can turn from the factory to neighborhood solidarities for assistance in their political efforts. The Mexicans are more territorially segmented, but they have strong ties through family and kinship that can be used by Mexican activists to mobilize their constituencies. Since the blacks are excluded from living in the mill neighborhoods and are thus residentially remote, they must rely on the grievance system in the mills to build the essential primary group loyalties required for political effectiveness.

Kornblum displays a deep sympathy for the real meaning of a "trade union democracy." It is not merely the formal elections but the system of coalition between ethnic groups, which, if it operates effectively, should insure a system of representation. The emergence of the blacks as the crucial element in the coalition building of union elections represents the latest stage of leadership succession in the long process of political change.

These same ecological patterns influence ward politics and the aggregation of organized labor interests into the national political system. They also help account for limitations in the influence of the trade union movement on organized partisan politics. Kornblum's approach to the question of the absence of a socialist working-class political movement reflects not only the economic incentives and rewards in the United States. It also reflects the organization of the local political ward that relies on trade union support but limits the penetration of the trade unionist into its organizational structure. The local political organization is a distinct political structure with a logic in part dictated by its particular linkages with municipal government. Participation and success in local politics draw activists away from the local trade union movement and, in turn, success in the trade union hierarchy serves as a barrier to participation in local and municipal partisan political activity. The result is that the trade unionists do not penetrate the rank of "professional" politics. Instead, there is endless bargaining between the two leadership groups.

The picture that Kornblum presents of the internal dynamics of the precinct and ward organizations calls into question much of the myth about local political organizations. He is describing a "machine" more representative of earlier times. The "machine" is hardly a routine bureaucratic apparatus. Within the political party organization, there is a constant group of insurgents—some with a labor background— who win or lose in the struggle for appointed and elected positions. The machine is also a device for balancing factions and accommodating personal ambition.

Machine politics—including labor machine politics—becomes less effective with the rise of literacy, the growth of broader perspectives among the electorate, and the capacity of the candidates to reach the citizenry directly through the mass media. Kornblum's analysis indicates that the blacks, both in trade union politics and in ward political organization, will contribute an element of continuity to the traditional practices of "machine politics," since their leaders are seeking to complete the process of ethnic succession.

However, the relations between trade union leaders and their rank and file, and the accommodation between professional political leaders and trade union activists, are under strain and have produced, in the closing years of the 1960s, outbursts of factionalism and insurgence comparable to those of the 1930s. The strain on union and partisan politics reflects the changed "gut" issues. For unionized workers, especially young workers, the issues of work discipline and patterns of authority in the workplace have become increasingly important. There is a new and powerful desire to be treated with dignity. They want to be more complete members of the mass society. But the backdrop of the politics is the threat of permanent inflation and the doubt whether existing political men can come to grips with the "new economic problems."

Blue Collar Community stands as a noteworthy example of the vigor and vitality through which the tradition of individually executed community studies perpetuates itself. This work represents a tremendous effort by a single sociologist; no doubt it made use of less manpower than that expended in a large-scale collective enterprise. If there is merit in the resistance to bureaucratic trends, including those in scholarship, this study validates the feasibility and fruitfulness of such resistance.

It represents an effort to objectify community research, for this type of participant research is fraught with hazards and methodological difficulties. There exists in the United States no intellectual center or university apparatus for institutionalizing and stimulating community research and for developing effective standards. There does not appear any likelihood that one will emerge in the near future. One could argue—but it would be in error—that the perpetuation of participation-observation research into community organization rests on the absence of organization and on individual impulse. In fact, it does seem that the community research based on participant observation has its own relatively self-contained traditions and culture. Its powerful intellectual natural history serves to connect new generations of practitioners. Its perpetuation and growth in recent years have been the result, in good measure, of student intellectual participation and initiative abetted by faculty interest.

Thus, for example, at the University of Chicago, William Kornblum's research is but one of a series of renewed efforts which have resulted in penetrating published monographs. They include George Hesslink's *Black Neighbors,* the study of the biracial county in South Michigan; Harvey Molotch's *Managed Integration,* an account of the efforts to maintain racial integration in the South Shore community of Chicago; and Albert Hunter's *Symbolic Communities,* a comprehensive overview of the ecological and normative patterns of the local community. Each of these topics was selected on the initiative of the sociologist during apprenticeship training. Although these new studies are linked to the community research tradition, they reflect individual choice rather than old-fashioned discipleship.

But the persistence of individual scholarship and effective participant-observer research requires more than stubborn student scholars who are prepared to resist modish trends and fads. The individual scholar in the field is subject to powerful distortions and self-selections in his data collection. Only a system of careful, systematic, and continuing supervision, comparable to that exercised by the training psychoanalyst, can offer a minimum guarantee for the essential struggle—if not achievement of a degree of objective detachment which, as William Kornblum demonstrates, is not incompatible with a sympathetic sense of understanding. In this regard, this particular research, and others of this variety, have benefited from the gifted intellectual presence of Gerald Suttles and his skills.

MORRIS JANOWITZ
The University of Chicago

Preface

The emphasis in this study on the contribution of community institutions to ethnic change in South Chicago owes much to the older traditions of community studies in Chicago. Early in the century, "Chicago School" sociologists viewed South Chicago as a typical "natural area." Its population of foreigners was locked in the area by the giant corporations of the steel industry; steel became a way of life for its families. W. I. Thomas and his associates studied South Chicago's Polish settlements as part of the city's "Polonia." Students of Robert Park and Ernest Burgess saw the immigrants re-creating the social structures of their European village societies in ethnic primary groups and neighborhood parishes. Pioneers in the new field of social welfare, such as Edith Abbott, Sophonisba Breckinridge, and Emily Balch conducted meticulous studies describing the grinding poverty of the tenement neighborhoods below South Chicago's "Satanic mills." This generation of social scientists viewed the ethnic neighborhood associations as local solutions to the social disorganization of peasant society in industrial America. They speculated that ethnic associations would advance the immigrants and their children toward eventual assimilation in a national culture. But further study of community organization and ethnic adaptation in working-class communities had to wait until a generation of American-born citizens matured in communities such as South Chicago.

Efforts since World War II to continue the "Chicago tradition" of community studies have involved a stronger recognition of political institutions in the community. With the exception of the pioneering work of Harold Gosnell, most of the earlier Chicago community studies tended to treat political processes as derivations of more "fundamental" processes such as invasion, succession, and dominance. Since the late 1940s, however, scholars who have continued in the Chicago tradition have focused explicitly on the role of local political institutions in linking groups within local communities to the larger society. Studies such as Janowitz's *The Community Press in an Urban Setting*, Wilson's *The Amateur Democrat*, Suttles's *The Social Order of the Slum*, and Wade's *The Urban Frontier*, have stressed the importance of political processes in shaping the course of intergroup adaptation in urban communities. Also, by studying political negotiations in a variety of institutional settings, from the more informal grouping of adolescents to the development of reform factions in urban political parties, these authors have recognized that local political processes are not merely a reflection of processes such as ethnic competition or industrial conflict. As Max Weber recognized earlier in the century, urban political institutions themselves often channel the course of structural and cultural change within communities. This study therefore seeks to view the issues of work and ethnicity in the light of the political institutions which both reflect and shape other communal institutions and sentiments. This is a point of view which seems especially appropriate for a community where local political institutions so clearly play a major role in forming the ethnic and class consciousness of its residents.

I was inspired and encouraged to conduct this study by Professors Morris Janowitz and Gerald Suttles while I was a Fellow of the Center for Social Organization Studies in the Department of Sociology, University of Chicago. My initial training and experience in the social sciences, I owe to Professors Bert Hoselitz and Aristide Zolberg, who generously gave me material and intellectual support whenever I needed it. Other faculty members in the Division of Social Sciences at the University of Chicago, particularly Arthur Mann, Richard Wade, David Street, Theodore Lowi, and Lloyd Fallers, were kind listeners and critics during the formative stages of my research. While at the University of Chicago, I received financial support from the Russell Sage Foundation grant to the Center for Social Organization Studies and the Ford Foundation, the latter through Professor Hoselitz's Center for Economic Development and Cultural Change.

Although she likes to deny it, Susan Kornblum is responsible for many of the insights reported here. While busy with her own studies in psychology, she enthusiastically became a blue collar wife and mother during our years in the mill neighborhoods. Much of whatever success I had in becoming a South Chicagoan is due to her good humor and her ease in making friends.

Hundreds of men and women in South Chicago, and many residents of other communities in the Chicago "steel belt" graciously allowed me to become a member of their social worlds. Almost without exception, they made me feel at home in their neighborhoods and their community institutions. As friends and informants they shared with me their lifetimes of experience in the community. Although I cannot do justice to the richness of their communal lives, I hope this study can begin to repay their kindness and their generosity.

Among my colleagues at the University of Washington, I am particularly grateful to Professors Michael Hechter and Guenther Roth for their valuable comments on sections of the manuscript. Finally, I wish to thank Carol Chase, Jerry Bardon, Beulah Reddaway, Lucille McGill, Katie Dudley, Ina Howell, and Barbara Gerhardt, not only for their typing and drafting skills, but for their patience and interest in this study.

I dedicate this book with love and gratitude to Martha, Daniel, and Peter Kornblum.

Introduction

The South Chicago Community

South Chicago is a large steel mill community within the city limits of metropolitan Chicago. Similar to steel-towns throughout the United States, South Chicago's population is predominantly working class, for the majority of its families live on incomes gained from blue collar work in local mills and related industries. Among the community's 90,000 residents there are enclaves of almost every major ethnic and racial group which settled in American industrial communities over the last century. Scots, Irish, and Germans were among the first settlers and builders of the steel mills in the last decades of the nineteenth century. Immigrants from Poland, Serbia, Croatia, Slovenia, and Italy, between 1900 and 1935, were the second major wave of immigration to the community. Now Mexicans and blacks are the fastest-growing population groups in the community. As generations of immigrant groups have matured in South Chicago the community has become highly specialized; in its blast furnaces and rolling mills it produces steel, and in its neighborhoods, its union halls, and its political clubs it creates blue collar Americans.

For many native Chicagoans the smoke stacks and blast furnaces of the area symbolize the city's industrial might. For others, the immensity of the mills and their outpouring of smoke and soot suggest the ruthlessness with which great industry consumes the city's working people. Intellectuals often remember South Chicago as a center of militant labor organization during the national steel strike of 1919. The infamous Memorial Day Massacre occurred here at the Republic Steel plant in 1937. Today, however, Chicago intellectuals are more likely to refer to the community's troubled history of ecological invasion, racial conflict, and sudden violence. Here is the site of the Trumbull Park race riots of 1954, of violent resistance to Dr. King's Open Occupancy marches in 1966, and of the mass murders by Richard Speck in 1966. In these episodes South Chicago is represented as the extreme of a working-class factory community whose "white ethnics" cling tenaciously to their private bungalows and provincial neighborhoods. In general, sympathetic and unsympathetic observers alike have neglected the cultural diversity of the people, and the complexity of the community institutions they have created, in favor of more facile general labels.

In this study of South Chicago it is not my intention to present it as a "typical" working-class community, since every community has elements of its culture and social organization which make it unique. The historical and contemporary study of a community which surrounds a heavy industrial concentration is a topic that warrants investigation in its own right. On the other hand, South Chicago's diverse population of blue collar ethnic groups and its range of community institutions are representative of a rather widespread pattern of working-class community organization in the United States. South Chicago is also the scene of a new transition, the large-scale entrance of blacks and Spanish speakers in the workplaces and institutions of the community. Here the object of the study is to determine similarities and differences between past and contemporary trends in ethnic settlement and succession. Finally, the trend toward suburban living among blue collar Americans may seem to have caused older mill communities such as South Chicago to go out of style. There is ample evidence, however, in the work of sociologists who have studied blue collar suburban communities that changes are not as far reaching as is often thought. Although these new suburban industrial communities need to be studied in more detail themselves, they often constitute a continuation and modification of settings such as South Chicago.

Over the South Chicago community, spanning the industrial towns of northern Indiana, stretches an elevated superhighway which allows the passing motorist to escape the network of tracks and bridges that carve up the workplaces and mill neighborhoods below. Similar freeways and viaducts efficiently carry the nation's traffic over equivalent sections of Detroit, Cleveland, Toledo, Pittsburgh, and eastern New Jersey, thus skirting the country's major concentrations of working-class communities and heavy industry. Bypassed in the development of metropolitan transportation arteries, traditional American working-class communities have also receded somewhat into the background in intellectual representations of American society. Images of a "post-industrial" society with computerized plant technology, airport architecture, service corporations, and a suburban labor force, increasingly replace the steel crucible and railroad car as symbols of American society. It is true that basic industrial production employs a declining proportion of the American labor force, but despite this decline, most of the steel, coal, lumber, cement, rubber, glass, and other primary manufactured products which Americans consume in increasing quantities is manufactured by over seven million working-class men and women who tend to live out their lives in blue collar communities like South Chicago. In the Chicago-Gary area alone, there are approximately 130,000 members of the United Steelworkers of America, AFL-CIO, who work in the production and processing of steel. Those who are employed in the production of steel from its raw materials generally live along the lower basin of Lake Michigan in "steel-towns" such as South Chicago, Hammond, East Chicago, Indiana Harbor, Chicago Heights, Calumet City, and Gary. Elsewhere in the region, steelworkers work in steel forges, rolling plants, wire mills, slag and ballast companies, canning plants, and fabrication shops. In these settings the workers are more dispersed in blue collar communities which have a wider economic base. These include the working-class Chicago neighborhoods along Division Street, North Avenue, and Kedzie Avenue, and "suburban" towns such as Cicero, Harvey, Blue Island, Joliet, and Kankakee.

In almost all these communities it is clear that the settlement of blacks and other minority groups is following an ecological direction established decades earlier by Irish, German, Serbian, Croatian, Italian, and Polish migrants. Like the Polish and South Slavic steelworkers with whom they work, and with whom they struggle to live, the blacks and Mexicans in these working-class communities do not normally dream of owning the steel mills or the railroads. Rather they wish to "make it" in the mills and factories as skilled workers and as managerial officials.

For every black person who succeeds in a governmental agency or an administrative hierarchy, there are many others who develop blue collar occupational careers in settings much like those presented in this study. For every elite black administrator there are hundreds of black neighborhood leaders who concern themselves with the unity of their local groups and who engage in cooperation and conflict with members of other such groups. Most of this activity passes unnoticed in the larger society, as the blue collar stratum of the society recedes from the

American consciousness. Nevertheless, conflict and cooperation are adaptive processes which continue to follow the patterns outlined in this volume.

It is true today, as it was in the nineteenth century, that the American working class is less politically unified than the blue collar stratum in other industrialized countries. Marx himself observed that status conflict among various racial and ethnic segments of the American working class tended to prevent the emergence of long-standing traditions of socialist organization and thought. In particular, working-class Americans have been preoccupied with establishing themselves in urban communities in which they could be certain of at least a modicum of security and comfort in return for their labors. Of course this stress on the security of their local places explains much of the violent resistance in white working-class neighborhoods to ecological invasion by blacks. All new groups have encountered such resistance, but the stigma which attaches to black skin in this society has made the white worker's fear of racial mixing even more deeply felt. Nevertheless, despite the often hysterical resistance to racial invasion in white working-class neighborhoods, it is also true that in communities such as South Chicago, Gary, Indiana, and even Newark the political organization of black residents has progressed to such a point that they have succeeded to positions of leadership in aggregations which include the leaders of white segments of the community. This suggests that we must look into what is often regarded simply as working-class "white racism." Having done so, one discovers processes which aggregate working-class whites and blacks in community institutions but allow them to elaborate their own neighborhood cultural traditions as well. Therefore, while racial and ethnic schism continues to divide the American working class when it is viewed at the national or even the metropolitan level, it is in the community institutions of this class that one finds the greatest promise for breaking down the caste barriers which have always given the lie to America's most cherished values.

Part 1

Ethnic Groups and Community Institutions

1

The Ecology of Neighborhood Settlement and Ethnic Change

The Mills and the Neighborhoods

The South Chicago area often seems little more than a grimy stretch of neighborhoods crowded between steel mills. The streets and houses are frequently coated with a layer of red mill dust, and the gases from the furnaces and coke ovens make the air over the community among the most polluted in the nation. Even more important than the industry's toll on the physical environment is the fragmentation of the area into well-bounded territorial settlements. Industrial land use tends to isolate the neighborhoods from one another by wide frontiers of impassable machinery and burning meadows. Also each of the South Chicago ethnic groups has attempted to segregate itself in one or more of these neighborhoods, a settlement pattern which adds the weight of local morality to the considerable physical distance between the neighborhoods. Thus the area appears to be a mosaic of neighborhood ethnic groups whose provincial residents defend their residential territories against the threat of new populations and new ideas. But this view neglects the processes which create community attachments that transcend the "primordial" ties of kinship, neighborhood, and ethnic descent.[1] It is in these community-forming processes that South Chicago residents establish their own versions of modernity and cosmopolitanism. And it is at the level of the community, rather than in the small neighborhoods or the larger "class structure," that local ethnic groups adapt the basis of their solidarity to meet the exigencies of the national society.

In South Chicago, the steel mills line the banks of the Calumet River, which runs directly through the area. Although the river is part of an essential lifeline to the orefields of Lake Superior, it also separates the neighborhoods from each other by drawbridges and dead end streets. Of course the mills and the river are not the only boundaries which isolate the residential settlements. Rail lines servicing the mills also impose impassable barriers between neighborhoods. The waste-dumping areas which light the night sky with bursts of red flame also form mountains of slag that break the human settlement pattern. Finally, Lake Michigan and the main highway arteries of Chicago form perimeter boundaries which isolate South Chicago from communities such as Pullman and Roseland across the major freeway.

At the mouth of the Calumet River lies the South Works plant of the United States Steel Corporation, the largest (10,000 to 12,000 employees) of the South Chicago mills. Crowded between the rail lines and mill areas of this fifteen-block complex are "Millgate" and "the Bush," two of the traditional mill neighborhoods of the area. Upriver from the South Works plant, beyond grain elevators, shipping docks, and smaller steel firms, is the Wisconsin Steel Works of the International Harvester Company on the western bank of the Calumet. The old neighborhoods adjacent to this mill are "Irondale" and "Slag Valley," two areas separated by an immense stretch of slag heaps and rail linkages. Directly across from this mill and its neighborhoods, on the east bank of the river are the Republic Steel plant and its satellite neighborhoods known as the "East Side." Somewhat larger than the other neighborhoods, the East Side is roughly divided into smaller neighborhoods by the three Catholic parishes, St. George, St. Francis, and Annunciata. In summary, if one were to travel through South Chicago along the river itself, there would be glimpses of all the scattered neighborhoods of the area, starting with the Bush and Millgate, continuing past Slag Valley and Irondale, and finally passing the parishes of the East Side.

In addition to the old tenement neighborhoods at the gates to the mills, there are newer settlements more peripheral to the industrial spine of the area. Some of these neighborhoods are clearly working-class areas of second settlement where the residents have constructed rows of one-family brick bungalows with picture windows facing on the streets. These neighborhoods have names such as Bessemer Park, Cheltenham, Veterans Memorial Park, and Fair Elms–East Side, names which reflect both the influence of the steel industry and the preference of stable working-class families to settle near the older mill neighborhoods of their birth. Other neighborhoods at the margins of South Chicago are newer, more middle-class areas which constructed on vacant prairies after World War II. These settlements

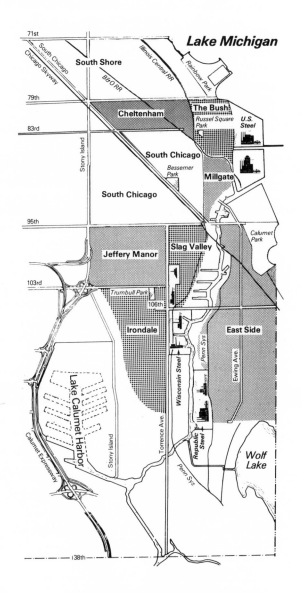

Figure 1 The major neighborhood areas, industrial land use patterns, and parks of South Chicago. Seventy-ninth Street marks the informal boundary between South Chicago and the more densely settled apartment house neighborhoods of South Shore.

have much less clearly marked boundaries, and their names often retain the labels given to them by the tract developers. Jeffrey Manor, Marrionette Manor, and South Shore Gardens are such neighborhoods. They occupy the northwestern border of the South Chicago area, the only portion of the community not clearly isolated from surrounding communities.[2]

The names by which residents identify their neighborhoods convey something of the strength of territorial sentiments in South Chicago. Bessemer Park, the Bush, Millgate, Irondale, Slag Valley, and East Side—these are clearly bounded neighborhoods, each with its public and parochial grammar schools, its neighborhood taverns and churches, its particular ethnic cultures, and its overshadowing steel mill. These neighborhood names, whose origins usually go back to the end of the nineteenth century, are frequently used in connection with other personal relationships. People whose families have been on intimate terms for one or more generations almost invariably stress the neighborhood dimension of their attachments when they say, "We grew up together in Irondale"; "I'm going to visit my kum [God relations] in Millgate"; "They were my compadres when we all lived in the Bush"; "We used to fight the Hunkies in Slag Valley." This stress on neighborhood affiliation is strongest among the working-class families who reside in the old mill neighborhoods and declines in the less provincial, more middle-class neighborhoods of second settlement. People who live in the Manors and South Shore Gardens place much less emphasis on territorial attachments, and they are in less agreement as to the boundaries of their neighborhoods. In general, however, when speaking to outsiders all refer to themselves as residents of South Chicago. But it is particularly in the ethnic mill neighborhoods of the area that one finds well-elaborated notions of neighborhood solidarity.

Ethnic Settlement in South
Chicago

The ethnic composition of the South Chicago community is the product of labor recruitment by the nationally based steel corporations. The first rolling mills along the Calumet River were constructed and manned largely by native Americans and Scandinavian or German immigrants and the largely northern European population of the mill neighborhoods remained concentrated at the entrances to the major workplaces of the community.

The steel mills began to recruit Poles—who invaded the South Chicago area—at the end of the nineteenth century. By 1930 the Poles were the largest ethnic group in South Chicago, with their ethnic institutions grouped around St. Michael's Cathedral in the Bush. In Irondale, Slag Valley, Millgate, and the north end of the East Side— all mill neighborhoods of first settlement—other representatives of the "new immigration" were establishing their settlements. Southern Europeans, particularly Serbians, Croatians, and Italians, invaded Slag Valley and Irondale about 1915. The Slovenes, who were recruited slightly earlier, settled in the neighborhoods of Millgate and the lower end of the East Side. Today Irondale and Slag Valley continue to include important segments of the Serbian, Croatian, and Italian populations, and these remain the dominant political groups here.

As early as World War I, the steel mills found it necessary to recruit Mexicans to fill the heavy demand for wartime labor. At this time a small enclave of Mexican families settled in Millgate. This enclave has since expanded and Mexicans have established a second neighborhood in Irondale. These separate residential areas create an important cleavage within the Mexican population. Politicians and political organizations attempting to gain Mexican support must engage in delicate negotiations calculated to avoid competition and conflict between the two Mexican neighborhoods. Because of their residential segregation, the relatively short duration of their settlement, and consequent lack of primary ties extending into other neighborhoods and mills, the Mexicans are the most isolated of all local ethnic groups.

The demand for labor during World War II did for the blacks what it had earlier done for the Mexicans. Subsequent federal legislation and the scarcity of new white laborers in the steel industry have vastly increased the number of blacks in the mills since 1945. The first black recruits to South Chicago's steel mills settled in Millgate, probably because it was the most deteriorated of the local neighborhoods and least resistant to their entrance. With some exceptions, black recruits to the mills have found it exceedingly difficult to establish residences in other neighborhoods because of strong resistance from the white residents. Thus a majority of black employees in the South Chicago mills do not live in South Chicago. At the same time the black enclave in Millgate has so deteriorated that black employees no longer seek it out as a place of residence. It has in the last five years received a heavy concentration of welfare families. Thus the blacks are unique among the ethnic and racial groups because they lack a cohesive residential base in South Chicago from which they may form primary ties and appeal to neighborhood loyalties. As will be evident throughout this study, this limits their influence in both union and local politics far more than would be expected on the basis of their numbers in the mills.

In addition to the major working-class groups upon which this study focuses, there are also smaller settlements of Czechs, Lithuanians, and Bulgarians settled in Millgate and adjacent South Chicago neighborhoods. Hungarians and some Russians were among the newcomers

Table 1

Patterns of Ethnic Settlement in South Chicago Neighborhoods, 1900, 1930, 1970, in Order of Importance

Neighborhood	1900	1930	1970
Bush	N.E., Irish, some Poles	Polish, N.E.	Mexican, Polish
Millgate	German, Scand.	S. Slav, Italian, Mexican	Mexican, black
Cheltenham	N.E.	N.E., Polish	Polish, some Mexican
Bessemer Park	German, Irish, Scotch	N.E., Polish	Polish, Mexican
Slag Valley	none	S. Slav, N.E.	S. Slav, N.E., Mexican
Memorial Park	none	N.E., S. Slav	S. Slav, Polish
Irondale	Irish, German	S. Slav, Irish	Mexican, S. Slav, black
East Side:			
St. George	German, Scand. some Slavs	S. Slav, Italian	Italian, S. Slav
St. Francis	German, Irish, Scand.	German, Scand., Irish	S. Slav, N.E., Polish
Annunciata	none	German, Scand.	N.E., Polish, S. Slav

NOTE: N.E. signifies northern European with no group necessarily dominant. S. Slav refers to Slovenes, Serbians, and Croatians, the major South Slavic groups in the community.

in Irondale at the end of World War I. In contrast to the working-class ethnic groups which were attracted to the community because of employment opportunities in the steel mills, other ethnic groups settled in South Chicago to do business there. Jewish and Greek merchants established stores in the center of the community along Commercial and South Chicago Avenues. And in the mill neighborhoods themselves, such as Irondale and Slag Valley, Jewish storeowners carried on their trade next to stores owned by representatives of the older ethnic groups. While their numbers were never very large in any of the various mill neighborhoods, these minor groups provided small voting blocks which were sought after by other ethnic groups. From the start they fitted into a system of political persuasion and influence based on multiple claims over people's loyalties. Also, their higher economic standing made them especially attractive in the negotiation of political constituencies. In turn they added to the cosmopolitan experience of the immigrants and their children for they opened neighborhoods to influences from other cultures. Weak minorities in neighborhoods dominated by other ethnic groups, the Jewish and Greek merchants were among the first of the new immigrants to appeal to broader loyalties than those of ethnic group and neighborhood enclave. As businessmen and as members of their own primary groups they lent their services to a community composed predominantly of other groups.

In general, the entire South Chicago area is honeycombed by neighborhoods which differ according to ethnicity. Included among its residents are Serbians, Croatians, Poles, Italians, Scandinavians, Germans, Mexicans, and blacks, who make up its main residential groups as well as the majority of employees in the mills. In addition there is further residential segregation on the basis of generation of arrival in the city, with some areas including a diverse population of second- and third-generation Americans. The tendency for second- and third-generation residents to move to the peripheral neighborhoods of the community increases the heterogeneity of residential settlements and creates the generational differences within local ethnic groups. Thus by 1970 scarcely a neighborhood in the community was predominantly occupied by a single ethnic group. This pattern of immigration and neighborhood settlement has increased the necessity of making appeals to groups on the basis of diverse loyalties rather than to the residents' more narrowly defined concepts of ethnic identity.

Managing Ethnicity

I moved to South Chicago—more specifically to an old mill neighborhood called Irondale—in the winter of 1968 and remained in the community with my family until August 1970. At first my plans were to study the Serbian and Croatian communities only, and the first six months of fieldwork were spent almost exclusively in the homes, taverns, churches, and mutual benefit societies of the Slavic immigrants. Living with first-generation immigrants was much like returning to the society which Chicago sociologists studied before 1921.[3] The Serbian and Croatian immigrants, some now elderly men and women, others recent arrivals, were repeating the well-known processes of immigrant settlement in industrial communities. They were busy forming "secondary associations," they were reading the immigrant press, or more typically they were listening to news of the old country on foreign language FM radio stations. The aged continued arguing political issues of World War I vintage, while disputes among the more recent immigrants were fought over World War II issues. Chetniks,

Ustasha, Domobran, Mihailovich Brigada, and even some Partisans—
one found the old sores of Yugoslav regionalism continually being
reopened in tavern fights and church schisms.

In general the material conditions of life for immigrants in Chicago
are incomparably better now than they were when Edith Abbott studied
the tenements of South Chicago, but the psycho-social effects of
immigration seem hardly to have diminished at all. Thus the South
Slavic immigrant generation was engaged in isolating itself within
ethnic associations that provide solace to those who have been uprooted
from their homes in Serbia and Croatia. For example, the largest
gathering of immigrant Serbians in South Chicago occurs, paradoxi-
cally, on the Fourth of July, when the immigrant settlers of the area
host a picnic for immigrants from the entire Chicago-Gary region. The
day reserved in the larger society for affirmation of American citizenship is a celebration for the culturally isolated Serbian immigrant
colonies of Lake Michigan.

Among second- and third-generation Serbians and Croatians I found
greater levels of involvement in the wider South Chicago community.
Native-born residents were actively cooperating and competing with
other ethnic groups in a variety of neighborhoods and local institutions.
Indeed, as I came to associate with second- and third-generation
adults, it became almost impossible to set Serbian and Croatian
ethnicity apart from the activities of native-born Poles, Italians,
Mexicans, and blacks in South Chicago neighborhoods. All these
groups manage their ethnic attachments within a diversity of primary
groups and institutional settings which may or may not include
members of other ethnic groups. Thus I soon found myself associating
with people in heterogeneous primary groups formed in the churches,
the steel mills, the local unions, and the ward political organizations of
the area. For example, one of the first primary groups to invite me to
join their company were middle-aged Serbian and Italian men who
directed the local union at the Wisconsin Steel Works in Irondale.
Shortly after we began associating together, this group invited me to
attend the annual South Chicago Humanitarian Award Dinner, an
affair which attracts all the organized groups in the area. During the
evening, the Serbian men at my table were careful to point out other
Serbians in similar groups seated elsewhere in the enormous hall where
the dinner was held. Italian friends in this group of local unionists also
introduced me to neighborhood Italians who attended the affair on
behalf of other organizations.

For some of the men and women I met that night, ethnic attachments were the sine qua non of their adult affiliations. People in

church groups or those attending as representatives of ethnic associations selected their primary groups almost entirely on the basis of ethnicity. In groups such as the one which had invited me, on the other hand, ethnicity was managed in such a way as to be one among many potential bases for friendship formation. Generations of neighborhood association, participation in steel mill work groups, activism in union or ward politics, these were also dimensions along which friendships could be formed. Here people would have to manage their ethnic attachments in various ways depending on the nature of solidarity in their primary groups. For some, such as the unionist and ward political groups, ethnicity and the claim to an ethnic following might be grounds for initial entry into the group. For others, such as those active in neighborhood voluntary associations in the newer residential sections of the area, ethnic attachments are a private matter, and group solidarity depends more exclusively on the shared attachments of residential propinquity. Thus as I came to participate in a much larger circle of adult primary groups, my own concerns began to focus on the various means whereby South Chicago residents manage their ethnic attachments. I learned that ethnicity is not just a persistence of the past but that ethnic identity may take its place among more modern criteria for forming personal attachments in contemporary communities.

In industrial communities such as South Chicago, ethnic adaptation occurs within the community itself and is not necessarily dependent on outside mobility. The processes which form heterogeneous adult primary groups cause ethnicity to be managed within a broader range of alternative social relationships. All the South Chicago ethnic groups offer the possibility for association within distinct ethnic cultures whose institutions create their own occupational opportunities and maintain unique customs and norms. Unlike the ghetto communities of many central city areas, however, industrial communities in metropolitan areas engage their populations in a cultural world which itself presents the first possibilities for ethnic adaptation. Whatever their ethnic affiliations, South Chicago people share the common culture of working-class America, and more specifically this is a culture which is largely shaped by the steel industry. Steel-making brings South Chicago people together in the world of work. Steel presents all the ethnic groups with similar life chances and common aspirations for future generations.

Steel as a Way of Life

I worked in the Wisconsin Steel Company, No. 3 (a fictitious number)

Mill, during 1969, and from the first day in the steel mill it was clear that it would have been impossible to understand the community or its people without working in the mills. As I became familiar with mill work, it also was evident how much of the time people had been talking about their occupational lives and I had not understood the language. Within a week all the comings and goings of humans, railway cars, and boats became intelligible; the open spaces and cramped neighborhoods fit patterns of land use determined by the steel industry; the temporal patterns of street life could be explained by the cycle of mill work; and the material life style of various neighborhoods fit patterns of seniority and skill inside the mills. In their leisure lives outside the mills, South Chicago families could attempt to segregate themselves within ethnic cultural worlds, or they might associate with diverse groups of neighborhood friends, but in every case ethnic segregation was limited by the more universalistic experiences of life on rolling mills, blast furnaces, coke ovens, ore docks, and the switchyards of the steel industry.

Space and time in South Chicago are organized in large part by the exigencies of steel production. Some neighborhoods are separated by mile-wide no-man's lands of scrap yards, slag-dumping areas, and the giant glowing mills themselves. Crowded at the entrances to the mills along the Calumet River, the neighborhoods are often hidden under clouds of sulfurous red smoke and dust. Here and there in the open industrial expanses there are clusters of taverns, inviting refuges against the bitter cold of winter and the humid heat of Chicago summers. The daily round of comings and goings in the taverns, and in the neighborhoods themselves, follows the three-week cycle of industrial shift work. Except in slack periods, the mills operate twenty-four hours a day, seven days a week, and the steelworkers normally work one of three eight-hour shifts, changing around the clock each week. Sundays and holidays are "premium days" when all are anxious to work at "time and a half" or "time and three-quarters." For this reason, most community events, from church picnics and family gatherings to political rallies, are scheduled to overlap with the shift work time schedules. Leisure time is carefully budgeted so that there is rarely a moment when some working people are not on the streets or in their front yards during a day off.

The material conditions for South Chicago families are also largely determined by the steel industry. Saturday after payday Friday is the primary shopping day when women and their husbands crowd the supermarkets and clothing stores of the area. Throughout the 1960s and into the early years of the new decade, wages in the steel mills were increasing to a point where the average yearly income had reached the long desired $10,000. But inflation during these years steadily eroded advances in hourly rates, and the family budgets of South Chicago residents also depended on long hours of overtime and premium pay. Skilled workers in the mills such as the elite rollers, heaters, and craftsmen could earn as much as $25,000 a year. At the other extreme, among the more numerous laborers and other unskilled categories, wages might be below $7,000 yearly. Thus in the old tenement neighborhoods of the area, where Mexican, black, and European newcomers now raise their families, money is tight and life for large families is hard. Life is easier in the newer South Chicago bungalow neighborhoods, but here also the well-paid rollers, railroad engineers, foremen, and other skilled workers seek every available opportunity for extra money to keep up payments on the mortgage, the central air-conditioning, the furniture, and the new car. Established families in the area can point to one or more of their members who have made it out of the steel industry and now own small businesses or hold jobs "with the city." But for every adult who succeeds in earning a living outside the mills there are many more inside the plants who dream of making a "killing at the track" and place their bets faithfully with bookmakers in the mills or at their local taverns.

After accumulating ten or more years of seniority in the mills, a worker finds it extremely difficult to locate equally well paying jobs elsewhere. Thus many wives supplement the family income through work in the grain mills and light manufacturing plants of the area. Other women commute daily to downtown Chicago for work in the offices and hospitals of the larger city. For their part, the men may add to the family budget and to its local prestige through activities in the unions, ward party organizations, or the various ethnic cultural institutions of the community. Of course the more roots a family has in the area, and the more its particular ethnic group has established its power in community institutions, the greater the opportunities for such mobility. Thus the steel industry creates a common way of life for South Chicago residents, but the formation of more general community institutions is equally dependent on the processes whereby families and ethnic segments of the population establish their reputations and prestige beyond the confines of their local neighborhoods.

Work Groups and Union Politics
in the Steel Mills

Two organizations are primarily responsible for aggregating groups of residents into community institutions: the ward political system and the

steel workers' labor unions. The pattern of residential segmentation in
South Chicago is due largely to the transportation arteries which service
the area's steel mills, but the influence of the mills is not just divisive.
On the one hand, concentration in the steel industry brings to bear on
local people a uniform body of national policies and legislative
enactments. The occupational concentration of residents in the mills
and the overall dominance of the steel industry are so great that no
resident can escape being influenced. Some of the influences are
relatively obvious: National Labor Relations Board (NLRB) policies,
presidential wage and price guidelines, national collective bargaining
agreements, federally sponsored occupational training programs, and
equal employment opportunity legislation. Other broad influences of
this character are more subtle: the residents' conception of steel as a
way of life, the shared tradition of labor-management conflict, and a
heightened awareness of how ethnic groups have been introduced into
the industry by distant and centralized authorities. Taken together, the
steel mills and national authorities determine the basic patterns of
daily life in South Chicago.

On the other hand, the residents also possess in their labor unions a
system of negotiation through which they can transcend the physical
and cultural isolation of their neighborhoods. Although employees tend
to work in the mill nearest to their place of residence, the mills draw on
the population from the entire area as well. Steel mills then bring
together the diverse elements of different neighborhoods into work
groups which in turn are aggregated in union politics. This pattern of
aggregation depends on no single principle but builds upon primary
relations and ethnic loyalties which are created in both place of work
and place of residence. Union politics is a source of lively interest in
South Chicago, drawing only slightly lower turnouts than ward politics.
The coalitions and constituencies which have developed over time range
across a multiplicity of definable groups: coalitions based on residential groups, on work groups, on ethnic groups, or some combination
of these.

The principal vehicle for constructing their coalitions is the work
group in the plant; this occurs, however, within a division of labor and
series of union rules which shape the activities of different work
groups. The ecology of the plant, the seniority system, and the "turn"
(alternating work shifts) create considerable variation in the influence
of different work groups on the formation of constituencies in union
politics. This negotiated aggregation which occurs in the mills and in
union politics tends to include unlikely partners. In the course of time,

blacks, Poles, residents of Millgate and the East Side, have all shifted back and forth between brutal enmity and mutual support. These dramatic shifts are due less to the composition of the work force than to the placement of different groups relative to the ecology of the plant, the seniority system, and the "turn." People's experiences in the work groups create precedents for ethnic change in an even wider set of primary groups in communal institutions.

Primary Groups and Negotiated Aggregations

South Chicago is a relatively old industrial community and its pattern of settlement has been determined largely by the recruiting policies of nationally based steel firms. The age of the neighborhoods, the generational changes, and the differentiation of the community along lines of religion, language, and organizational affiliation has produced a widespread network of primary relations and groups which tie the area together like a web that must be rewoven at each ward or union election. The basic unit of this community solidarity is the primary group that is reconstructed throughout the life cycle of residents in the community. These primary groups are developed on multiple principles of affiliation: ethnic and neighborhood descent, common participation in a street corner gang, patronage of a local tavern, participation in precinct organizations or union caucases, and friendships in the mills. Sometimes a single group will combine members who are all related to one another through separate circumstances. Once formed these affiliations may lapse because of changes in residence, work, or any number of circumstances, only to be reconstructed at a later period.

Occasionally this reconstruction of primary ties is quite instrumental, as in the case of people entering precinct, ward, or union politics. On the other hand the majority of the residents reconstruct or let lapse their primary ties as they fit into the family cycle and the pattern of residential invasion and change. As people lose old neighbors, they may seek out friends from past periods who are relocated in still other neighborhoods, while their children are being incorporated into a more strictly ethnic street corner gang. Young married couples may restrict their range of primary ties because of the immediate burdens of work and child-rearing, only to expand them at a later time as their family responsibilities diminish. Involvement in union or local politics may draw people into new primary relations and enlist them in new organizations. Throughout this flux of expanding and contracting primary relations, a large number of these primary groups remain available to be drawn into communal organizations and especially into ward politics. The multiple basis upon which these primary groups are constructed and reconstructed requires that they be enlisted into local politics by multiple appeals. Among the appeals that local leaders can make are those to ethnicity, neighborhood solidarity, religion, union membership, and the expressive symbols of "good government." Probably the most important of these is ethnicity.

Before Mexican, black, and European newcomers can settle as equals in the area's newer neighborhoods they must join aggregations of people whose personal attachments span the moral and physical frontiers of the older ethnic settlements. The new primary groups formed in local political institutions are such aggregations, and it is through the activities of political primary groups that the respectability and solidarity of entire ethnic generations in communities such as South Chicago are forged. The negotiations which form new primary groups, and the ethnic adaptation which these groups effect, vary somewhat in each neighborhood. Nevertheless, there are a number of general patterns which may be observed. Among the older white ethnic groups, such as the Serbians, Croatians, Italians, and Poles, political primary groups attract a diverse membership, and in so doing they establish the social settings in which the residents negotiate precedents for cooperation behind heterogeneous leadership groups. It is in such groups that the residents first manage their ethnicity within a broader range of personal and civic attachments. Among the more recently established groups, such as the Mexicans and blacks, political primary groups tend to focus their activities inward, on the internal politics of their ethnic groups. In this case political primary groups usually act to bridge the internal cleavages which prevent even the group's mere entry into political competition in the community.

The South Slavs: Serbians, Slovenes, Croatians

The people of South Slavic origin often use the term "Hunkies" when speaking of themselves as an ethnic group, but even this suggestion of solidarity is problematic. Whatever unified ethnic identity they share is subject to continual maneuver and negotiation. Although they have lived for three generations in the community, the Serbians, Croatians, and Slovenes have tended to maintain the animosities which still divide them in modern Yugoslavia. In addition, they have created new distinctions out of their common and often conflicting experiences in the United States. The groups initially settled in adjacent neighborhoods, and in the early years of their settlement they shared common neighborhood institutions. Similarities in language made it possible for Serbian, Croatian, and Slovene steelworkers to bed and board together in common quarters, usually at the back of one of the large corner taverns in their new neighborhoods. Such taverns served as the common house, the social and political meeting place, the bank, and the sometime funeral parlor for all the men and what few women were settled in the neighborhood.

As the number of South Slavic immigrants increased, and as they began to form families of their own, the need for separate cultural institutions in the neighborhoods became more apparent. This situation is exemplified in the following account by a church leader whose parents were among the first Croatian settlers in the community.

Before 1921 the Croatians here in South Chicago were part of the old church in Millgate that our parents built with the Slovenian people. For about fifteen or twenty years we were all in the same congregation. When the two groups began getting bigger there was more and more argument about who would be the leaders. You know all us Hunkies were always fighting, especially about what was going on in the old country. The Serbians and us used to fight at picnics, and I even have pictures of the Serbian volunteers parading through the community on their way to fight for the Serbian king in World War I.

Maybe part of our problem with the Slovenians was that our groups were getting too big for one church. Anyway we had different languages and customs too. It was just that the Slovenians had got there before us and had made a place for us to come in on. Some of this has even continued today. You know old K——, the undertaker? Well his father ran one of the biggest taverns and boarding houses during immigration. They were Slovenians, but plenty of Croatians and Serbians lived there when they first came to South Chicago. Lots of our parents and some of us kids had our weddings at his place. Now the son is burying the folks his dad married off.

When churches split there is always bad feeling. There's still Croatian families who don't get along too well with the Serbians, but things aren't like they were. We'll back the same Hunky politicians, and even the church people are getting along better.

Although they often remained hidden beneath the surface of community life, the memory of conflict and schism usually required at least two generations of political negotiation to erase. When church schism drove them apart, the Slovenes kept the old church and the Croatians established a new one in a mill neighborhood on the other side of the river. Since their numbers never matched those of the

Serbians and Croatians, the Slovenes were later obliged to share their Catholic church with the growing Italian settlement in their neighborhood. At the same time the Serbian families in Millgate began to seek space to build a new church and to establish a new settlement in the less densely settled prairie sections of the area. By the end of the Great Depression the Serbians, Croatians, and Slovenes had established themselves as separate cultural groups with separate neighborhood institutions in South Chicago.

Today, in their cultural institutions, particularly the churches, taverns, and fraternal-benefit associations, the South Slavic residents of the area keep alive Old World traditions which have long since disappeared in modern Yugoslavia. Also, the political cleavages which continually threaten the stability of Yugoslavia as a nation are nurtured in Slavic neighborhood areas. Thus when new immigrants from Serbia and Croatia arrive in South Chicago they find that what passes for Serbian or Croatian identity among the native-born and older immigrant generations is a combination of antiquated cultural practices, kinship ties, and peer friendships formed in South Chicago's neighborhoods and steel mills. The new immigrants, often referred to somewhat derisively as "DP's," contribute to the vitality of these South Slavic neighborhoods, but cultural and political differences between newcomers and native-born add generational conflict to the already complicated course of South Slavic ethnic relations. In general the new immigrants reject the older versions of Serbian or Croatian ethnicity in order to form their own local associations and to elaborate cultural expressions of their experiences as immigrants. On the one hand, this rejection is an added source of tension and conflict among the South Slavs. On the other hand, it adds to the already rich traditions of music, food, dance, and fraternal association which these blue collar ethnic groups maintain in the community.

The ecological patterns of Serbian and Croatian settlements in South Chicago are quite similar to those of ethnic groups which are their historical contemporaries. Both the Serbians and the Croatians continue to maintain their dominance of Slag Valley and Memorial Park, the mill neighborhood area they settled early in the century. Also, a large proportion of their numbers are still homeowners in adjacent neighborhoods of first settlement such as Irondale. Within this traditional neighborhood base the groups maintain the primary social and cultural institutions of their ethnic groups. These institutions include a "national" parish of the Catholic church for the Croatians and a large Serbian Orthodox church for the Serbians. Both are congregations numbering over fifteen hundred families, and like the neighborhoods themselves they help preserve the ethnic roots of Croatian and Serbian Americans who have settled in communities throughout the Chicago-Calumet region. Alongside the churches there are numerous taverns, restaurants, and other small business establishments such as funeral parlors and attorneys' offices. These are generally owned by neighborhood leaders whose ethnicity has become closely connected to their business lives.

Elsewhere in the community, in its neighborhoods of second settlement, Serbians and Croatians of the second and third generation participate in networks of primary groups in which ethnicity is only one among a number of possible elements of solidarity. These are the groups of neighbors and friends who manage the precinct work, the neighborhood improvement associations, the Labor Day parades, the Little League teams, the church committees, the tavern groups, the bowling teams, the card circles, and all the other primary group activities of such neighborhoods. In consequence, when South Slavic political leaders attempt to enlist the support of their ethnic peers here, they must fashion appeals combining ethnic pride with these more diverse dimensions of solidarity. In the old neighborhoods, political leaders still gain support by appealing to sentiments of ethnic solidarity and to the ambitions of the ethnic group for succession to power in local institutions. But to those in the newer areas of the community, people who are now members of heterogeneous neighborhood primary groups, the ethnic leaders must also base their appeals on their own prestige in the larger community. Thus whatever overall solidarity there is in the community's South Slavic population is created in the course of political competition in community institutions.

During my years in South Chicago, Serbian labor leaders and Croatian ward politicians were quite successful in competing for power in major union and party organizations of the community. "Hunky" solidarity figured quite prominently in the negotiations of primary group coalitions during the often bitter struggle for power in mill unions and ward precincts. Indeed, this ethnic solidarity grew largely out of the needs of politicians to gain the support of Serbian, Croatian, and Slovene activists in local political primary groups. But to win power in South Chicago's community institutions requires more than the unification of any particular group. Thus Serbian and Croatian political leaders must also enlist the support of adult leaders in primary groups for which ethnic descent is not the sovereign basis of affiliation. To do so these ethnic politicians must compete for recognition accord-

ing to more universal values of prestige as they are defined in the larger
community. It is through this political competition, which on the one
hand mobilizes a seemingly antiquated ethnic solidarity, that ethnic
leaders at every level of politics learn to play down their ethnic
attachments in favor of personal and civil ties to neighbors and
workmates.

Poles: A Gerrymandered
Ethnic Group

Poles of first-, second-, and third-generation nativity have long consti-
tuted the single largest ethnic group in South Chicago. In addition to
St. Bronislava, the Polish "national" parish in the Bessemer Park
neighborhood area, Poles have almost entirely dominated a large
territorial parish, St. Michael's Cathedral, at the South Shore entrance
to the community. Since the center of Polish settlement in South
Chicago is nearest to the middle-class, lake-front communities along
Lake Michigan, many educated Chicagoans have associated the Poles
with the entire South Chicago area. In fact, the situation of intense
ethnic pluralism which makes processes of negotiated aggregation so
apparent in the community is due in large part to the inability of the
area's Poles to overcome the severe physical and political segmentation
which divides their population. Also their traditional neighborhoods
are located in the area which has had the greatest invasion of black and
Mexican newcomers. Thus the Poles are often viewed as the stereotypical white ethnic group which violently resists the settlement of lower
status newcomers. In reality such resistance is a general phenomenon
throughout the South Chicago area. Only the numerical importance of
the Poles and their location in the direct path of racial invasion have
caused them to be singled out for their racism.

The Polish population of South Chicago has never attained the
political power or degree of prestige in community institutions that its
numbers alone suggest it could. As explained in the following passage
from an interview with a Polish ward political leader, the Poles have
been gerrymandered into two political wards, the Seventh (South Shore)
and the Tenth (South Chicago).

We've been split into the two wards since about 1928 and this has hurt
us in the community quite a bit. The Irish and others have run the city
for a long time. They haven't wanted us out here to take over in South
Chicago.

Getting split up in politics makes it hard to bring the people together.
When our families move from the Bush and Bessemer Park to new

places on the East Side it's more of a jump for them than it would be if
it was still the same ward committee in both places. Also people start
going in all directions in order to get something going for themselves.
You have a fairly good number of Polish businessmen in South Chicago
who are Republicans. Republicans don't do too bad sometimes.
They're not really important since the Democrats still control all the
clout, but the Republicans still pick up plenty of crumbs.

Most of us have stayed as Democrats all our lives. We've maybe not
done as good as we could, but there are plenty of people like old L——
who's been the state representative from this district for years and
years. He's another good example of what I'm saying though. He was a
boxing champion and that's as important as the fact he's Polish. He
even changed his name when he was fighting to make it sound Irish.

Another reason the Polish population of South Chicago never won
quite its share of power and prestige in the community is that of all the
white ethnic groups here the Poles are the most residentially segmented. In addition to the large Polish neighborhoods in the Bush and
Bessemer Park, there is another largely Polish complex of neighborhoods on the extreme southern edge of the area. This neighborhood
area, referred to as Hegewisch by the residents, is a small island of
working-class bungalows surrounded by acres of industry and open
marshland which effectively isolate it from the other South Chicago
neighborhoods. Hegewisch is one of the most isolated urban neighborhoods in Chicago, and from the perspective of ethnic relations this
division of South Chicago's Poles between southern and northern ends
of the community represents ethnic segmentation at its most extreme.
The neighborhood institutions of Hegewisch mirror those of the Polish
neighborhoods in South Chicago proper. There is some contact
between the two Polish populations, but in general Poles in the two
areas see themselves as quite distinct descent groups with different
local histories and different communal concerns. This heritage of
segmentation has been reinforced through an additional political
gerrymander which recently placed the population of Hegewisch in the
Ninth Ward, while the main settlements of South Chicago were always
included in the Tenth Ward. Thus the only local institution which
brings the two Polish populations together on a regular basis is the steel
industry.

Only in the mills and in local union politics do Polish steelworkers
from the two ends of the community come to enter into joint
negotiations as Poles in which they form coalitions with representatives
of other ethnic groups in the industrial labor force of the area. In
consequence of this, Polish unionists have had relatively more success

in their political competition than have the Polish precinct captains and ward politicians. Also, as a gerrymandered ethnic group some prominant Poles have flirted with the Republican party as a means of improving their political position in the community. In general this has tended to divide the Poles further and make their unification behind a solidary political leadership more difficult. The overall consequence of this relative political impotency is that as Poles of the second and third generation move into the heterogeneous neighborhoods of second settlement in the area, their ethnic affiliations bring them little status or recognition. More than is true for the other white ethnic groups they must relinquish their ethnic affiliations as they join adult primary groups which form around neighborhood association. Such is not true, for example, of the South Slavs or the Italians, since these groups have developed traditions of joint "ownership" of local neighborhoods and maintain long-standing coalitions among their leaders.

The Italians

Like the Poles and the South Slavic ethnic groups, the Italians of South Chicago are divided into discrete neighborhoods and this segmentation has made their overall solidarity problematic. The main Italian settlements are located in two neighborhoods, one in Irondale and the other in the oldest section of the East Side. As a result of this spatial fragmentation the Italians have had to participate in a range of negotiations with representatives of other neighboring ethnic groups in order to win their share of power and rectitude. In general the organization of their settlements is based around rather large extended families of Italians who trace their descent from the same villages in southern Italy. Like the Poles, they become affiliated with territorial parishes of the Catholic church and often gain considerable local prestige for their church participation. On the other hand, in South Chicago as in other working-class communities with sizable Italian settlements, the Italians gain some solidarity from their reputed ties to the underworld "syndicate." As a group, however, they receive little material reward from such reputed underworld attachments. Nevertheless, the Italians are somewhat overrepresented among the area's small bookmakers and corner businessmen.

As neighborhood businessmen some Italian families have established rather widespread prestige in the old neighborhoods. Thus Italian neighborhood leaders tend to circulate more freely among the area's adult primary groups than do any of the leaders of other white ethnic groups discussed here. It is for this reason that although their numbers

are smaller than those of the other ethnic groups who were their
contemporaries in immigration, the Italians often figure more centrally
in the negotiations which form political primary groups in community
institutions. For example, in Irondale the Italians negotiate precinct
level coalitions with Serbian activists who share common histories in
that neighborhood. Likewise, on the East Side, the Italians figure
predominantly in the formation of heterogeneous coalitions of neighbors. In general the Italians play an instrumental role as negotiators
who circulate among the area's segmented white ethnic groups. On the
other hand, their allegiances to the parochial values of the local
neighborhood limit their ability to make appeals to the newer groups
in the community, particularly to its Mexican and black populations.

The Mexicans: The
Acceptable Newcomers

The Mexicans of South Chicago are on the verge of becoming full
participants in the negotiation of primary groups in community
institutions. Over a generation of residence in the area the Mexicans
have had to concern themselves largely with the organization of
communal institutions such as churches and informal mutual benefit
associations within their own neighborhoods. Segmented into two main
settlements, Mexicans in Millgate and Irondale continue to duplicate
their communal institutions and to compete with each other for
leadership of their population in the area. Thus up to the time this
study was conducted most of the negotiations of new primary groups
among the Mexicans took place within the Mexican neighborhoods
themselves. As Mexican unionists and ward political leaders began to
compete for recognition in the institutions of the wider community,
animosities stemming from years of competition between the Mexican
neighborhoods was a continual source of cleavage, a situation
explained by a prominant Mexican professional.

I would say our biggest headache, the thing that keeps us from getting
better established in the community, is that we do a lot of fighting
among ourselves. Take the two main Mexican neighborhoods in
Millgate and Irondale. There's always arguing and competing between
them. Even though we have big families with branches in both
neighborhoods it hasn't seemed to make much difference. I suppose
it's a natural thing, but we're always coming up against it.

Fights between the neighborhoods really begin as kid's stuff. The
Mexicans here spend more time with other Mexicans than with anyone
else. So the kids go to dances where they get into fights or arguments

with other Mexican kids. It doesn't matter to them that they're all
Mexicans, what matters is that there is a group from Millgate and one
from Irondale or somewhere else. So they make these distinctions, they
fight, they compete, and it continues like that into the next generation.
I see this type of thing happening in Mexican communities all over the
city. I know we'll have to overcome this before we get anywhere in
South Chicago.

It is widely recognized among leaders of the older white ethnic
groups that the Mexicans are critical to the future of the community.
Although there remain neighborhoods, especially on the East Side,
which resist the settlement of Mexican families, there are other
neighborhoods where it is clear to all concerned that the increasing
presence of Mexican families serves to stem the wholesale exodus of
white families. One commonly hears the opinion expressed among
white families in these neighborhoods that "the Mexicans are helping
to keep up the neighborhood but when their turn comes to sell houses
they'll sell to blacks in a minute." In other words, many of the
neighborhood's older white residents perceive the Mexican settlement
as a transitional one to the eventual dominance of the area by blacks.
This recognition of the Mexicans' intermediary position in the community's future stability lends credence to Mexican ambitions that their
numbers alone would not warrant. For example, in local union politics
the Mexicans rarely account for more than 15 percent of the labor force
in any major mill, but as a "swing" group between the whites and
blacks, the Mexicans are able to become prime movers in the negotiation of leadership primary groups. Their ability to act in this capacity is
predicated on high levels of solidarity and unity behind a set of leaders
in the unions and in the Mexican precincts. Unfortunately such unity is
often problematic, and the processes of primary group formation
among Mexican neighborhood leaders usually hinge on attempts to
negotiate aggregations of leaders who can represent the interests of
more than a single Mexican neighborhood, or more than a single
segment of the Mexican labor force in the mills.

The Blacks: Limitations of
Negotiated Aggregation

Thus far in its history, the processes which have brought other groups
into community institutions have failed the black population of the
area. The black settlement in Millgate dates back to World War I, but
the black families have generally been excluded from the negotiations
which brought their white contemporaries to prominence in community
institutions. A history of discrimination in mill hiring, exclusion from

union membership, and inequities in the real estate market made it almost impossible for blacks to enlarge their neighborhood settlement in Millgate. Nor were they able to move outward from that neighborhood of first settlement as they experienced occupational mobility inside the steel mills. Therefore, the black settlement in Millgate steadily lost its most stable and talented families to settlement outside the community. Over time the black neighborhood institutions in Millgate developed to serve a dependent lumpen proletariat of unemployed, aged, recent migrants and welfare families. Thus when a slate of steel unionists led by black workers finally succeeded to power in the South Works, the plant directly adjacent to Millgate, that election generated little enthusiasm among the neighborhood's black population. As one of my informants expressed it during the campaign, "You see how it is in this neighborhood. There ain't no union for the guys who work these corners."

The growing black population of South Chicago now resides in the newer and more middle-class neighborhoods of the community's western frontier. This black population represents the southward extension of Chicago's "black metropolis." It is not a specifically steelworking population as are the whites who dominate the traditional mill neighborhoods of the area. Nevertheless, the black invasion of South Chicago is also bringing numbers of working-class black families into neighborhoods such as Irondale and the Bush. Most white residents perceive that the racial composition of these neighborhoods is destined to change in the next decade. One continually hears gossip about this or that block where "they are already moving in." And, in general, in the white neighborhoods adjacent to these racially changing areas there is a new sense of pragmatism in discussing the future of community institutions. Leaders of the older white ethnic groups increasingly recognize the necessity of negotiating with leaders of black primary groups in the mills and the neighborhoods.

Blacks compete more and more as powerful actors in negotiating aggregations of leaders in the local unions and in South Chicago ward politics. Although the races may never form stable, integrated settlements, blacks and Mexicans certainly will share neighborhoods in the decades to come. Serbians, Poles, Italians, and Croatians who remain in other mill neighborhoods are increasingly forced to share their power and prestige with talented black leaders. Of course none of this change takes place easily. Political mobilization, the formation of unified political primary groups, and competition among such groups are often marked by hatred, violence, and the bitter frustration of defeat. On the other hand, for all the groups which have made their histories in South

Chicago, succession to power after generations of struggle is a prize
worth taking with immense pride.

Neighborhood and Community

Social change in South Chicago is mediated through the joint processes
of segmentation and aggregation. Segmentation of the population
according to ascribed statuses has allowed generations of new immigrants to establish their families in the area's local neighborhoods.[4]
Street corner primary groups, *Landsmannschaften*, tavern friendships,
ethnic parishes, and fraternal benefit societies all segregate South
Chicago's population in a segmental structure of equivalent ethnic
primary groups. Were it not for additional community-forming
processes, the area would remain fragmented in a series of often hostile
ethnic territories. But the adult members of these segmental ethnic
groups also meet in genuine communal institutions. Leaders in the steel
mills, in the local unions, and in the ward political organizations
negotiate aggregations of people from the various ethnic segments of
the area. Succession to power and respectability in community institutions depend on the negotiations which form new primary groups and
which break down social barriers in ethnic neighborhoods.

The unionists who compete for power in steel locals, the precinct
activists who mobilize the political aspirations of their neighbors, the
tavern owners who nurture tavern friendship groups, these and similar
actors negotiate new aggregations of residents which bridge the ethnic
territorial segmentation of the area. These new groupings of South
Chicago residents emerge in the processes of competition in communal
institutions. They are negotiated aggregations because they come about
through direct political conflict and cooperation rather than in
"underlying" processes such as competition for territorial dominance.
The steel industry and the patterns of settlement in mill neighborhoods, as presented in chapters 2 and 3 of this volume, create the
ecological potential for ethnic aggregation in community institutions.
Nevertheless, the breakdown of segmented social structures and the
aggregation of groups according the more broadly defined criteria of
commonality grow out of competition for political influence in broader
communal institutions. Parts III and IV of this study show that the
competition for succession in local unions and in ward party organizations is a motive force behind many of the adaptations of ethnic social
structure in this industrial community.

From this perspective the community's complex system of culturally
distinct neighborhoods, its heterogeneous industrial workplaces, and

its boundary-defining communal institutions offer a micro-level view of the perplexing issues of tradition versus modernity in contemporary society. South Chicagoans are not just "white ethnics" who strive to preserve the provincial values of little neighborhoods against outsiders whom they perceive as threatening. They are also leaders and followers at the local level who act in a political ecology which has all the main configurations, in much simplified form, of political struggle in larger societies. Perhaps this statement could be made about almost all local communities, but South Chicago's particular characteristics make it an especially appropriate choice for a study of racial and ethnic change in blue collar America. Because it is centered upon a base of heavy industry and because its cultural groups are representative of the industrial Midwest, this study of South Chicago should help fill a number of gaps in our knowledge of contemporary life in all such urban manufacturing communities.

Commenting on the fascination which Chicago intellectuals have always held for their city, Richard Wright observed in his preface to *Black Metropolis* that "Chicago is the *known* city; perhaps more is known about it, how it is run, how it kills, how it loves, steals, helps, gives, cheats, and crushes than any other city in the world." Wright gives much due credit for this knowledge to writers such as Carl Sandburg, Nelson Algren, James Farrell, and Theodore Dreiser, but he reserves even more admiration for Robert Park, Louis Wirth, Robert Redfield, and E. Franklin Frazier, the social scientists who "relied upon the city for their basic truth of America's social life," and who were "not afraid to urge their students to trust their feelings for a situation or an event."[5]

Although Wright's statement is generally true even today, the classic period of "Chicago School" social science itself did not produce any notable studies of industry or of industrial communities such as South Chicago. In fact from all of pre-World War II American social science, W. Lloyd Warner and Leo Strole's Yankee City series and Helen and Robert Lynd's *Middletown* and *Middletown in Transition* remain the most widely cited works on industrial communities. Neither of these extraordinarily valuable series studied an industrial community within a larger metropolitan city. On the other hand, the general empirical and theoretical work of this earlier generation of American sociologists still provides many of the analytical constructs necessary for a contemporary community study such as this one. Prominent among these are the concepts of the "natural area," "ethnic succession," "community status," and "the primary group."

South Chicago is a natural area according to every criterion of Park and Burgess's famous theory. Perhaps most important, the dominance of the steel industry in the area stimulates the emergence of "its own peculiar traditions, customs, conventions, standards of decency and propriety," and even to some extent produces a specialized language of its own. Each of the never ending stream of new immigrant groups has had to assimilate aspects of its own culture to the overriding culture of this steel community. Every new cultural group has had to overcome the disorganizing experience of resettlement. Each has had to reorganize its social structures for succession in the "secondary associations" of the community.

What earlier Chicago studies tended to neglect, however, is that each new group's succession to local prestige and power, and even to better jobs, education, and housing does not come naturally through ecological processes or individual adjustment alone. The relative success of different cultural groups in American communities is highly dependent upon their success in political negotiations and competition in political institutions. This is an orientation which did not emerge strongly until after World War II with the publication of studies such as Nathan Glazer and Daniel Moynihan's *Beyond the Melting Pot,* and Robert Dahl's *Who Governs?* The Glazer and Moynihan study is particularly concerned with a macrosociological analysis of assimilation and class mobility in New York City's major minority groups. In contrast, South Chicago offers the opportunity to examine processes of ethnic political negotiation at closer range in a community with a much less complex order of classes and status groups. In this study of blue collar ethnicity it is possible to devote more analysis to the effects of industrial occupations, neighborhood social organization, and primary group formation.

Studies of working-class communities in the United States and Europe have often focused a great deal of attention on the role which primary groups play in forming the social structure and the morality of urban neighborhoods. W. F. Whyte's *Street Corner Society*, Herbert J. Gans's *The Urban Villagers*, and Gerald Suttles's *The Social Order of the Slum* are important American studies in which the male peer group is the major unit of analysis. Each of these authors, Suttles in particular, is concerned with the processes which combine, or fail to combine, adolescent and adult primary groups into larger institutions. Studies by Elizabeth Bott, Michael Young, and others have signaled the importance of kinship-based primary groups in English working-class communities. Although all these studies have analytical frameworks and empirical findings which make each unique, the authors have all documented the persistent efforts of working-class people to form deep communal roots. Thus each has questioned the assumption of Durkheim and others that with industrialization "the provincialism of the parish vanishes never to return." It remains then to study the conditions under which primary groups may be the vehicles for social change as well as the guardians of traditional virtues and provincial morality.[6]

The outlines for pursuing this goal are suggested in Edward Shils's essays, "The Study of the Primary Group" and "Primordial, Personal, Sacred, and Civil Ties."[7] Primordial attachments are those which are based on perceptions that people have prior claims to one another's loyalty and trust, as is the case in primary groups organized according to notions of common descent. Such groups as families, adolescent corner gangs, and adult neighborhood peer groups, commonly analyzed in the studies previously mentioned, tend to exclude the possibility of primary relations among people of obviously different descent, such as blacks and whites. But South Chicago, like so many other working-class communities, is now witnessing the rapid arrival of black and Mexican newcomers. Also, in this community ethnic and neighborhood primary groups are basic units of local social organization. The question here is whether the organization of primary groups according to the primordial sentiments of kinship, ethnicity, and neighborhood descent precludes the possibility that blacks and whites may never live more or less as one people in the community. Of course the ability to answer this question depends in part on how well one can understand the processes which have allowed the various white ethnic groups of the community to live together over the generations. In general the residents' notions of prior attachments are subject to continual negotiation and modification. Likewise, the organization of primary groups based on more personal friendships is an outcome of the processes which bring people of diverse cultural backgrounds together for partisan political competition in civil institutions.

2

Mill Work and Primary Groups

For steelworkers from the Bush, Irondale, Slag Valley, the East Side, or Millgate, the steel plant is the milieu which presents the greatest opportunity as well as the necessity to form personal attachments transcending the moral and physical boundaries of neighborhoods. Seniority and skill are the main criteria in making work assignments, and attachments formed over a lifetime in the mills often cut across the racial, ethnic, and territorial groupings which may divide men in the outside community. In the multitude of work groups which the functional and temporal division of labor in the steel industry necessitates, the workers form loyalties more broadly defined than those of their locality groups outside the mills. Certainly there are instances where outside sources of tension and cleavage threaten the smooth operation of an industrial plant. The overwhelming trend is for men to have to live with those tensions but sometimes accommodations are made which pave the way for negotiated aggregations to emerge in which steelworkers of diverse backgrounds form primary groups in the rank and file and in the union.

This same "knitting" of racial groups in industry has been noted by Hughes. Gouldner also points out that "the patterns in the plant (gypsum) paralleled those found in the community. Young versus old, Oscar men versus Tyre men, farmer against villager, and more recently veteran against non-veteran. These were gentle tensions, barely rippling the surface, but noticeable to the observer." As in Gouldner's gypsum plant, the profound differences in the community are much moderated in the steel mills. They are manageable ripples though not nearly so gentle as those observed by Gouldner. The greater disturbance produced by these cleavages in the Chicago steel mills indicates the seriousness of the divisions which are being bridged.[1]

The white ethnic steelworker routinely works next to black men from the South Side ghetto; the Mexican worker from Millgate shares a locker room with Serbian steelworkers from Slag Valley. Yet the degree to which common work experiences provide the basis for primary group formation transcending communal cleavages is problematic. White workers on the East Side or in Irondale may spend their entire occupational careers working with black men and still bar blacks from their neighborhoods. Mexicans from Irondale gain intimate knowledge about their Serbian workmates from the same neighborhood, but after work the two groups drink in different taverns. On the other hand, it is possible for a black worker to gain a reputation as a leader not only among other blacks but with his white co-workers as well. For example, the industrial community in the steel mills is one in which black workers routinely achieve positions of political responsibility as grievancemen and local union leaders.

In considering a steel mill as a moral community in which prejudices and cleavage brought in from outside are ameliorated or exacerbated, it is necessary to look at the ecology of work groups in the plant, the authority system of the turn, the grievance system, and the demands which the union places upon work groups in union politics. The way in which all these conditions coincide can best be seen in a case study of Mill No. 3 of the Wisconsin Steel Works.

Steel Mill No. 3

Wisconsin Steel's No. 3 Mill is a typical steel rolling mill located in Irondale. Although this is the only mill I worked in, my contacts with steelworkers in other mills and departments of the Wisconsin Steel Works, as well as in other plants in the area, would bear out these observations on work groups. Thus the observations recorded here, although confined to one rolling mill, were found to have analogies in the experience of respondents from a variety of steel industry work settings.

No. 3 Mill is a sixteen-inch rolling mill built in 1920. Rolling mills, in general, are the last major productive unit in the steel-making process, which begins with the blast furnaces and coke plants and continues to the open hearth and basic oxygen furnaces where steel ingots are produced. Ingots are reheated in the blooming mill, where they are shaped into square billets for use in the rolling mills. From the blooming mill the billets are shipped to rolling mills where the steel is again heated for shaping into any number of finished products, from steel wire to structural steel girders and metal plate. All these productive units of the steel plant are linked by a system of wide- and narrow-gauge rail spurs, and in the Gary-Calumet area all basic steel plants are fed raw materials from the Great Lakes orefields and the coal regions of southern Illinois.

No. 3 Mill is called a "merchant mill" because it produces flat and round steel of fairly narrow gauge, a product which may be sold to steel warehouses where steel products are retailed. Despite its name, however, most of the customers who buy steel directly from No. 3 Mill are large manufacturing concerns in the automotive and farm implement industries. Other types of rolling mills produce steel plate, steel tubing, structural steel, or sheet steel. No. 3 Mill, then, is somewhat unusual in the Gary-Calumet steel industry because it produces a great variety of special rolled steel products including some which are quite difficult to roll, such as plowshares and grader blades. These products are difficult to produce because they require high-carbon steel to be forced through complex roll passages in order to shape the desired product. Specialty products such as these require veteran work crews who can set up the mills rapidly and with a minimum of wasted or scrap steel. For this reason the Wisconsin Steel Company advertises itself as "Creative Steel Bar Specialists."

The advantages which other steel companies gain in producing large quantities of a single product, such as sheet steel of one size for the automotive industry, No. 3 Mill makes up for by servicing a large number of orders for a diversity of products. More than in other plants, therefore, the process of continuous production must be halted quite frequently in No. 3 Mill for changes in the machinery of the mill. To remain competitive, such changes must be made rapidly, and thus the normal emphasis on teamwork and intergroup cooperation which characterizes the steel industry is even more important here. This has direct bearing on the present study, for the more often the process of production is halted and rearranged, the more visible are sources of tension and conflict in the work process.

*Residential and Ethnic
Distribution of the Employees*

A steel mill is a communal institution to the extent that the men who work in it also live in the surrounding mill neighborhoods. The upper echelons of managerial personnel, the supervisors and the foremen, do not normally live in the South Chicago community. In fact as early as 1901 observers noted the absence of managerial officials from the South Chicago mill neighborhoods.[2] In general the mill supervisors, personnel officers, and plant managers live in suburban communities to the southwest of the steel neighborhoods, in communities such as Park Forest and Beverly Hills.

Table 2				Ethnic Distribution in No. 3 Mill Hierarchy (Percent)		
	N.E. & Irish	S. Slav.	Italian	Black	Mexican & Other Span.	(N)
Plant supervisors ...	100	...	...	...	...	(7)
Mill foremen	33	58	...	8	...	(12)
Crew chiefs	25	62	12	...	...	(8)
Rank and file	5	19	5	33	37	(550)

The residential distance between managers and blue collar workers also corresponds to clear ethnic differences among the personnel. Table 2 shows that the plant supervisors are still overwhelmingly of northern European origin. Even after two generations in the plant, the southern European groups have only recently succeeded to middle level managerial positions as foremen. It is important to note that in this capacity they continue to work directly on the line of production and generally follow the same temporal cycle of work as do the rank-and-file workers. This general pattern of ethnic clustering also applies within the blue collar stratum of the plant's labor force. Thus table 3 reveals that while blacks and Mexicans are represented in all the occupations considered here, they are clearly overrepresented in the lower status occupations of chipper and laborer.

Table 3					Ethnic Distribution in Four Rank-and-File Departments (Percent)		
Skill & Dept.	N.E. & Irish	Polish	S. Slav	Italian	Black	Mexican & S. Slav.	(N)
Mill	13.8	23.9	19.5	5	22.4	15.2	(138)
Loading ...	10.0	12.0	14.0	15.0	19.0	30.0	(100)
Chipping ..	0.3	0.3	0.2	0.2	40.0	52.0	(281)
Labor	0.0	9.0	9.0	0.0	67.0	12.0	(31)

With the exception of black steelworkers and those of northern European origin, the majority of rank-and-file steelworkers and their union officials do live in the South Chicago mill neighborhoods. The Italian and South Slavic workers are concentrated in Irondale, Slag Valley, and the East Side. The latter is the neighborhood of second settlement for these groups, as well as for Polish steelworkers from South Chicago proper. The Mexicans in No. 3 Mill are most likely to live either in Millgate and South Chicago proper or in Irondale, a reflection of their segmentation in the outside community. And as would be expected, only a small proportion of the black workers in No. 3 Mill live in the community, in Millgate, while the majority commute to the mill from more distant neighborhoods in Chicago's black community. The seniority of black workers is highly correlated with the distance they live from the plant. Generally the younger workers tend to live in Woodlawn and black neighborhoods to the north of South Chicago, while older and more highly paid black steelworkers tend increasingly to live in the newly opened neighborhoods in Roseland and areas to the west of the Calumet Expressway along Ninety-fifth Street.

In summary, with the exception of black workers and supervisory personnel, No. 3 Mill's labor force is recruited largely from the mill neighborhoods of South Chicago. Far from representing the separation of place of work and place of residence, the steelworker's occupational world is to a large degree an extension of his community environment. Since the majority of his workmates live in the mill neighborhoods of South Chicago, a man's performance at work is also a communal performance; there is a high chance that the South Chicago man's actions in the mill will become part of his reputation outside the plant. Also, if the work force of No. 3 Mill is considered in the aggregate, there should be ample opportunity at work for men from the various South Chicago mill neighborhoods to form attachments with men of the same or differing ethnicity in other local neighborhoods.

Black workers are the major exception to these observations. Since they usually do not come from steel-mill neighborhoods in South Chicago, and are not concentrated in mill neighborhoods of their own—those who live in Gary, Indiana, for example—a black worker's behavior in the mill does not reflect directly on his reputation in the community. Of course, black workers are often regarded as a cohesive group by foremen and others responsible for the overall occupational community in No. 3 Mill, but the solidarity of blacks must emerge in the plant itself if at all. There is no prior residential basis for solidarity among black workers as exists, for example, among Serbian steelworkers who have grown up together in the neighborhoods at the gates to the plant. This situation is reflected quite directly in the climate of ethnic and racial relations which one encounters in No. 3 Mill.

The Climate of Ethnic and Racial
Relations in No. 3 Mill

The participant observer in No. 3 Mill immediately encounters a bewildering emphasis on ethnic, territorial, and racial attachments in the steelworker's occupational world. The first question addressed to a new man whose communal attachments are not obvious is What are you? meaning what is your ethnicity and where do you come from in the area? This is important information because one soon learns that an assumption governing relations in the mill is that men of the same race and ethnicity will stick together despite conflicting expectations which may emerge in the work process. It is considered "normal" for the Polish to defend their compatriots in a conflict, for Mexicans to prefer to work with other Mexicans, for blacks to spend their leisure time at work with other blacks. And a favorite topic of conversation at work centers on the interpretation of events on the basis of racial and ethnic stereotypes: Polish workers are considered to be less intelligent than others; Mexicans and blacks are thought to be lazy; southern whites are considered heavy drinkers; Italian and "DP" Slavs are called penny pinchers. These stereotypes are continually being invoked in explanations of an individual's behavior, or in favorable comparisons between someone's actions and what would have been expected of him according to the racial or ethnic stereotype. "For a Pollack he's no dummy," "That nigger works like a white man," "He's the most generous Guinea you'll ever meet"; these are the daily currency of conversation in a situation which brings men together across ethnic and racial boundaries.

The blunting of ethnic tensions over years of common occupational experience is seen in the custom of face-to-face, joking relationships over ethnic differences. Among some white workers it is permissible to make jokes about another's ethnic status. Polish, Serbian, and Italian workers will engage in joking contests in which ethnic stereotypes are made fun of. This is less common between Mexicans and other white ethnic steelworkers. When Mexicans come from the South Chicago mill neighborhoods and know Serbian and Italian workers as neighbors, the same joking relationships are found, but between Mexicans from outside the community and others such face-to-face release of tension is less common. Finally, the racial cleavages in the mill are more tension-laden than any others. Whites and blacks make use of racial and ethnic epithets in private, but in situations of overt conflict between white and black steelworkers these epithets are used as insults of last resort. When men begin calling each other "white mother-fucker" and "nigger bastard" in the open, nearby men will break in and separate the antagonists, for fighting is the next step in this escalation of tempers.

During my fieldwork in No. 3 Mill, I encountered innumerable situations of conflict between white ethnic workers, blacks, and Mexicans in which it appeared quite certain that had these sources of communal cleavage not divided the men it would have been possible for them to settle their differences themselves. As a foreman I was continually called in to settle disputes and work stoppages in one or two crews who were protesting a grievance against another crew. The cases which came to my attention most often involved groups of black workers who were protesting their treatment by heterogeneous groups of Italians, Serbians, and Poles, although there were also examples of unresolvable conflict between groups of white workers of different ethnicity. Invariably these disputes arose out of problems in the division of labor which create breaks in the flow of material between segmented work groups. But ethnic and racial differences between the groups often make it impossible for the work groups involved to arrive at mutually satisfying accommodations without recourse to a supervisor.

While instances of racial and ethnic conflict abounded in No. 3 Mill, and will be treated more systematically in succeeding chapters, instances of actual physical conflict were rare. Fighting is not taken lightly either by supervisory personnel or the rank-and-file workers, and the uncontrollable loss of temper which ends in violence is strongly proscribed. Thus veteran workers in No. 3 Mill speak disparagingly of another mill in the plant (No. 8 Mill) because of the number of fights which occur there. The explanation offered for this unusual situation of hostility hinges on the fact that No. 8 Mill was built only five years ago. This suggests that the common culture of a steel mill emerges only over time, as various subgroups seek to negotiate arrangements which will allow the smooth ordering of age, racial, and ethnic differences. The logical beginning in the search for such arrangements is in the various work groups which constitute the functional division of labor in the plant.

The Ecology of No. 3 Mill
Work Groups

The steel industry, along with industries such as chemicals, oil-refining, and instruments, includes a balanced distribution of skill categories. In contrast to the automobile industry, in which the majority of work is performed by assembly line labor, steel production necessitates a wide range of work groups at different skill levels. There are few instances in the steel industry of assembly line work, and a great many examples of group machine tending and skilled work-group operations. In addition to the occupations directly related to the production of steel, the mills employ all the major categories of craft workers, including machinists, brick layers, carpenters, and electricians. These craft occupations normally are not employed in the direct line of production but serve in maintenance capacities.[3]

On the line of production itself, the first distinction is made between workers "on the mill" and those "on the floor" of the plant. The former include all the work groups employed at the furnaces, roll stands, and shears through which hot steel passes in the rolling process. Men on the floor are those employed in the capacity of loaders, machine operators, chippers, inspectors, and laborers. In both areas of the mill it is important to note that, with the exception of certain machine operators, all the work done on the line of production involves work groups rather than single workers. The greatest amount of face-to-face interaction at work occurs in these work groups, and it is therefore appropriate to compare the effect of different work groups on the conduct of ethnic and racial relations in the mill.

The work groups which will be compared here include mill hands (workers on the mill), loaders, laborers, and foremen. Each of these groups is represented in the direct line of production and all (with the foremen excepted) are considered either semiskilled operatives or unskilled labor. Each of the work groups is organized according to a skill hierarchy (here the laborers are an exception) in which the leader of the group is termed a crew chief and has the longest seniority and greatest skill in the group. Figure 2 outlines the place each of these work groups occupies in the rolling mill.

Work groups whose relationship to the ecology of the steel plant is such as to encourage the development of primary attachments among men are also most likely sites of change in the degree of cleavage between ethnic, racial, and neighborhood groups in the mill. Independent of whatever conflicts and solidarities the men bring with them to the plant from their neighborhoods, the type of attachments they form in their work groups depends on the location of the work group in the process of steel production, the actual work the group does, and the group's relationships with foremen and other figures of plant authority. Work groups in which the majority of workers are newcomers to the plant form weaker attachments and antipathies than groups in which the men have been together for fifteen or twenty years. Similarly, work groups which perform dangerous work, or work which is quite central to the production of steel, form stronger attachments than groups in which the work is merely tedious. The status of a work

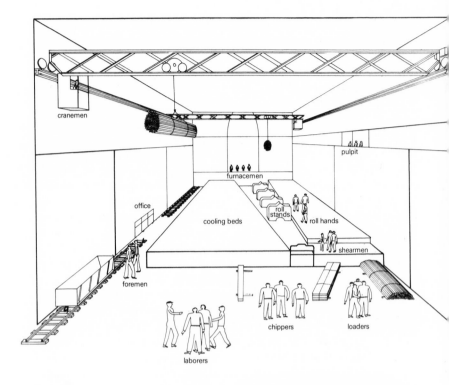

Figure 2   Scheme of No. 3 Mill, showing the
physical scale of the workplace as well
as the approximate spatial position-
ing of each of the work groups discussed.

group in the organization of the "turn" is also an important determinant of the degree to which primordial cleavages may be modified at work.

The Turn and the Foremen

The turn refers to the set of work groups organized under the supervision of a team of foremen. In the steel industry the turn is the basic unit of the temporal division of labor, for since steel is produced twenty-four hours a day, each turn must alternate in sharing the hours around the clock. Thus the steelworker's hours change each week, from the day shift to the swing shift, or "the three to eleven," and finally the night shift, from eleven at night to seven in the morning. Once he settles into a work group the steelworker may remain on the same turn for years, always working through the temporal sequence with the same co-workers and foremen. Since the division of labor segments them from other work groups in the same plant, the foreman becomes an extremely important link in defining the workers' relation to groups whom they encounter only indirectly or meet for fleeting moments before and after work hours. The foremen's relationship with a group may account in large part for both the group's internal solidarity and its reputation among other work groups on the turn.

The Work Group in the Mill

In No. 3 Mill the relationship between a work group's role in the ecology of the steel mill, and the modification of ethnic, racial, and neighborhood cleavages is best seen in three work groups, the laborers, the mill hands, and the loaders. Each of these work groups differs in the primordial cleavages it faces and the types of aggregations which are negotiated within the group. Age and racial cleavages divide the laborers; the majority of young laborers are black while the majority of older laborers and supervisory personnel are white. And among the black laborers there is another dimension of cleavage between young men who are gang members and those who are not. In the case of the mill hands and the loaders the cleavages are more complex; in their work groups there are divisions among blacks and whites as well as ethnic and neighborhood cleavages.

Over the work group's history, modification of these cleavages may range from increased exacerbation of tension and conflict to the formation of interracial and interethnic friendships which carry over to the outside community. For their part the laborers remain badly divided among themselves and from other work groups in the mill. The mill hands are a mixed case, for the nature of their work allows men of differing ethnicity and race to work on quite amicable terms; but at the same time the development of deeper friendships among men may be inhibited in the work process. Finally, the loaders' work encourages the development of attachments among workers which may be extremely close and frequently extend outside the plant to unite families of differing ethnic and neighborhood affiliations.

No. 3 Mill Laborers

The laborers who work in No. 3 Mill are divided into three subgroups. First are those who work at various jobs on the finishing end of the mill. This group is organized into a pool of unskilled workers, most of whom are relatively new to the mill community. Every day at the beginning of each new shift, the foremen on duty assign these laborers to the various jobs in the mill which require laboring work. Some men assist operators on straightening machines, others assist the shear crew at the end of the mill, and still others work at various operations which involve inspection and preparation of the steel for shipment to the customer or to other locations in the plant.

The second laborers' group is composed of older men who work on the chipping beds. The chippers' job requires that two-man teams use electric grinders and electric chisels to remove surface impurities from various steel products. In No. 3 Mill four pairs of chippers work on every eight-hour shift. Normally they are older men who have remained in the labor category because the chipping department traditionally pays quite large piecework incentive bonuses. Also, unlike the general finishing end laborers, the chippers work in their own section of the mill—the chipping beds—and they are not subject to continual reassignment by the foremen as are the general laborers.

The third important group of laborers are referred to as the "light duty men." For the most part they are older steelworkers, usually over the age of forty-five, who have suffered disabilities either through injury or ill health and have too many years of seniority in the plant to seek more suitable employment in another plant but too little seniority to take their pensions. Some are walking reminders that despite elaborate safety programs, the production of steel continues to take a toll on fingers, arms, and eyes, to say nothing of lives. In No. 3 Mill a man with one arm delivers intraplant mail, another fellow with too few fingers to perform his skilled job is given odd clean-up tasks, and one who has suffered a heart attack assists in the foreman's office. Still other light duty men work as laborers, along with the "new hires" in the mill, with the understanding that the light duty men will aid in the organization of the laborers' work but will not perform any heavy tasks.

As the preceding description would suggest, all three of the laboring groups are among the lowest status workers in No. 3 Mill's occupational community. Of the three the general laborers are clearly the lowest of all, for the jobs of the other two groups have features which compensate for the very low levels of skill entailed. The chippers are able to earn as much as more highly skilled workers on the mill because of the favorable terms of their incentive system. The light duty men do not earn much more than the general laborers, but they receive informal rewards owing to their role in the mill's network of communications.

Light duty men are scattered through No. 3 Mill's labor force because of the benevolence of management and often at the insistence of local union officers. Deprived of their full physical capacities, as well as their job security, the light duty men as a rule make up for their loss of status by becoming carriers of gossip and rumor between work groups and between territorial units of the entire steel plant. Unfortunately their excellent knowledge of No. 3 Mill's "ropes" and of the personalities of the plant's managerial personnel is available only to men of similar communal backgrounds. In general the men who manage to become placed on light duty assignments after personal tragedies also tend to be those from the ethnic and residential groups represented in the South Chicago mill neighborhoods. In consequence of this, the groups which are most in need of the information which the light duty men could provide, that is, the groups of new laborers who most typically come from outside the mill neighborhoods, are deprived of this information. To understand why this is true and significant one must examine the background and social organization of the general laborers and chippers in further detail.

Laborers: Race, Gang
Membership, and Work-Group
Solidarity

The solidarity which emerges among the general laborers is a product of the antagonism they all develop toward the No. 3 Mill foremen. Over time the rural-urban cleavages dividing the young black laborers are replaced by hostility toward the white foremen who assign the laborers their tasks and act as straw bosses in overseeing the performance of these tasks. Over 90 percent of the current group of general laborers in No. 3 Mill are young black workers from Chicago's South Side. Despite the common racial and age characteristics which this group of young men share, the organization of their work in No. 3 Mill hampers the emergence of strong personal ties in their work groups. No sooner are friendships formed than they are broken by changes in work assignments. Foremen and other supervisory personnel regard the young black laborers as a homogeneous group and attribute collective solidarity to them, but in fact this is not the case. As newcomers to the steel mill, and strangers to each other, the young black workers' groups are no more cohesive than an equivalent group of white workers would be. Indeed there are numerous sources of tension and disunity which divide the black general laborers. The most common is the tension between men from the rural south and those who have grown up in Chicago and are members or affiliates of the South Side's major youth gangs.

Gang membership itself does not cause visible tension between members of rival gangs who work in the mill. Rather, the "street wise" style of dress and speech of the gang affiliate marks him off from the southern migrant with only a few years of residence in Chicago. Southern black migrants, who have not been socialized through adolescence into the major gang networks, are intimidated by the suggestion of gang activity which appears throughout the plant. The bathrooms of No. 3 Mill, for example, are covered with epithets common to the Blackstone Rangers and the Devil's Disciples, two major black gangs. Much of this graffiti repeats the wall slogans used to mark off turf in the gang neighborhoods. "Mightly Black P Stone" on one wall is countered by "Stones Ain't Shit, D's Run It" on another, as members of the rival gangs carry their neighborhood opposition into the steel mill. But occurring on neutral territory, and among young men who do not know one another's reputations from their neighborhoods, this opposition never assumes more serious proportions than joking and signifying. Yet this level of gang activity is sufficient to cause the southerners to request assignments with men of similar background rather than chance being placed with Chicago-born black laborers who they feel are likely to make trouble for them if only by teasing their "country" mannerisms.

The sense of racial consciousness and solidarity which eventually transcends this rural-urban cleavage is created in the mill itself. Most often it arises as a result of the black workers' negative experiences with white foremen. Only the laborers, who do not work at a fixed place in the mill and whose work is not ordered by the flow of steel from the mill, are subject to the direct orders of the foremen. In addition to the racial hostility which young blacks bring initially to the plant, their dependence on orders from the foremen creates a situation in which the white foreman becomes the stereotypical example of "the man," the objectification of everything which is hateful about being a new black worker in a white-dominated setting. The laborers usually work on the "finishing end" of the plant where steel which has already been rolled is inspected and prepared for shipping. Since the operations which they perform are not central to the production of steel itself, the laborers' work is often given low priority by the foremen. Consequently the latter feel free to shift the laborers from one task to another, often with no explanation. Convinced that their work is of little consequence, the laborers resent the foremen's insistence that they continue working on what often seem to be "make work" tasks.

The foremen return the black laborers' hostility in kind. Even without the racial cleavage dividing the two, the laborers would be the foremen's primary "problem" at work because they are relatively new men who require direct supervision and training. Compounding the socialization issue with severe racial tension creates a situation in which the foremen come to view the black laborers as dangerous. Here differences in age, race, and authority combine to create severe strain in the occupational community of the mill, as for example in the following comment which is characteristic of the foremen's perception of the laborers.

(Milan, 45, white, Serbian from Slag Valley.) One of these young shines is going to kill a foreman someday soon. You can see it in their eyes, those black bastards. It used to be nice to work here, now with all these young niggers coming into the mill you never know what's going to happen. You take your life into your hands to tell them to do something. Half the time they stink of booze and they act like animals. Someday soon one of them is going to pull a knife on a foreman, that's the kind of garbage we're getting in here. You hardly ever see any white kinds coming into the mill anymore. When they do come in they're retards like young P—— and S—— there.

The foreman who expressed these attitudes was not considered by the black workers to be among the worst of those who directed their work. Unlike some who make it a practice to stand in surveillance over their work groups, this foreman showed a greater respect for the black workers' ability than is apparent in his comment. Milan was among those who adopted the practice of "contracting" with the laborers, that

is, he told them what he considered a fair day's work and allowed them
to determine their own pace. Among foremen who defined their role as
involving more direct supervision of the laborers, anti-black sentiments
were more virulent than the general fear and concern over loss of status
which Milan's comments suggest. Even the most skillful foremen often
found themselves acting out their part in the self-fulfilling prophecy.
The foreman's perception of the black laborers as a danger to his safety
and the blacks' anger and resentment often result in serious conflict
between the groups, as illustrated in the following example.

Milan (the same foreman quoted earlier) has been disturbed by two of
the black laborers, Josephs and Albert, who normally work on his turn.
They have been in the mill for almost a year and are among the highest
in seniority of all the young laborers. Both are Chicago-born, and
accustomed to street life, which they complain they miss when they
work evenings or nights. The two have become close friends in the mill
and often spend time together outside. Albert is small and well built.
He was a boxer for a while, to which the scars over his eyes attest.
Josephs is tall and thin and wears a goatee which gives his face a
Mephistophelian appearance. Both men are frequently absent on
week-end turns, and on other occasions have come to work noticeably
drunk.

Milan has had a hard time with the mill hands' crew chief (the roller)
because of Josephs and Albert. As senior laborers, Milan must send
them up to the mill on roll changes, but the chief roller has asked him
not to send them because they kid around too much. At the same time,
Tony, one of the cranemen on Milan's turn, has been needling him
about his relationship with the pair. Both Tony and Milan were boxers
in their youth in Irondale, and the craneman delights in describing to
Milan how well Albert moves his hands when he shadow boxes in the
mill. Josephs and Albert have become symbolic of Milan's feelings
toward the black laborers. He calls them Mau Maus and says he
intends to get them out of No. 3 Mill even if the higher management
will not back him up.

This Friday night the incident occurred which precipitated hostility
between the foreman and the two black laborers. Josephs came to work
somewhat late and told Milan that his friend Albert would be in
somewhat later. Milan told Josephs that Albert would be sent home and
that he should not bother coming in at all. Josephs began to protest,
waving his arms and stamping his feet in frustration. Milan threatened
to send him home also. Josephs became more angry and said, "No
white motherfucker is going to talk to me like that." Milan then told
Josephs to go home, "get your clothes and get out of the plant, you're
not working tonight. I'm going to file a discipline report on you." On
this note Josephs stalked off to the other end of the plant where he
began talking to the other black laborers. Milan then went to the

foreman's office and called the security guards to come and take Josephs from the mill. Furious, Josephs ran out of No. 3 Mill toward the cafeteria where he was picked up by the plant guards and escorted to the gates.

The assistant grievanceman, who was working that night on the mill, told Milan he would file a grievance with the union on Josephs' behalf. This assistant grievanceman, a veteran black mill hand, will be supported on the issue by the chief grievanceman for No. 3 Mill. Unfortunately for Milan, the latter is also his brother, and this new case will further aggravate a relationship already strained by the opposition into which their mill roles cast them.

Since their dealings with the foremen are so often marked by opposition and hostility, as seen in the preceding case, the young laborers must turn to some other group in the mill for socialization into the mill community. The nearest and culturally most congenial group of more experienced men are the chippers.

Laborers and Chippers

The chippers, the majority of whom are black or first-generation Mexicans, earn an hourly salary as well as an incentive bonus based on a piecework rate. When material is readily available and easy to work with, the chippers may earn as much as more highly skilled men in the plant. On the other hand, if the steel is difficult to work because of its shape, carbon content, or temperature, the chippers may prefer to do very little work. The men see no point in working hard if they can earn an hourly wage and there is little incentive bonus to be made. Therefore on days when the material is difficult to work, the chippers read newspapers, take long breaks, and cook food in the wood-burning stoves (salamanders) which are placed throughout the mill wherever men are not near enough to hot steel to be warmed. The foremen refer to this practice bitterly as "the chippers' " barbecue.

Over an average of five years or more experience in the mill, the chippers have learned a number of strategies with which to neutralize the foreman's influence over their work situation. In No. 3 Mill the chipping beds are located at the entrance to the mill where wandering supervisors are likely to see them. Thus when company executives are in the plant it is relatively easy to make the foremen look bad by making a show of taking it easy at those times. Chippers frequently punish foremen through the use of this and related devices to make the latter "look bad to the men across the street."

In their contact with the chippers the laborers also learn strategies with which to begin neutralizing the foreman's influence.[4] The chippers teach the laborers where to hide in the mill when they are tired, how to slip away from the workplace for an early quitting time, and what levels of output are considered minimum on various laboring jobs. When the laborers accumulate a year or two of seniority in the mill, they may have the option to earn relatively high pay immediately by choosing to work on the chipping beds rather than take the slower but ultimately more satisfying and profitable route to jobs in steel production. Since they are isolated from the production workers by the ecological arrangement of the plant, the black laborers have fewer opportunities to form attachments with the older and highly influential black workers "up on the mill." In consequence, the young black workers rarely learn about the more positive aspects of careers in the mill. Also the ecological separation of young laborers and experienced black mill hands presents serious obstacles to black unity in union politics, a subject which will be treated in a later chapter.

In summary, the laborers' status in the process of steel production, the fact they are strangers to each other and to the older workers when they enter the plant, and the racial antagonism which marks their dealings with the white foremen, all lead them to develop solidarity in opposition to the authority structure and overall culture of No. 3 Mill's occupational community. This racial solidarity is sufficient to ameliorate certain cleavages such as the tension between rural migrants and urban gang members, but it is insufficient as a basis of respect among workers to create primary relations in their group which could extend beyond the workplace itself. After work the young laborers generally go their separate ways, to their own neighborhoods of Chicago's black metropolis, and only the small percentage of men who will remain in the plant for over five years will have the opportunity to move into jobs such as exist "up on the mill" where it is easier to develop close personal attachments among workmates.

The Men on the Mill

In contrast to No. 3 Mill laborers, the men who work "up on the mill" have opportunities to develop friendships which cross ethnic and racial boundaries. The overriding ethic of the mill work groups rests on competence, not only at a specific task or set of tasks, but at fitting those tasks into the effort of the entire mill crew. Teamwork requires that men know where their tasks fit into the larger scheme of production, they must be willing to sacrifice their own efficiency for the greater efficiency of the larger unit. In comparison with the laborers, whose relationship to the production process is both marginal and highly individualized, the mill hands are part of a complex team effort in which they perform as total personalities before a large audience of peers. In due course the work performance of men who also live in the mill neighborhoods becomes the substance of a reputation in those neighborhoods. For men who are not from the mill neighborhoods, the knowledge which they gain about one another's characters and competence may supersede racial and ethnic stereotypes.

The merchant mill usually must change the size and shape of its product continuously. Since size changes may delay steel production for as long as five hours, the speed with which workers can "change over the mill" becomes an extremely important factor in the unit's productivity. At all times the operation of the rolling complex—called "the mill"—takes precedence over any other operation, such as loading or finishing steel which has come off the mill. When the mill is not operating because of size changes or roll changes, the primacy of steel production on the mill becomes even more apparent. If necessary, all other work in the plant may be halted while men on the mill monopolize the large overhead cranes to perform necessary operations. In consequence of this the workers on the mill crews pride themselves as much on their ability to change over the mill as they do on their total steel output. The need for speed and close cooperation during roll changes places a premium on teamwork and thus unifies the four subgroups which constitute the functional segments on the mill.

When the mill is operating at full tilt, slamming hot steel at thirty to forty miles an hour through the roll stands, there is little need for communication between furnacemen, operators, mill hands, or shearmen. The furnacemen push the white-hot steel billets out of the furnace at the prescribed intervals; operators twist handles and push buttons to guide the ever lengthening ribbon of steel back and forth through the passes at each roll stand; the mill hands walk between their stands to make sure there are no imperfections being rolled into the clean steel; and the men at the shear clip off the proper lengths of bars or flats to complete the customer's order.

When the mill is down for roll changes, the level of cooperation and communication necessary between groups is intensified. The men at the furnace must estimate how long the mechanical changes will take so that they can regulate the temperature of the steel in the furnace. If the furnace becomes too hot, the steel billets may become melted or fused, causing long delays while the men struggle to unclog the ovens. If the steel is too cold when the mill is ready to roll again the billets will jam in the roll stands and cause trouble for the roll hands. In changing the mill, the mill hands must cooperate with the overhead cranemen as they open the huge roll sets, remove the rolls, and replace them with ones of different sizes. A delay at one roll stand during this process can be multiplied at each of the others if the cranes are not kept moving rapidly. Similarly, the shearmen must finish cutting the steel from the previous order which is still cooling on the hot beds, and they must oversee the changing of the shear knives for the new order which will be coming through the rolls shortly.

The test of how well a mill crew operates comes when the first billets are pushed through the newly adjusted passes. If all goes well only a few minor adjustments will be required to begin rolling at full speed. If the steel is difficult to roll and major changes must be made on the roll stands, additional tons of steel will become scrap bars unfit for sale to the customer. Thus the rating of a mill crew is based not only upon how fast the men change the mill but on how little scrap is produced. Mistakes are easily translated into dollars lost for the company and for the men.

During the complicated procedures of changing the mill, each mill hand performs his tasks in full view of the others on the mill and the foremen as well. A man reveals much of himself while he deals with the various problems which arise on the job, and these glimpses at his personality become the substance of a reputation among his workmates on the mill. How patient is he when "breaking in" a new man? Does he toady to managerial officials when they stop to ask questions? Does he attempt to cover up or shift the blame for his own mistakes? Will he back down in an argument with foremen or another worker? Most important of all is the question of how well he performs his job. Even without the various problems which may arise, nothing reveals more about a steelworker to his co-workers than the skill and finesse with which he carries out his routine work. These measures of a man's character permit the mill workers to form attachments among themselves which transcend stereotypical racial, ethnic, and occupational differences.

Skill, Seniority, and Ethnicity
on the Mill

The history of recruitment policies in South Chicago's steel mills has caused differences in seniority and skill among mill workers to be compounded with racial and ethnic divisions. The Wisconsin Steel Works pursued a highly discriminatory hiring policy before World War II, and as a result almost all the workers now on the mill who were hired between 1920 and 1943 are from South Chicago neighborhoods and are of white ethnic backgrounds.[5] The great majority are of Polish and Yugoslav descent, and for the most part they are the second-generation sons of fathers who also worked in local steel plants. Approximately one-third of the men of southern and eastern European descent who came on the mill after 1951 are in the so-called DP group, and almost 90 percent of the men of eastern European origin who came on the mill in the 1960s are first-generation immigrants. Black workers were not hired in No. 3 Mill until World War II, and many blacks who were "moving up on the mill" in the forties were "bumped" down again by demobilized white workers who returned to claim their jobs after 1945. As table 4 indicates, the next cohort of black workers was hired in the Korean War period (1950–54) as the supply of white workers once again became limited. Another hiatus in the access of black workers to mill jobs occurred between 1954 and 1964, but in the mid-1960s, with American entry into Vietnam, black workers again broke into mill work in large numbers. Mexican-Americans follow almost the same pattern as do the blacks, although they are less likely to seek jobs on the mill for reasons which will be discussed later.

Table 4

Seniority, Ethnicity, and Race in No. 3 Mill, 1970 (Percent)

When Hired	N.E. & Other White	Polish	S. Slav	Black	Mexican	(N)
1920–24		70	30	0	0	(5)
1925–29	18	63	18			(11)
1930–34	40	26	33	0	0	(15)
1935–39	16	25	50	8	0	(12)
1940–44	0	28	17	39	22	(18)
1945–49	14	57	0	14	14	(7)
1950–54	0	10	5	70	10	(20)
1955–59	23	17	17	22	21	(17)
1960–64	33	33	6	13	2	(15)
1965–69	0	19	15	59	7	(39)

This history of hiring policies at the Wisconsin Steel plant, which is typical of the industry as a whole, has resulted in quite definite cohort patterns on the mill, and in the No. 3 Mill occupational community in general. The men with greatest seniority, largely those of South Slavic and Polish ethnicity have succeeded to jobs as operators. These jobs place them above the mill itself in "pulpits" at least two stories above the roll stands, where they control the flow of steel through the mill. In the mid-range of the seniority scale, among the roll hands and furnacemen, there is a high degree of ethnic and racial heterogeneity.

Here it is not uncommon for black roll hands to be in positions of authority over two or three white assistants. At the lowest levels of seniority on the rolling complex the large majority of youngest workers are black or Mexican.

Since the oldest workers sit high above the mill and watch everything that occurs there, this group is highly influential in the communications network of the entire plant. Foremen often rely on the pulpit workers for information about incidents on the mill. On the other hand, the day-to-day interaction on the mill itself is conducted between extremely heterogeneous groups of workers, and the potential difficulties which their ethnic and racial differences might cause are generally muted by the teamwork ethic.

During roll changes racial and ethnic cohorts are crosscut by the formation of work teams in which high seniority black workers often assume positions of responsibility and leadership. When the mill is operating smoothly a different situation prevails. Here the men have work stations which separate them somewhat; it is difficult for them to see each other over the geysers of steam and water which explode from the roll stands as bars of steel hit them; and it is impossible for them to hear one another over the din of heavy machinery. Conversations are out of the question when the mill is running, and so the men develop elaborate hand signals in order to communicate over distances greater than a foot or two. These conditions allow the mill hands to withdraw from personal relationships without damaging the effectiveness of the crew during roll changes, and if he so desires a man may spend his entire occupational career without necessarily forming close relationships with his co-workers. Thus the mill work setting is one in which men have the option, once they have demonstrated their competence, of becoming close or remaining distant from their fellow workers more or less at their own discretion. Furthermore, differences in skill and seniority do not often become sources of potential conflict between ethnic or racial groups on the mill.

Status distinctions based on the skill hierarchy on the rolling mill are muted by the position of mill work in the status system of the entire mill. Nominally all jobs on the mill are considered unskilled or semiskilled when compared with craft occupations, but in the rolling mill it is generally recognized that the mill hands are on an equal footing with all but the most experienced millwrights and electricians. First, while the mill hand may have no generalizable skills, he is intimately familiar with the idiosyncrasies of a particular mill. This is a familiarity which may take years to acquire, depending on the range of sizes and shapes of steel rolled and on the age of the mill. Old installations such as No. 3 Mill are said to be held together with "baling wire and spit." The machinery seems to have a personality of its own and the men who coax steel through it know they cannot easily be replaced with new men. This contributes to an egalitarian spirit among mill men of different seniority; all are pitted together against the whims of a cantankerous old steel mill.

A second feature of the mill hands' work which contributes to egalitarianism on the mill is the danger and discomfort which the work entails. Veteran mill hands frequently talk to newcomers about the old days of steel production when hot steel had to be turned with hand tongs by "catchers." As inheritors of the old catchers' jobs, the modern mill hand must use hand tools whenever the ribbon of red steel jumps from the rolling bed in what is called a cobbel. The danger of cobbels, which if they struck a man would cause serious injury or death, prevents non-mill hands from walking on or crossing the mill in other than protected walkways. This is especially true of upper level managerial personnel who are frequently unfamiliar with the safe areas of the mill and are not usually dressed to go near the intense heat of the hot steel. In consequence of this, the raised rolling complex becomes the private domain of the mill hands, much as the mine becomes the exclusive domain of the miner, and the egalitarianism which characterizes the miners' occupational culture is also found among rollhands in a steel mill.

The combination of narrowed skill hierarchy, emphasis on teamwork competence during roll changes, long average length of tenure, and common access to a personalized domain creates a spirit of egalitarianism and accommodation among mill hands which generally overcomes potential cleavages based on race and ethnicity. Evidence that this is so can be found in the political coalition which directs union politics in No. 3 Mill.

Negotiated Aggregations
on the Mill

The group of men who have run successfully for leadership of the union's grievance system in No. 3 Mill is an extremely heterogeneous aggregation of Serbians, Italians, Poles, and black mill hands. A Serbian has been the undisputed leader of this group for over nine years, but his success is due in large part to his ability to negotiate an aggregation composed of popular men from the roll stands, the furnace, the shear, and the pulpits. His fellow political activists are among the most respected men in their various work groups, and over years of common experience in the mill this heterogeneous aggregation of mill activists has become a primary group which defines its solidarity upon grounds of common fate and mutual respect rather than any prior criteria such as ethnicity, race, or neighborhood affiliation. The black, Serbian, Polish, and Italian men who control the grievance system in No. 3 Mill meet in a yearly cycle of extra-mill events such as wakes, retirement parties, union-sponsored social affairs, and informal gatherings at neutral taverns, i.e., those which are not identified with a particular ethnic or neighborhood segment in South Chicago.

Events often occur in steel plants in which an aggregation of men such as this one will have its solidarity severely tested. The following example, which continues the episode of conflict between black workers and white foremen is typical of the strains which routine incidents in the mill community may provoke in negotiated aggregations of steel workers.

When Milan (the foreman) sent Josephs (the black laborer) out of the plant under escort of the security guards he precipitated a serious grievance claim in No. 3 Mill. The assistant grievanceman in the mill that night was Johnson, a black roll hand who had been recruited by the Serbian grievanceman in the mill. Johnson, a burly senior roll hand with the reputation among black workers for "not taking any shit," confronted the foreman outside the latter's office after the incident. With much show of anger Johnson informed the foreman that he would file a grievance claim against him on Josephs' behalf. Inside the foreman's office, away from the public scrutiny of the men on the mill, the assistant grievanceman was obviously quite ambivalent about the Josephs case for he had had trouble with the young black man himself. On the other hand, the black workers felt that Josephs had been another victim of the foremen's bigotry, and they were expecting Johnson to represent their views.

Grievances in a plant are filed by the chief grievanceman rather than an assistant, and Johnson reported his version of the incident that morning when Pete, the Serbian grievanceman for the entire mill, came to work that morning on the day shift. Now the Serbian union activist in the mill was on the spot because many of the foremen and older white workers who sided with the foremen were men he had grown up with in South Chicago, and some were his ethnic peers. In fact the foreman, Milan, is his brother. Nevertheless, with a big union election due in a few months, the grievanceman could not afford to offend the black leaders in the leadership group. Over the years Pete worked hard to bring the most respected black roll hands into this group of activists. Many of them were now spending time at union-related social affairs, and an incident such as this could split the blacks from the other men. Thus Pete immediately sided with his black assistant and made a show of strong protest against the foreman on Josephs' behalf despite the further damage this action would do the grievanceman's reputation among his Serbian peers in the neighborhoods outside the mill.

Despite the grievanceman's firm action on the black laborer's behalf, the incident almost seriously weakened this aggregation of union activists. Johnson, the black assistant grievanceman, resigned his position a month after the incident, with the explanation that "it's too much pressure from all sides. What do I need that trouble for, man? I'll still support Pete, but he's gonna have to find another assistant for our turn. These white foremen just ain't ready." Rather than attempt to convince another of the black roll hands in his group of union activists to take the assistant's position, Pete appointed a young worker of Italian background who had grown up in Irondale, the neighborhood at the gate of the plant. This was a strategic appointment because the new assistant was younger than the black mill hands in this group of activists, and the new assistant will have to defer to them on many occasions both at work and in social situations. On the other hand the new assistant is well liked among Serbian and Italian residents in Irondale, and his appointment will bolster the group's sagging reputation in that mill neighborhood.

Work groups such as those on the mill may stimulate the development of negotiated aggregations among men of diverse backgrounds, but the preceding case suggests that such negotiations are subject to a wide range of pressures which arise not only at work but in the lives of men outside the plant. The mill is a favorable setting for aggregation across primordial barriers because it is possible for the mill workers to arrive at personal adjustments which are rather fluid. A mill hand may change the degree of his involvement with an aggregation of union activists, for example, without necessarily endangering the solidarity of his work group. Similarly, the leaders of negotiated aggregations which arise among mill hands may react to outside pressures by shifting roles in their group with little danger to the steady flow of steel through the mill. The same cannot be said of work and social relations among the loading crews where personal relationships are central to the operation of the work group, and thus the development of personal ties among workers is much more of an "all or nothing proposition."

The Steel Loaders

The loaders in No. 3 Mill are an example of what Mayo called a "natural group" in industry. Attachments in the loaders' groups become quite close.[6] Men frequently spend their leisure time with one another outside the plant, and this intimacy leads to an emphasis on the recruitment of men from the mill neighborhoods whose backgrounds are compatible with other crew members. Blacks and other outsiders to the mill neighborhoods have a difficult time gaining acceptance and forming primary relations with fellow workers on the loading crews. The intimacy of attachments on the loading crews, which outsiders find difficult to share, arises necessarily out of the organization of the loaders' work.

Working in small groups of seven to nine men, the loaders compete against the clock to move as much steel out of the plant as possible within the limits of their own comfort. On the rolling mill the worker is involved in the technology of steel production; he learns to manipulate an overpoweringly large yet delicate complex of machinery. The loader on the finishing end of the mill, on the other hand, is involved in a quite different aspect of the steel industry, namely, the articulation of the mill with outside markets. Loaders must be guided by monthly shipment quotas, inventory stocks, orders past due, and customer complaints. Thus where the mill man's concerns lead back into the steel plant, to the blooming mill and basic oxygen furnaces which supply his product, the loader's work is not so contained. The loader's concerns lead beyond the mill to the rail yards and truck warehouses. And although his work cannot lead him as high in the skill hierarchy as mill work can, the loader may use his knowledge of the steel business in applying for jobs with outside shipping contractors, a possibility which increases the loader's leverage with management.

The mill crew gains its solidarity and status from its central position in the production of steel but the loaders gain theirs from the importance of shipping in the business end of the industry. A good shipping department can mean the difference between profit and loss for an entire steel plant, and, at the same time, shipping is the most problematical step in the long chain of activities between the initial order for steel and final delivery. Railroad cars may be held up en route to the mill, trucks may be delayed while other orders are filled, and in the meantime tons of steel may be buried under more current orders coming off the mill. In consequence of the anxiety which surrounds the shipping process, the loaders are in a position to demand informal concessions from management which the technological constraints of the mill workers' jobs would not allow.

Most of the concessions granted to loaders by management officials involve informal controls over the work process which allow the loaders autonomy in budgeting their time during the workday. Additional concessions stemming from control over the work process allow loaders to accumulate large orders of steel for premium days such as Sundays and holidays when incentive rates are highest. These concessions in turn serve as the basis of cohesion and leadership in the loaders' work groups.

Leadership and Work-Group Solidarity

In the merchant mills loaders work in small groups of seven to nine men under the direction of a chief loader and a foreman (who usually has other responsibilities in the mill as well). Although the chief loader usually has at least fifteen years of seniority in the plant, his crew changes composition fairly rapidly through transfers into other locations in the plant. Normally labor turnover in work groups is a problem for management to ponder and solve, but in the loaders' case it is the chief loader, himself a rank-and-file worker, who must attempt to maintain a cohesive work group despite outside competition for his men.

Successful chief loaders use two tactics, good pay and good times, to maintain cohesion in their work groups. High incentive bonuses (good pay) and freedom to create leisure time (good times) through control over the work process are the fruits of concessions from management. But in addition to leisure time the loaders must attempt to create a milieu in the work group which facilitates the development of primary attachments between men on the crew. Whenever possible therefore the chief loaders attempt to compose a work crew of men who get along well with each other. This in turn leads them to encourage men with common community backgrounds to join the crew. A brief example of the content of communal and primary ties in the loaders' work crews is found in the following case of a craneman who wished to leave the loading crew.

Tony, the craneman, and his chief loader, Phillippe, were second generation Italians from South Deering. They had known each other since childhood and now both were in their mid-fifties. After a divorce and remarriage, the craneman moved to a nearby Indiana town, while Phillippe remained with his family in his father's two-family house in South Deering. Although they had spent their entire occupational careers at Wisconsin Steel, their current association spanned the last thirteen years of employment. Aside from their intimate knowledge of each other's life situations, the two men maintained a relationship at work which required the utmost in cooperation.

The overhead craneman rides in a cab about two stories above ground level, while on the floor the loaders direct him to bundles of steel which they chain to the boom of his crane. Through years of working together Tony and Phillippe had learned to anticipate each other's moves, and to work with such efficiency that a useless lift—to move a bundle which might have been left untouched—was cause for good-natured argument during breaks. Through their efficiency and leadership Phillippe's crew usually came out with the highest weekly incentive bonuses.

During their breaks, when the loading crew gathered in their shanty over lunch or coffee, the craneman often joked with the assistant loaders as they released the tension which had accumulated during the previous work period. Normally such tensions resulted from the loader's directions which move his men into "setups," situations which monopolize the use of the crane and which insure the greatest number of loaded bundles upon which incentive bonuses are based. Philosophical debates between Phillippe and his assistants, as well as Tony, who sided with the assistants, usually centered on the question of money in the scheme of human values. The assistants argued that Phillippe pushed them for nothing since despite all his money he had little to spend it on.

Two months before an opening for a craneman on another crew was to fall due, Tony began to suggest to the crew that he might bid for the job. Although no one seemed to believe him, his possible departure became the subject of long debates in the loaders' shanty. The younger men could not believe the two men would split so abruptly. But throughout the discussions Phillippe remained rather tight-lipped, suggesting only that if Tony left the crew he would make less money on the new job. To me, privately, he expressed the hope that Tony would stay with him, but he never said this directly to the craneman.

As the time for Tony to make his bid approached, it became clear that the decision was an extremely difficult one for him. He could speak of nothing else. Although he attempted to shrug it off, foremost in his mind was his long relationship with Phillippe and the strain his departure would create. On the other hand, he reasoned, since they were both Italians and had grown up together they would always remain friends. Why leave Phillippe and create the strain in the first place? Tony most often said it was because Phillippe "was too hungry for the buck," and it was unpleasant to work with him. But the loader he would work with was also a hustler so this explanation seemed to lack substance especially as grounds to end a relationship of thirteen years.

Two weeks before the time came to make his bid date Tony began announcing repeatedly to the entire crew that he would indeed take the new job. At the same time he began to show a new reluctance to smooth over the usual tensions in the crew. Phillippe also shifted his position, first, by implying that there were other good cranemen in the mill, second, by playing more of a conciliatory role with his assistants. While the two remained friends their feelings had cooled perceptibly.

It was common knowledge that next to the man he would replace on the other crew, Tony was easily the best craneman in the mill. Nevertheless he never confronted Phillippe with this fact. By the time it became appropriate for the craneman to bid for the new job it was clear that he would do so, and under Phillippe's leadership the crew had already begun to adapt to his departure.

Shortly after the arrival of the new craneman, a Mexican who was quite friendly with the young assistants, Phillippe began placing this man in situations where he had to perform as a socio-emotional leader in the manner of his predecessor. Tony, from his place with the new crew, expressed a combination of guilt toward Phillippe and pride that after thirteen years he had acted on his own. And after work, when the young loaders debated the merits of the case in their taverns, it was clear to them that the craneman's decision was more than a simple question of improving his conditions of work.

Blue collar work often involves men in what they consider to be serious value decisions, especially where work relationships are carried to the outside community. As the preceding example suggests, the steel loaders hardly enjoy the mill hand's option to limit the degree to which they develop personal attachments to their co-workers. The organization of the loaders' work and the composition of their work groups make it almost mandatory for them to form primary attachments with their workmates. And the fact that loaders are so often recruited from the nearby mill neighborhoods ensures that performances at work come to constitute the basis of reputations outside the mill.

Ethnic and Racial Aggregation on the Loading Crew

The paradox of the loaders' situation is that the necessity which they feel to form primary relationships also tends to limit the ability of the group to overcome racial divisions. Most loading jobs pass on to men with local ties in the outside mill neighborhoods, and black workers who come from beyond the area are at a disadvantage in competing for these positions. The Mexicans, on the other hand, are now neighbors of the older Italian families from the mill neighborhoods. Since many of the Italian men have secure positions in the loading department, the young Mexicans are able to use their neighborhood acquaintances in moving more freely on to the loading crews. These informal patterns of recruitment and the pressures in the work group to maintain close relationships may create quite severe difficulties for the black workers who do become loaders, as the following field notes will show.

Phillippe's loading crew, which is mainly recruited from among the Italian and Mexican residents of Irondale, also includes two black workers, Virgil and Michaels, who are on the crew because their seniority made it possible for them to bid for and obtain slots on the crew despite the chief loader's objections. In fact, Michaels, the older of the two, has enough seniority to make him assistant loader under Phillippe. When the latter has a day off, Michaels assumes command of the loading crew.

Virgil, the second black man on the loaders' crew also has over ten years of seniority on the loading department, but his lack of education makes it impossible for him to bid for more responsible jobs on the crew. He cannot read or write much more than his own name, and in a job where it is necessary to read order forms he is at a loss. Virgil remains at a low level job on the crew where he seems content to act as the group's clown. He enjoys pretend fights in which he shouts at the other Mexican and Italian loaders, calling them "motherfuckers" and insulting their ethnic groups. In return the Mexicans and Italians may call him a "black sonofabitch," an indication of the comparative ease with which Virgil and the white workers interact.

Michaels is in a far different position in the group because he must compete for its leadership. As assistant loader he is second in command under Phillippe, and Michaels is often expected to take direction of the crew in the former's absence. Directly under Michaels are the young Mexican assistants who like the senior men all come from Irondale. The young men find it difficult to take orders from the black assistant loader. The tight control which Phillippe exerts over his men, in part because of his ethnic status in Irondale itself, completely dissolves when Michaels is in command. There seems to be nothing he can do to prevent the men from simply taking it easy when he is leader. Invariably this results in fights between Michaels and those under him, particularly with Ringo, the Mexican loader with the next longest seniority on the crew after Michaels. Ringo and the black loader are continually at each other's throats, and while the Mexican man receives a good deal of support from his Irondale neighbors, Michaels has no one to turn to for support on his side. Privately, there is much speculation that Michaels will leave the loading crew to join another one elsewhere on which there are more black loaders; Michaels himself feels this is most probable. "Those guys ain't ready to take orders from a man like me, you know. That Guinea [Phillippe] works them like dogs and when I'm in charge they take it out on me."

In summary, the loaders' case is one in which the organization of work around an active group leader and the operation of a reward system which places a premium on close attachment ties within the group provide the impetus for the selection of men according to particularistic criteria. Their work also encourages the emergence of primary bonds between men in the work group. These primary groups often meet outside the plant and they are the source of friendships which bridge ethnic and residential barriers, such as between groups of Mexican and Italian workers. But men who do not share the localistic ties which serve as a basis for cohesion in the loading crew must either develop special, noncompetitive roles for themselves, or, as in the case of Michaels, eventually they will be eased out of the crew.

Conclusion: The Mill and the Wider Community

The steel mill has been viewed in the preceding pages as an occupational community in which a great diversity of status groups must reach accommodations allowing men to cooperate in spite of their ethnic and racial differences. In the mill community men not only produce steel, for which they must interact as workingmen with limited roles in the division of labor, but bring into the mill all the primordial cleavages which separate them outside the plant. Cleavage along dimensions of age, ethnicity, race, and neighborhood are combined in the mill with segmentation arising out of the division of labor. In general there is little reason to believe that all work groups in a modern industrial setting should exert equal influence over modification of ethnic and racial cleavages. The comparison between status cleavage on the mill and in the steel-loading crews offers an indication of the extent to which variations in the division of labor influence the emergence of personal relationships which bridge ethnic and racial division in work groups.

There is no unilinear progression over the careers of steelworkers toward the diminution of primordial cleavages. Rather, the formation of coalitions of workers of diverse neighborhood, ethnic, and racial background varies greatly depending on the work group's position in the ecology of the steel mill. Aggregation of status groups in the No. 3 Mill range from the formation of racial solidarity which begins to unite rural and urban black workers to the emergence of inter-ethnic primary groups among Mexicans and Italians, and finally to the negotiation of interracial leadership coalitions which direct the entire labor force in union politics. Thus the work group is the most important vehicle in constructing aggregations of workers which may later appear in the outside community.

Beyond the influence of particular work groups, the entire labor force of No. 3 Mill participates in an occupational community. This is a community in which during careers spanning twenty-five or thirty years in the mill the workers learn the details of each others' personal lives, and this information is used in the management of relationships both inside and outside the plant. Between men with widely divergent communal backgrounds, such as blacks and white ethnic steelworkers in No. 3 Mill, the same situation prevails but to lesser degrees. When white and black steelworkers labor together over long careers in the mill, they no longer must rely in their dealings with each other on the stereotypes which govern relations between whites and blacks outside the mill. Men from interracial work groups routinely share wakes, funerals, retirement parties, weddings, and a host of family activities over the course of their lives in the mill. And out of this interaction between peers of different races comes the possiblity that black men may be treated not only as peers but as leaders in competition among peers.

The steel mill is also a political community; through their unions, rank-and-file steelworkers select men whom they wish to lead them in the union. Thus the work setting where men establish personal reputations transcending primordial boundaries is also the site of competition for leadership and the honor which leadership carries.

Certainly there are severe limitations on the extent to which common participation in an occupational community can bring ethnic and racial groups together. In No. 3 Mill the young black workers develop their solidarity in opposition to the foremen and the older white workers with whom the foremen associate. Even the black mill hands leave work and go to segregated black neighborhoods where they do not normally associate with other steelworkers or their families. Some black workers will enter the negotiation of political primary groups in union politics, but the process is a long and painful one. The importance of ethnic definitions in the mill community also serves to reinforce ethnic attachments for the white workers in South Chicago neighborhoods. Serbians, Italians, Poles, Mexicans, all the ethnic groups which meet in the mill, become aware of cultural differences between them and learn to apply those distinctions in their communal lives as well. On the other hand, ethnic definitions in the mill are much more flexible than they tend to be in the outside neighborhoods. Mexicans are grouped together by other workers despite the fact that there are severe territorial cleavages in their groups outside the plant. Similarly the Serbians and Croatians, both immigrants and native Americans, are grouped together as "Hunkies," and this establishes the basis for new solidarities among South Slavs which never existed before. In general there are personal attachments formed in the mill and carried outside to the mill neighborhoods. These attachments establish the basis for inter-ethnic associations in neighborhood and community institutions.

3

Primary Group
Formation in Mill
Neighborhoods

The conditions of life in South Chicago's steel mill neighborhoods have improved considerably since the first decades of this century when men worked in the mills six days a week for twelve hours a day. In the 1920s and 1930s, settlement workers and Chicago sociologists fretted over the area's sagging frame tenements and boisterous saloons. Since World War II many of the old houses have been torn down and replaced by rows of brick bungalows, the single-family dwellings which symbolize advancement over one's childhood condition. Elsewhere the old tenements whose frame construction has remained solid have been covered with synthetic siding and otherwise made ready to receive a new generation of steelworking families. But despite material changes in the style of life, one need only look eastward down any street to find a steel mill blocking the horizon, and it is the mill which continues to shape the course of human relationships in the outside community. The demand for labor in the mills brings ever new cultural groups into the community. This demand also creates the conditions for ethnic and racial succession in the mill neighborhoods and, sometimes, for the violent resistance to that succession.[1]

In his foreword to Wirth's *The Ghetto*, Robert Park observed:

> Our great cities turn out, upon examination, to be a mosaic of segregated peoples—differing in face, in culture, or merely in cult—each seeking to preserve its peculiar cultural forms and to maintain its individual and unique conception of life. Every one of these segregated groups inevitably seeks, in order to maintain the integrity of its own group life, to impose upon its members some kind of moral isolation; so far as segregation becomes for them a means to that end, every people and every cultural group may be said to create and maintain its own ghetto.[2]

Although there is little argument with the intent of this statement, it must be taken as the ideal-typical view of a process which is limited in various ways in different types of urban settlements. In the case of neighborhoods which surround heavy industrial complexes, a new group's attempts at "moral isolation" are countered by a range of processes which take the group in another direction.

In a typical mill neighborhood, such as Irondale at the gates of the Wisconsin Steel plant, bonds between people formed at work are carried into the outside neighborhood. Friendships and animosities formed in the steel mill interact with ethnic and residential attachments to create a neighborhood ecology of primary groups. These primary groups, in turn, create the institutions of the neighborhood, its church congregations, its tavern cliques, and its political associations. The membership of the groups reflects a range of individual solutions to the dilemma of ethnic isolation versus occupational integration. These primary groups, in which the members "reconstruct" a history emphasizing commonality rather than differences, may then be enlisted into broader aggregations which are negotiated in the political organizations of the workplace and the community.

The physical structure of the neighborhoods, with their corner stores and taverns, their stoops and alleys, and their public places which must be shared, produces a style of "back fence cosmopolitanism." This neighborhood ecology allows the occurrence of processes whereby primary ties are reconstructed. Much of the day-to-day interaction among adults involves inter-ethnic contacts. For men this occurs at work, as well as on the walk through the neighborhood on the way to and from the mill. For women every trip to the corner store, the laundromat, or the bakery is an exercise in contact between different ethnic backgrounds. Thus the Italian owners of a corner grocery learn some Spanish in order to converse with the new arrivals, just as a generation ago they learned some Serbian, which they still use with the old people and the young Serbian immigrant families.

As he walks through the neighborhood, or sits with his family and visiting relatives on his front stoop, the mill worker has a chance to judge his fellow worker as a neighbor and as a man. Criteria such as how he raises his children, how he maintains his house, how he bears misfortune, and how friendly he is in his coming and going may be more important considerations in the long run than ethnicity. Years of work in the mills bring men to form particularistic judgments of one another which may transcend ethnic stereotypes. Perhaps the most important dimension of such judgments, reflecting the weight of the

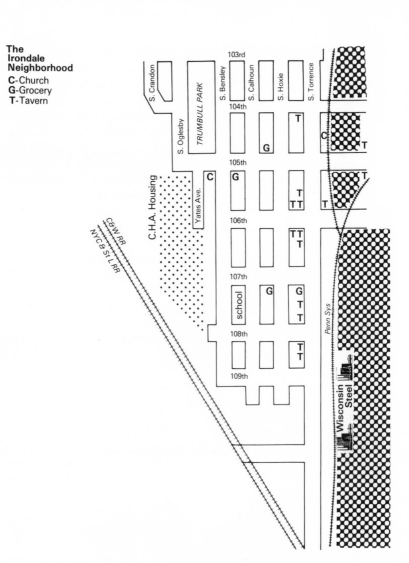

**The
Irondale
Neighborhood**
C-Church
G-Grocery
T-Tavern

Figure 3

The Irondale neighborhood. No block is more than a ten-minute walk from the gates of International Harvester's Wisconsin Steel Works.

work experience, is the comparison between a man's behavior inside and outside the plant. Much of the talk in the steelworker's tavern, for example, centers on the reputations of people in the neighborhood. For men the common theme is "What's he like on the outside," or "What's he like at work." On the other hand, should he so choose, the steelworker and his family may spend a lifetime of association in the exclusive company of ethnic peers. This pattern of cultural isolation in the midst of residential heterogeneity can also be found in South Chicago neighborhoods such as Irondale.

Life Cycles and
Neighborhood Settlement

In Irondale, as in any of the other discrete mill neighborhoods in South Chicago, the occupational distribution is largely responsible for patterns of ethnic residential settlement. For example, between 1915 and 1940 Serbians and Italians were attracted by employment opportunities in Irondale's expanding Wisconsin Steel Works. For Mexicans from Texas and Mexico, this pull into the neighborhood occurred with most force from 1945 to the present. Each of these groups was attracted away from the more important neighborhoods of first settlement in South Chicago proper.

As Serbians and Italians, and later Mexicans, moved into the frame tenements between 106th and 109th Streets, the Irish and northern European residents, who had been the original settlers in what was an industrial village, began to build new homes below 106th Street. Many families also contributed to the eastward migration of second-generation people across the Calumet River to the East Side (see chap. 1).

Table 5   Residence and Ethnicity: Wisconsin Steel Works, No. 3 Mill, Loaders and Mill Hands, 1969 (Percent)

	N.E. & Irish	Pole	S. Slav	Italian	Black	Mexican
East Side	42	17	32	39	0	0
Irondale	3	6	18	30	0	25
Slag Valley	0	2	18	0	0	8
South Chicago proper ...	0	37	14	13	8	45
Hegewisch	3	21	4	4	1	2
Outside...............	52	17	15	13	91	20
Total	100	100	100	100	100	100
(N)	(31)	(48)	(43)	(21)	(72)	(53)

Table 5 shows that the place of residence of the labor force in No. 3 Mill now corresponds closely to the general pattern of dispersion of ethnic groups from neighborhoods of first settlement. The Mexican steelworkers are clustered in Irondale and South Chicago proper, both neighborhoods of first settlement for this group, and they have not yet begun to move in large numbers to the traditional neighborhoods of second settlement such as the East Side.

Within a given mill neighborhood the pattern of ethnic residential mobility most commonly follows a direction away from the older tenements along the river or adjacent to the mills. This pattern of population movement is similar to the old expansion of immigrant groups beyond the "zone of transition" in the inner city. In Irondale it might be expected to result in a concentration of new Mexican families in the more rundown southeast corner of the neighborhood. Moving northwest, one finds this concentration of Mexicans giving way to Italian and South Slav residences and finally to a more heterogeneous area of the latter groups plus Irish and northern Europeans. In fact the neighborhood settlement pattern shows a less marked tendency for groups to move from older to newer areas within the neighborhood than one might expect. This is due to the fact that second-generation Serbian, Italian, and Mexican families often remain in Irondale in houses inherited from their parents, which they renovate. Therefore, while the South Slav and Italian direction of settlement has been generally toward the north, many members of those groups have remained in or very near their original family dwelling.

Despite the residential integration characteristic of steel-mill neighborhoods and the cosmopolitanism which such integration fosters, door-to-door heterogeneity need not imply that a given neighborhood cannot be perceived as "belonging" to a particular ethnic group. Serbian and Italian residents of Irondale reminisce over the early period of their settlement in the area when they had to "fight the Irish on the corner of 106th and Torrence." Similarly the Mexican families now moving from the old tenements into private homes remember when they too had to prove their fighting ability against Serbian and Italian boys, as well as against the remaining Irish and northern Europeans. Today, however, the southern half of Irondale is considered by many of its residents, and particularly by community activists in other neighborhoods, to be "mainly Mexican."[3]

Violent Resistance to
Negro Settlement

Irondale is notorious throughout Chicago's black community for its history of resistance to Negro settlement. In 1954 five black families moved into the Trumbull Park Housing Project on the northwestern corner of the neighborhood. Organized as the South Deering Neighborhood Improvement Association, many of the white home owners in Irondale staged six months of sporadic rioting and bombing in an effort to drive out the black families. The housing project has traditionally been isolated from neighborhood life since its construction in the 1940s. Residents of the neighborhood refer to it as "the rock" and often gossip about the reputed loose morals of some of its welfare families. Inclusion of blacks in the project seemed to many Irondale home owners to be the final threat to the neighborhood's tenuous safety and solidarity. Nevertheless, the residents were by no means unified in their anti-black sentiments, and despite months of violence, the families remained in the project. Since 1954 the black population of the project has tripled, but blacks have not been successful in moving into the private homes in the old sections of Irondale.[4]

The precedent for collective action against a perceived threat, and the hard feelings and tensions which the Trumbull Park riots created, continue to play a significant role in the social life of the neighborhood. On the one hand, the failure of its leaders to drive out the black families led to the eventual discrediting of White Citizens' Council politics in the neighborhood. During the 1968 presidential campaigns, only fifteen residents came to the Improvement Association's headquarters for a George Wallace rally. Those who did come heard a former leader of the 1954 events say, "This is the chance we've been waiting for since Trumbull Park. Where is everyone?" The subject of the riots is a source of deep embarrassment to many older residents of the neighborhood, and those who participated in the riots would not speak to me about them until I had lived in the neighborhood well over a year. On the other hand, participation in the riots for some men who were adolescents at the time continues to be a source of their local reputations. Thus, one of the popular figures in some Irondale circles is referred to as "the Bomber" by friends and acquaintances.

Of greater significance is the effect which the riots had on Mexican residents of the neighborhood. As the newest and lowest status group in the neighborhood, the Mexicans were frightened by the 1954 events. Nevertheless, as Irondale Mexicans have moved into commanding positions in neighborhood churches and political organizations, they have been required to uphold the traditions of racial exclusion which were established in the Trumbull Park riots. As will be evident later, this has created serious constraints on their ability to enter into the negotiations of larger groups of activists outside their neighborhood.

Corner Groups and
Neighborhood Identity

Perhaps the most compelling influence on the ethnic identity of an urban neighborhood is the composition of its adolescent street corner groups. Since most child-rearing families in Irondale are now of Mexican background, it is not surprising that street corner youth groups are predominantly Mexican and that the officials of community agencies perceive the neighborhood as "Mexican." There are, of course, non-Mexican adolescents, particularly in the northern end of the neighborhood. Generally these boys "hang out" with the Mexicans, if they associate in neighborhood groups at all.[5]

Between 1930 and 1940, when the majority of Serbian and Italian men in the neighborhood were adolescents, a similar situation prevailed. Young adolescent groups, limited to specific street corners, tended to be either Serbian or Italian. Sometimes they were heterogeneous enough to be prevented from having a clear ethnic identity. In consequence, disputes between corner groups were often defined as occurring between competing corners within the neighborhood, rather than between territorial segments of particular ethnic groups.

Late adolescence, and the more serious sexual contacts which mark this stage in the life cycle, is associated with increasing ethnic segregation of corner groups. Mexican children in Irondale graduate from the local street corners within the neighborhood to the main corner near the commercial center of the neighborhood. Adolescents who finish high school, and particularly those of Serbian and Italian background, tend to find their way into heterogeneous and less territorially defined groups formed on the basis of church and school participation. For those who do not finish high school, or who do not continue education after high school, the army or early marriage serves as the demarcation between street corner society and adulthood.

The first years of work in the mills, marriage, and early child-rearing, all bring a man and his family into the adult society of Irondale with its networks of occupational, family, and ethnic attachments. Although much more could be said of the adolescent years which shape a person's primordial attachments in the neighborhood, it is the adult experience, both in the mills and in the neighborhood, which is of most interest here. In Irondale and other mill neighborhoods, the local taverns are centers of informal organization for adult men from the neighborhoods. Consequently, the tavern is a neighborhood institution in which reconstructed primary groups may be formed.

Neighborhood Institutions:
The Tavern

The steelworker from Irondale who wishes to "stop in" at a tavern on his way home from work is presented with a wide variety of theoretical choices, for between the residential streets and the mill there are at least seventeen taverns. Included in this array are three Serbian steelworkers' bars which cater mainly to elderly men, four Mexican ethnic taverns, and an assortment of establishments which serve diverse occupational or youth groups. The owners of these establishments are often neighborhood leaders either of a particular ethnic group or neighborhood association or local political organization. Thus, events occurring in the taverns are distinctly communal in nature. This is in marked contrast to what Cavan observed in San Francisco: "In general, the rightful biographies of patrons in public drinking places can be held private, so that they are nobody else's business, or they can be created fictitiously on the spot out of almost nothing."[6] Such is not the case in Irondale's neighborhood taverns. On the contrary, they function as informal social clubs where everyone's biography is common knowledge.

Earlier in the century the steelworkers' tavern was most similar to the English working-class pub as described by Young and Willmott, or as portrayed in innumerable novels of the first half of the century.[7] As in England, the worker brought home his pay on Friday, often after cashing the check at a local tavern. After peeling off the house money, taking a much reduced wad for himself, he left the house to join his friends in the comfort of the man's world. Today, men over forty or fifty invariably include reminiscences about life in the taverns in the stories of their childhood in the mill neighborhoods. They remember that their immigrant fathers often worked seven days a week under the worst conditions and it seemed that only the beer and whisky could bring rest from that killing routine. Someone will remember carrying a full pail of beer, covered with a tray of pretzels, home from the corner tavern to his father. Another offers a directory of all the saloons which have vanished from Torrence Avenue or South Chicago Avenue, or the Strand.

Those who have made a serious study of their local taverns over the years, and especially people who have worked in or owned a tavern, remember that South Chicago until a few years ago boasted establishments which were world famous. Peckerhead Kate's was one everyone remembers; Kate served the ore boat sailors, herding them to her home at closing time and back to the tavern in the morning. Joe Higgens served everyone, including the biggest politicians, and he kept a big sign over the bar, "This Is America, Love It or Leave It." Their reputations were carried all over the world by the seamen, and these taverns were at least the rivals of the famous places on the Great Lakes, from Big Tit Irene's in Ashtabula to Indian Sadie's in Green Bay.

Today this picture is less common except among the newer arrivals such as the Slavic immigrants, the Mexicans, and the blacks. While he may become nostalgic over the memory of the old taverns, the blind pigs, and the brothels of his youth—or, increasingly, of his father's youth—the contemporary steelworker and family head does not fit the stereotype of the gruff worker in T-shirt and hard hat who slugs shots of whisky and fights with his pals. In contrast to the construction worker who shifts his place of employment continually, rarely works in his own neighborhood, and often cannot change into "street clothes" before coming home, the steelworker almost never leaves his plant in work clothes. To do so is almost a sure sign that a man is new to the mill and does not yet have a locker where he can shower and look "decent" after work. By the same token, the drinking done in most steelworkers' taverns is quite sedate and controlled. Except on payday, when the taverns may be crowded, the typical Irondale bar is a rather quiet place where men enter and leave with little fanfare. Talk is moderated and usually revolves around gossip concerning neighbors and workmates. Although a large number of men in Irondale continue to "stop in" after work, television, better housing, and the auto, which can take the family away for a weekend or evening, all claim their share of a man's time.

In the first stage of family formation, before all the children are in school, South Chicago men tend to become absorbed in the household routine of responsibilities. They have little time or money to spend relaxing with their old friends. Often men in this situation will "stop in" for a minute on the way home from work, but an evening out with old friends is hard to come by. Thus, in addition to the army and the disjunction in neighborhood affiliations which military life causes, family formation is another period in which men drift away from their adolescent corner groups. In the majority of cases, therefore, the local taverns serve men whose attachments have been reconstructed on a combination of earlier residential and generational ties, plus new attachments formed in the mills.

Irondale's Tavern Culture

Taverns in Irondale vary according to the nature of their patronage. In one generation a tavern may serve the members of a particular cohort of an ethnic, occupational, or residential group. Or, depending on the initiative of the owner, it may attempt greater flexibility by changing atmosphere and clientele as the residential and age characteristics of its potential patrons change. And in some cases taverns cater to a different clientele during any given day or week.

The Workingman's Tavern

The occupational or workingman's tavern in the South Chicago area is typically located at the mill gates or on industrial corners somewhat isolated from local neighborhoods. These taverns are patronized by groups of men, and in some cases women, who represent segments of work groups in local mills and business establishments. Small groups from different work settings and different occupations share the same tavern without necessarily forming a larger collectivity. One typical occupational tavern which I frequented catered to employees from two nearby steel mills, railroad men who served the mills, and men and women from a nearby grain mill. These populations are represented in the bar by single people and small groups of friends from work. While most of these regular patrons know one another and frequently sit with one another if the tavern is crowded, occupational segmentation is often maintained.

Here the hours kept by the manager are usually determined by the work schedule of the patrons, and it is not unusual for the bartenders to close well before the legal closing time if their "regulars" have departed. Most of these taverns have buzzer locks on their doors so that if the bartender is alone at night in the tavern, he can refuse to admit anyone whom he does not know. The early closing common in workingmen's taverns is usually compensated for with an early opening to catch men on their way home after the night shift. "Stopping in" is common even among men who are the lightest of drinkers because after working through the night, one is freqently wide awake at 7:00 A.M., and nothing brings on sleep as well as a shot or two of whisky with beer chasers.

The Ethnic Tavern

The ethnic taverns of Irondale, in contrast to the rather narrow use which characterizes occupational taverns, most often serve a number of functions for their particular ethnic group. Without conscious effort to adapt to the changing needs and fortunes of the ethnic group, these taverns will pass through the life cycle of a given ethnic generation, beginning as the noisy base for young men as they move from late adolescence into adult status, and ending as the sad retreat of a handful of widowers and pensioners. The more enterprising tavern owner with an ethnic clientele often attempts to make his establishment the informal organizational headquarters of the group, or at least a faction of it. This necessitates the improvement of the premises so that it can appeal not only to the men who stop in after work or to the street corner crowd but to the wives and families of more mature segments of the group as well. Success at such an endeavor is often due to the prestige of the tavern's owner, including his or her leadership in other ethnic organizations or in larger community institutions.

The ethnic taverns in South Chicago neighborhoods such as Irondale are the meeting places for various segments of local ethnic groups. There are Serbian, Croatian, Mexican, and Polish immigrant taverns in South Chicago where little or no English is spoken. The taverns which serve second- or third-generation ethnic segments frequently preserve cultural forms which have all but died out in the old country. For example, musicians in some of the Serbian and Croatian taverns perform tamburitza music. The fine wooden tamburitzas they use have been replaced in Yugoslavia by accordions and electric guitars. The tunes and lyrics of their songs were either popular in Yugoslavia forty or more years ago or were written (in Serbo-Croatian) about the immigrant experience in America at the turn of the century. Serbian and Croatian tamburitza bands travel throughout the ethnic colonies of the United States, bringing news to South Chicago people about their cousins and ethnic peers in Pittsburgh, Aliquippa, Steubenville, Hibbing, and other industrial areas where South Slavs settled. Thus, when a group from the ore fields of Minnesota plays in a local Serbian tavern, the establishment will be packed with second- and third-generation Serbians from the Chicago-Gary region who have come to dance the *kola* and to renew their ethnic ties. But despite the vitality of these blue-collar cultural traditions, the number of Serbian ethnic taverns has declined from a period in the 1950s when there were twelve tamburitza taverns in Irondale and Slag Valley alone, to a point where there are only three or four such taverns in all of South Chicago.

Except among the Mexicans and postwar Slavic immigrants, the purely ethnic tavern in Irondale is an institution on the wane. The ambiguity of ethnic territorial boundaries—when compared to more ethnically segmented areas of the city—makes it difficult for a tavern to cater to an ethnic clientele only. At the same time, attempts by enterprising owners to serve more than one ethnic group often end in failure. Thus, in the Bush, a neighborhood quite similar to Irondale but adjacent to the South Works of United States Steel, a middle-aged owner of Croatian descent attempted to open a night spot which catered to young Croatian immigrants and Mexicans, both from the South Chicago area. Since South Slavs and Mexicans frequent the same taverns in many local neighborhoods, this experiment seemed not too large a risk. There are definite cultural affinities between the groups, including appreciation of each other's music, soccer playing and interest in this game, and a liking for each other's food. But as the owner began to introduce entertainment on the weekends, he also drew a crowd from far-flung neighborhoods in the area. Gradually the climate of inter-ethnic respect declined, particularly after a number of fights over women, and this eventually forced the tavern's closing. Taverns which successfully cater to more than one ethnic group almost invariably limit their clientele to men from one or two nearby neighborhoods.

The Neighborhood Tavern

True neighborhood taverns, those which cater to clients living in the immediate vicinity without selection by occupation or ethnicity, are most often found in neighborhoods of second settlement, or in the new sections of old neighborhoods. Nevertheless, a number of old corner taverns in Irondale and similar locales do function as public houses. These taverns usually have the oldest histories of serving a diversity of neighborhood groups.

Typically, the corner taverns in the old neighborhoods of South Chicago, such as the Bush, Millgate, Irondale, and Slag Valley, were owned before prohibition by metropolitan breweries and managed by local beer distributors. At the height of immigration, such locales served as the headquarters of particular regional groups of immigrant men, who looked upon the proprietor as the broker between themselves and the strange world of the Americans. While some of these taverns still perform this function, by renting rooms to single men from Mexico and Yugoslavia, more typically they have become corner taverns which host a heterogeneous neighborhood clientele. These taverns are the places where transients in the neighborhood will most likely stop. The seamen, the truck drivers, and the construction workers who come only periodically to the mill neighborhoods quickly learn which taverns are most hospitable to strangers.

Bottle gangs and buckets of blood. Each mill neighborhood, and Irondale is no exception, supports one or more disreputable taverns which serve what local residents call the "bottle gangs." These are groups of alcoholics, frequently men and women, who have lost control over their drinking habits and can no longer patronize the neighborhoods' respectable establishments. Such taverns are continually subject to license revocations owing to the number of fights which occur in them. Their owners are frequently cited for violations of "dram shop" ordinances which place responsibility for overconsumption on the bartender as well as the patron. Irondale residents refer to one such tavern in their neighborhood as "The Bucket of Blood" or "The Saber Room." Although they often complain bitterly about the existence of such places in their neighborhoods, South Chicago residents are aware that the owners of disreputable taverns usually have sufficient political "clout" to prevent license revocation except under the most severe pressure. Thus, one notorious tavern in another South Chicago neighborhood was not closed until it was revealed that Richard Speck had become intoxicated there prior to his murder of eight nurses near the South Chicago hospital.

In summary, Irondale's taverns present the adult resident with a diverse choice of affiliations, and by "making the rounds" of taverns in the neighborhood, it is possible to maintain one's contacts with a set of primary groups which have selected their members on the basis of occupational, ethnic, or neighborhood attachments. Relatively few of the taverns are pure types; rather, they reflect tendencies to specialize in function. Except for the few taverns which become the headquarters for specific ethnic segments in the neighborhood, or which become the after-work meeting place for specific occupational groups, the distinction between occupational and ethnic taverns should be thought of as a continuum, for many tavern owners consciously attempt to increase their business by appealing to a diversity of neighborhood groups. In general, the taverns are the locus for primary group activity which exists outside the home. In their homes, blue collar families most often associate with relatives and friends of long standing who are free to drop in at almost any time. Invitations to other neighborhood friends are reserved for special occasions in the life cycle, such as marriage, birth, death, or important holidays during the year. Thus the tavern is among the most important of neighborhood institutions where people can form and maintain friendships with others whom they know well but may not associate with at home. This is especially true of friendships formed at work which may reach across ethnic or territorial divisions in the neighborhood or the larger community.

Ethnicity, Work, and
Primary Groups

In general, the longer a group has lived in the South Chicago neighborhoods and worked in the steel mills, that is, the greater its generational depth in the community, the wider the range of choice its members will have for affiliations in neighborhood primary groups. Third-generation Serbians, for example, may belong to a great diversity of tavern primary groups if they so choose. On the other hand, it is not uncommon for second- and third-generation Serbians to prefer to remain in the exclusive company of their ethnic peers. At the opposite extreme, black steelworkers are generally barred from residence in the mill neighborhoods, and blacks must limit their affiliations to racial peers and others who share attachments which grow out of the work experience.

Where Black Workers Associate

Pure occupational taverns in Irondale are located in somewhat neutral territory, away from distinct residential neighborhoods and close to the mill gates. An indication of the territorial neutrality of such establishments is the pattern of tavern frequentation of black workers from the mills.

Since the Trumbull Park riots, black workers employed in Irondale's Wisconsin Steel plant have been discouraged from associating in taverns adjacent to the residential section of the neighborhood. In most cases the discrimination is quite overt; "Members Only" signs posted at the entrance to many taverns are sufficient to discourage any but the most well-known black workers from entering. Where black workers do drink, therefore, is normally an indication that the establishment has little residential or ethnic identity and that it caters primarily to occupational groups. It is a sufficient but not necessary criterion, however, for many taverns whose trade is almost exclusively occupational do not normally encourage black patronage.

Since black workers are an increasingly important proportion of the mill labor force, the tavern owner who can afford to attract black workers is in an enviable position. Thus, some taverns at the gates of

South Works compete for the patronage of black workers, and only the Polish ethnic taverns discourage their trade. Farther south, in Irondale and East Side, an establishment which would serve black men requires, in addition to a neutral location, the ownership of someone well established in the neighborhoods, whose adherence to parochial values is beyond question. Thus the tavern in Irondale with the largest and most regular black clientele is owned by a man whose credentials in Irondale are impeccable. An established businessman and former president of the Neighborhood Improvement Association, he is the classic example of the leader who can afford to deviate from the social world of his neighborhood peers.[8]

Generally, however, such deviance is narrowly proscribed. During the Trumbull Park affair two local taverns which had been serving blacks were bombed, and although the climate of racial tension in the neighborhood has improved remarkably, the memory of such severe sanctions dies only with the generation which invoked them. Nor do black workers feel comfortable entering in large numbers even the Irondale establishment which seeks their trade. The quiet atmosphere and predominance of white patrons does not encourage the ethnic idiom or the bittersweet humor of black occupational groups. Thus in the tavern which they frequent, black workers usually drink with white workmates or in pairs. Larger black groups wishing to drink and carry on conversations among themselves will buy package liquor and drink in cars parked outside the tavern. It should be noted that this too is occupational drinking. After leaving work, black work groups must either disperse to all corners of the South Side black metropolis or choose to relax immediately in the local places they have come to know over the years. And as would be expected on the basis of the mill's occupational ecology, and the drinking habits described here, young black workers rarely frequent the local white taverns.

Where White Workers Associate

For Mexican, Slavic, and Italian workers from Irondale, the choice of tavern associations frequently represents a balancing of primordial and occupational ties. Through his choice of taverns, a worker can associate exclusively with ethnic peers, with members of his mill work group, or with a heterogeneous group of neighborhood peers. More likely, he will circulate among these tavern primary groups according to his mood during the yearly cycle of events in the neighborhood and the mill. Even in one evening, visits with two or three tavern groups in the neighborhood may bring the worker from the society of his ethnic peers to that of his mill friends. Depending on his particular work situation, there may be much or little overlap between ethnic and occupational attachments. Thus, conflict or cooperation between mill work groups is one of the primary explanations for patterns of tavern association outside the plant.

Work groups which quarrel and fight inside the mill, usually because of segmentation caused by the division of labor, often segregate themselves outside the plant. In No. 3 Mill, for example, relationships at work between the loaders and the men at the shear are often quite tense. So are relationships between crane operators and machine operators, and between foremen and many other rank-and-file groups. As one would expect, these groups associate among themselves in different taverns after work. Even in cases where men in the different work groups share common ethnic and residential backgrounds, conflict between their work groups tends to outweigh these prior dimensions of solidarity. Thus in Irondale, the Mexican loaders and a number of their Italian workmates frequent a tavern which is owned by two of the neighborhood's Mexican political leaders. Here is a case of mixed occupational and ethnic use; the tavern's ethnic identity is strongly Mexican, but it is used by a number of distinct occupational groups, and friendships which arise in the tavern are not limited by ethnicity. For their part, the Mexican shearmen patronize a tavern which earlier in the neighborhood's history served as the headquarters for young, second-generation Serbian men. Although they are now in their fifties, some of the original Serbian patrons continue to frequent this tavern. Since they are mill men and work quite closely with the young Mexican shearmen, and all live in Irondale, this explains their affinity and their ability to associate in their tavern. Finally, the foremen from No. 3 Mill rarely stop in at Irondale's taverns at all because they are likely to meet men with whom their relations are quite tense. Thus, the foremen choose taverns more distant from the Wisconsin mills, in other mill neighborhoods, where they are often joined by older crew chiefs and "key men" from the rank and file.

As these examples indicate, the division of labor inside the steel mill limits the degree to which an ethnic group may become segregated in the neighborhoods outside. On the other hand, the process of ethnic "moral isolation" is not fully mitigated by the force of work-group solidarities. There are taverns in Irondale which cater mainly to Mexicans, and ones which continue to thrive on a Serbian or generally Slavic clientele. Nevertheless, tensions between members of different work groups create small factions within neighborhood ethnic groups, and these may then be aggregated into larger constituencies in institutions such as the labor union and the ward political organization.

Aggregation of neighborhood groups for political action is made possible, in part, by the networks of affiliations which work groups establish outside the mills. In the case of South Chicago's Mexican population, for example, the ethnic group is divided into competing territorial segments living in Irondale and Millgate. Conflict between the Mexicans from these neighborhoods is most severe among adolescent youth groups and would continue throughout the life cycle were it not for the influence of work groups which span this territorial cleavage. Among the Mexican shearmen, blast furnace workers, and inspectors in No. 3 Mill, were men from Irondale and from Millgate. They often met in occupational primary groups in Irondale taverns after work. It is from this group of Mexican men, and others like them in different neighborhoods, that the leadership of the entire ethnic group is recruited. Such leaders must be able to pass comfortably across the frontiers of ethnic territories, and it is the base of affiliations created in the mill and in the occupational taverns which first makes this possible in an ethnic generation.[9]

*Tavern Affiliation and
Reconstructed Primary Groups*

Not all tavern affiliations develop into actual primary groups. Especially in these occupational taverns, where the segmentation of the workplace is maintained, men may frequent the same establishment for years without developing close attachments to all the "regulars." Even where such attachments do not develop, however, people who frequent the same taverns cannot help learning enough about one another's biographies and characters to establish a personal basis of trust. Also many of the primary groups active in the larger institutions of the community are composed of men who first formed reconstructed primary groups in neighborhood drinking establishments but who no longer frequent these establishments with great regularity. In general, the processes whereby primary ties are reconstructed occur to varying degrees in all the taverns discussed here.

The most limited form of primary group reconstruction takes place in the ethnic taverns. Here people with generally similar ethnic backgrounds form friendship groups in which cleavages based on age, generation in the neighborhood, or old country animosities may be bridged. The example of a popular Serbian tavern serving the Irondale–Slag Valley neighborhoods is a case in point.

Branko's in Slag Valley is one of the most popular Serbian taverns in South Chicago. On the weekends it is always jammed with groups of second- and third-generation Serbians. Most have grown up in the area, but many now come from distant suburban communities to see people from "the old neighborhoods." The newer immigrants are referred to here as DP's, and while they are welcome at Branko's, they have little affinity for the remnants of turn-of-the-century Serbian culture which this tavern preserves. The regulars at Branko's know hundreds of tamburitza songs, and they shout their requests to the band in Serbian. Though most do not speak the language fluently, many of the second-generation people have visited Yugoslavia and have improved upon the language they spoke with their parents.

The tavern is the informal headquarters for a number of Serbian primary groups. Those who are active in the magnificent Serbian church choir, or in the governance of the church, are especially likely to meet there during the major Serbian holidays. Serbian men who have become friendly in the mills or in ward politics are regular weekday patrons. This group organizes trips to Las Vegas that provide adventures which can be rehashed for months afterwards. Although most of the people in these groups have known each other since childhood, their primary attachments are continually being reconstructed after breaks in the life cycle. Paul, a third-generation Serbian who now works at U.S. Steel, recounted his experience as follows:

When I got out of the army in '67, most of the guys I hung around with in the neighborhood were gone; you know, to school, or they was still in the army, or they're married. For a while I was pretty unhappy. Here I am in my own neighborhood, you know, I know everybody, but I got no friends. I was working on the ore dock at South Works and I met Jim, who I knew from Slag Valley, but he was older than me. I used to hang around with his younger brother. Anyway, Jim was divorced, so we started going around with Pete and Joe and their wives and their wives' girl friends. Sure, I'd like to get married and all, but right now things are fine this way.

All the people in Paul's group are Serbians who have family histories in South Chicago neighborhoods. When they get together with larger Serbian groups in the taverns, for example, their joking conversation shows to what extent old animosities within their ethnic group have been eased. They often tease each other about the provincial origins of their families. Some have parents or grandparents who originally came from the Serbian province of Lika, others came from Montenegro, and still others may have had a Croatian parent. Now they can joke about these origins, but in their parents' generation these were differences that were thought to matter a great deal.

Primary groups formed in occupational taverns usually bring people together who have more diverse neighborhood backgrounds than is the case in the ethnic taverns. Here people perceive their commonality as growing out of years of shared experience in the workplace, and in the neighborhoods. They tend to play down the ethnic differences which separated them at other periods in their lives. One popular occupational tavern in Irondale offers examples of the processes of primary group reconstruction which occur in such places.

Mike's, in Irondale, draws a large and diverse crowd which includes workers form Wisconsin Steel and other nearby plants, railroad men who switch steel in and out of the mills, and men and women from a nearby grain mill. Certainly the largest crowd gathers on paydays, and when they are on the day shift, the steelworkers or railroad men may not be seen except on that day. Also not all the groups which meet at Mike's share equally in the tavern's company. Some work groups, especially those including blacks, usually keep to themselves, although the life histories of the men in these groups is common knowledge throughout the tavern.

Many events occur during the work year which draw the diverse occupational groups together in the tavern. The derailment of a gondola inside the mill, for example, will result in much joking between steelworkers and railroad men after the shift. The discussion is not always lighthearted, however. Explosions in the grain mill and at the steel furnaces, crane accidents in the rolling mills, shipping accidents on the Calumet River, and severe winter storms through which all must suffer are the subject of long analysis after the event. Industrial accidents, layoffs, and wildcat strikes occur regularly in the workplaces; the tensions and emotions they generate are relived and relieved in the tavern.

Attracted to the tavern through their work groups, many of the people at Mike's develop common interests which take them beyond the occupational world. Thus, men arrange fishing trips to Wisconsin and often their families accompany them on these excursions. Quite frequently, members of groups which meet in the tavern are enlisted into union or ward political institutions. Ralph, a Polish-American railroad man, explained how this occurred among his friends.

I'm not the kind of person who likes to talk about work after it's over. What I like is politics. You take Tom, though, he's one of those guys who can talk forever about railroading, and Mike [the tavern owner] gets worked up about the Serbian churches and the arguments they have with the DP's. Of course Mike loves ward politics, and me and him brought Tom into the organization as a precinct captain when he wanted some favors for his mother's building on the East Side. Now with us and some of the Mexicans in here who work precincts in Irondale you have a group of people who know the politics of the ward real well.

Common to all the primary groups which form in neighborhood taverns is an emphasis on shared experiences which bring out commonalities among the group's members and play down their differences. Thus, while men in a group of precinct workers may be of quite varied ethnicity, and earlier in their youths they may have jealously guarded their ethnic territories, now they have reconstructed renditions of their pasts in which they describe common experiences in the neighborhoods and their institutions. Thus, it is on the basis of appeals to these reconstructed pasts that these groups may be aggregated into the unions and the ward political organizations of the larger community.

Part 2

Negotiation and
Succession in
Local Unions

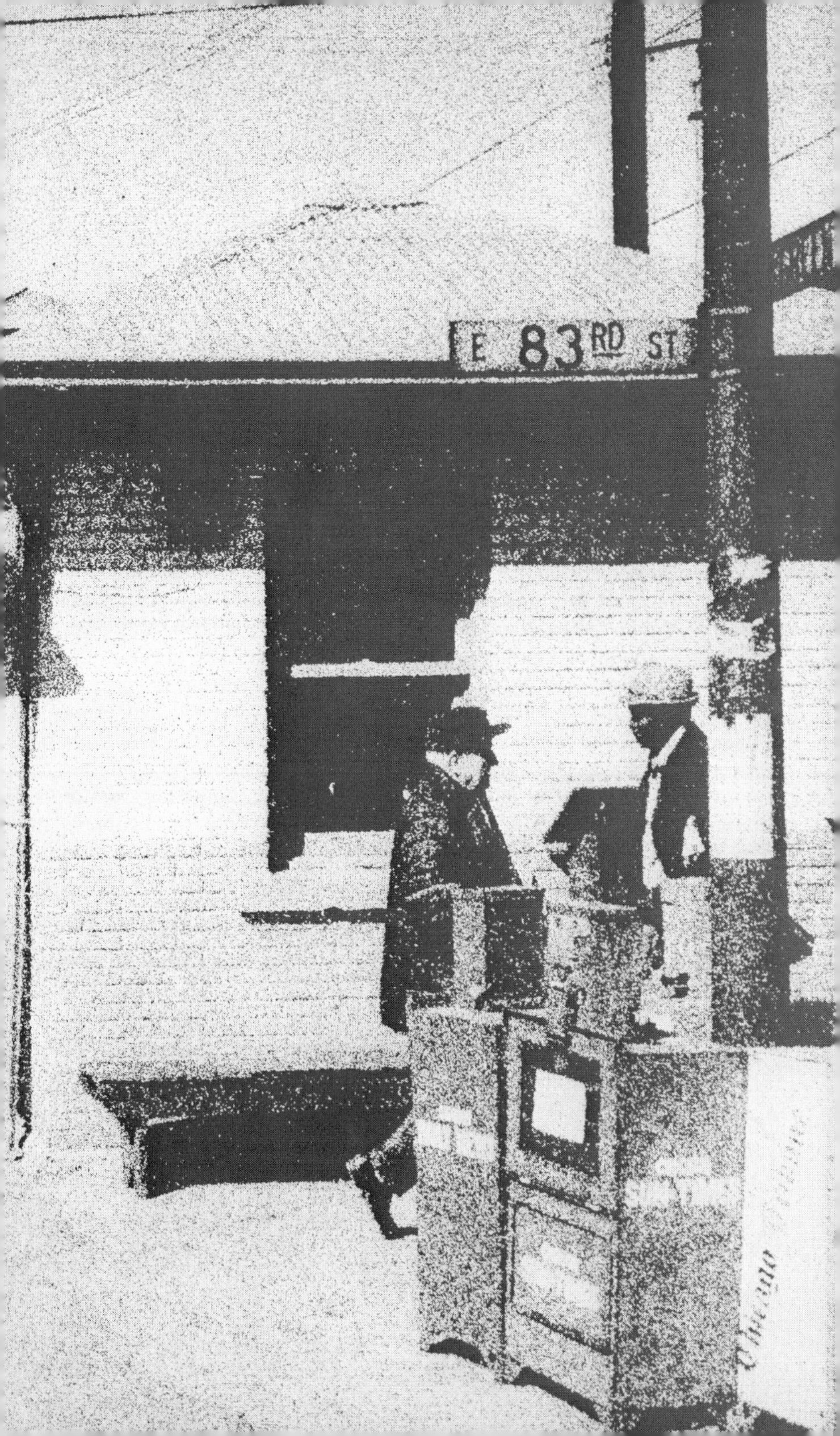
E 83RD ST

Outsiders to industrial communities often judge local labor unions according to their feelings about the development of the national labor movement since the 1930s. The industrial unions have discouraged many intellectuals who once saw in them the hope for a working class which would be conscious of its common interests and would select leaders who could best articulate those interests. In general, the disappointment over the unions' failure to unify blue collar America behind socialist or progressive political programs has resulted in an ignorance of the role local unions do play in the life of working-class people. More specifically, most observers have neglected the unions' success at forming communities in the segmented industrial areas of the country. It is true that local unionists operate within limits established by the relationship between national corporations and union bureaucracies. Also, in South Chicago as in most industrial communities, the early histories of labor-management conflict established patterns of local union politics which persist today. Even in South Chicago's "glorious" decades of labor organization, politics in the steel mills often combined well-articulated class issues with an overriding concern for ethnic and racial mobility through union leadership.

The preoccupation of South Chicago unionists with ethnic and racial politics can hardly be dismissed as "false consciousness." Rather, it is part of the overall political process whereby common class interests are eventually identified. Throughout the 1960s and early 1970s, at all levels of the labor movement, unionists have been hard put to protect improvements in the workers' level of living against the inroads of inflation. Conflict arising out of technological unemployment, layoffs, "piecework" incentive rates, industrial safety, and debates over American foreign policy also divides the allegiances of workers and unionists alike. But in the heavy industrial areas of the United States, the local unions are also community political institutions whose roles are not limited to issues of the workplace. Thus, in South Chicago the diverse steelworking groups which have settled in the area enter negotiations in union politics which aggregate the leaders of racial and ethnic segments of the mills and the mill neighborhoods.

Each group that competes in South Chicago union politics faces somewhat unique organizational problems, problems which largely arise out of the ecological situation of its members. But once they are formed, aggregations of unionist leaders may become agents for further ethnic adaptation in the South Chicago community. The manner in which this happens varies from one local union to another, depending on its neighborhood history as a community-forming institution. The role of unionist aggregations in the larger community also varies from one ethnic or racial group to another, depending on the group's stage of settlement in South Chicago and surrounding areas.

4

Local Unions and Their Neighborhood Histories

The political processes which now aggregate neighborhood and occupational primary groups had their antecedents in South Chicago's history of class conflict and industrial organization. Mill workers organized local labor unions at the turn of the century, and these were among the first truly communal institutions to develop in the area. The unions' primary purpose has been to protect the class interests of workers and their families, but since their beginning they have also played an important role in forming a community out of the congeries of South Chicago ethnic groups and industrial neighborhoods. Drawing their membership from the diverse population of ethnic, territorial, and occupational groups in the plants, the unions soon became the site for political competition among various blue collar ethnic segments of the area. Thus, while union leaders were often divided on issues concerning the protection of class interests, none could remain aloof from the negotiations among primary groups formed in the mills and in the mill neighborhoods.

In addition, each of the three major steel corporations had its own methods for dealing with labor strife and union organization. Labor policies which the companies elaborated earlier in this century have produced remarkably persistent differences, both in the nature of aggregations negotiated in the unions, and in the class content of South Chicago union politics.

At the Wisconsin Steel Works in Irondale and Slag Valley, local union politics is strictly a neighborhood affair. Today, just as in the early 1900s, the union is controlled by a primary group of Serbian, Italian, and Mexican men from Slag Valley and Irondale. Politics in the union revolves around questions of which leaders of new groups in the mill and in the neighborhoods should be admitted into the union's

92

leadership clique. Groups not brought into the aggregation of neighborhood leaders who control the local union attempt to negotiate their own constituencies to wrest control of the union. It is generally conceded that the prize sought is as much leadership in the neighborhoods as it is control over the union.

At the Republic Steel local union, on the East Side, a different situation prevails. In this neighborhood of second settlement there tends to be more indifference about who runs the union. Competition for leadership on the East Side bears little relation to politics in the union. Although local men generally win union elections, the neighborhood seems largely unfazed by the often rancorous campaigns being waged inside the mill. Ethnic unionists from the East Side frequently compete against progressives, whose roots in the labor movement originate not from the neighborhood, but from the left political wing of the CIO.

Finally, the South Works in South Chicago proper, is a mixed case in which unionists find it difficult to separate the aggregation of local groups from appeals to the class interests of those groups. Owing to its size, and its long history of labor organization, leaders at South Works have always had to work especially hard to form aggregations of activists from the many segments of the mill's labor force. Because of its power among the various steel locals in Chicago, some South Works unionists have become quite active in the politics of the larger community. Others find that the complexity of negotiations inside the plant prevents them from gaining reputations outside the workplace and the union.

There is a risk in bringing out differences among these local unions, for each is governed according to the same CIO principles, and all of their leaders are among the political elite of the community. Also, these local unions are all limited in the extent to which they can win concessions from the management of the national corporations whose local workers they represent. Nevertheless, the unionists themselves place importance on these differences, and their perceptions often have consequences for the role of the unions in the community. The Wisconsin Steel local is, in fact, an independent union and not affiliated with the United Steelworkers of America, AFL-CIO. Thus union activists from South Works and Republic Steel refer to it as a "company union" and often deride the status which Irondale residents confer upon its leadership. In turn, the Wisconsin leaders take pride in their autonomy and see the CIO unionists as subordinate to national labor figures. Likewise, men from the large South Works local frequently see themselves as the only important labor leaders in the community, and this may offend men in the smaller Wisconsin and Republic locals. Despite this bickering, however, the unionists all refer to themselves as "labor leaders." They are aware that their role, and the role of their unions in the community grew out of a history of hard and often bloody confrontations with the management of the steel mills.

Corporations and Community, 1890–1919

The influence of the large steel corporations on community formation in South Chicago was generally negative. On the one hand, some attempts were made to improve the conditions of life in the mill neighborhoods, particularly to "Americanize" the foreign workers entering the plants in large numbers between 1890 and 1921. On the other hand, company policies and practices with regard to labor organization were often directed at attempts to increase the cleavages and animosities between groups in the area. Where these groups did succeed in forming communal institutions, they most often did so out of opposition to company labor practices.

The steel-towns on the outskirts of Pittsburgh, Chicago, and Cleveland were not nineteenth-century industrial communities such as described by the Lynds and by Lloyd Warner. Unlike Middletown and Yankee City, the mill towns in metropolitan areas lacked the well-integrated status systems, extending from entrepreneurial families down to those of the marginal worker, in which owners of local firms could exert moral suasion over their employees on different levels of the town's stratification system. It is true that from 1870 to 1930 the steel industry went through the transition from family to corporate capitalism. But this transition did not significantly increase the social distance between managers and workers, for even in the period of family ownership of the mills, the owners were absent from the mill communities. Thus one of the first Ph.D. dissertations in American sociology noted the complete absence of entrepreneurial and managerial families in South Chicago.[1] From the vantage point of working people in the industrial enclaves of metropolitan centers, the shift in ownership of capital could only be perceived through change in the policies of managers who had never been part of the local status hierarchy.

In an address to the presidents of subsidiary companies in 1919,

Judge Gary, president of the United States Steel Corporation, stated the ideal goals of the company's welfare policy.

Make the Steel Corporation a good place for them to work and live. Don't let the families go hungry or cold; give them playgrounds and parks and schools and churches, pure water to drink, every opportunity to keep clean, places of enjoyment, rest, and recreation; treating the whole thing as a business proposition, drawing the line so that you are just and generous and yet at the same time keeping your position and permitting others to keep theirs, retaining the control and management of your affairs, keeping the whole thing in your own hands, but, nevertheless, with due consideration to the rights and interests of all others who may be affected by your management.[2]

In keeping with this policy, U.S. Steel and other companies in South Chicago did improve sanitary conditions in the plants, and did support the building of schools, parks, ball fields, libraries, and YMCAs in the mill neighborhoods. Likewise, the companies began supporting teams and bands, and also began offering stock subscriptions to the employees. Further analysis of these programs, however, shows that those who benefited most from them were the lower level managers and the highly skilled native Americans in the plants. Immigrant workers and many less skilled native Americans were unlikely to benefit from these programs because they were still working for twelve hours a day, six or even seven days a week, and their wages were well below the national average for industrial workers.

The Twelve-Hour Day, the
Seven-Day Week

The issue of extremely long working hours was a major bargaining point in the great steel strike against U.S. Steel in 1919. Exactly how many employees worked the twelve-hour day was itself a subject of controversy during the period. A fact-finding committee sponsored by the Interchurch World Movement found that approximately one-half of the workers in basic steel were subject to the twelve-hour day, and of these another half worked seven days a week. In weeks when these workers shifted from nights to days they worked a continuous twenty-four hours. Judge Gary himself admitted that many workers did put in twelve-hour days, but he claimed that 34 percent of all employees worked approximately eight hours per day, 39.5 percent of the employees worked ten hours per day, and 26.5 percent worked the twelve-hour turn. He also claimed that "the seven day week has been eliminated."[3]

Data from the United States Bureau of Labor show that the weekly hours in the industry were decreasing from 1910 to 1919, approaching an overall average of sixty-five hours per week. But departments which bottlenecked the flow of steel out of the mills, notably the open hearth departments where iron was converted to steel, still regularly worked the twelve-hour day, and often the seven-day week. It is also true that such departments hired a disproportionate number of immigrant workers in areas such as South Chicago.[4] On the basis of these and similar figures, the fact-finding committee concluded that the average immigrant worker would find it extremely difficult to avail himself of the opportunities for "Americanization" which the steel corporations did provide in his neighborhoods. Even today, the union, the ethnic associations, and the informal meeting places for workers are much more attuned to the temporal cycle of work in the steel industry than are the educational and welfare institutions which are managed by middle-class employees who work a standard nine-to-five-hour day.

Table 6   Average Weekly Hours in the Open
                                     Hearth Furnaces, 1913–19

Occupation	1913	1914	1915	1917	1919
Stockers	100	99	99	100	96
Stock cranemen	100	99	98	98	91
Charging machine operators	100	99	100	99	94
Ingot strippers	100	100	100	93	88
Laborers	100	91	93	98	95

Americanization and the Ethnic Groups

Whenever they were faced with "labor troubles" in the mills, the corporate executives did their best to increase tensions between ethnic groups in the mill neighborhoods. At the same time they used their influence with "responsible" leaders of the ethnic groups to influence clergymen and editors of the immigrant press to join the cause of 100 percent Americanism and disavow the "labor agitators" in their midst.

During the 1919 strike private labor spy agencies were hired to monitor the activities of the labor leaders and to influence the men to come back to work. One such spy, hired by the Sherman Service to work in South Chicago, turned over his correspondence with the service to Chicago labor officials. Among his correspondence was a communication warning him that there was enough ammunition stored in the plant of the Illinois Steel Company at South Chicago to "shoot down every striker like a dog" and dictating the following actions.[5]

OCTOBER 2, 1919

8A 563-D
Rep. -----

DEAR SIR:
WE HAVE TALKED TO YOU AND INSTRUCTED YOU. WE WANT YOU TO STIR UP AS MUCH BAD FEELING AS YOU POSSIBLY CAN BETWEEN THE SERBIANS AND ITALIANS. SPREAD DATA AMONG THE SERBIANS THAT THE ITALIANS ARE GOING BACK TO WORK, CALL UP EVERY QUESTION YOU CAN IN REFERENCE TO RACIAL HATRED BETWEEN THESE TWO NATIONALITIES: MAKE THEM REALIZE TO THE FULLEST EXTENT THAT FAR BETTER RESULTS WOULD BE ACCOMPLISHED IF THEY WILL GO BACK TO WORK. URGE THEM TO GO BACK TO WORK OR THE ITALIANS WILL GET THEIR JOBS.
DAILY MAXIM—SENT TO EVERY REPRESENTATIVE TODAY:
CONSERVE YOUR FORCES ON A SET POINT—BEGIN BEFORE THE OTHER FELLOW STARTS.

REMAIL

It is difficult to measure the effectiveness which such agitation had in the mill neighborhoods. If this and similar pieces of evidence are any indication, one must assume that the labor spy companies operated from extremely faulty intelligence. The main divisions between workers at the Illinois Steel plant, which later became the South Works of U.S. Steel, were between Poles and northern European ethnic groups. The numbers of Serbians and Italians at that plant were always much less important than they were in the other major factories of the area. Despite their general ineptitude both in sponsoring Americanization programs and in fomenting tensions between various ethnic segments at the mill gates, other labor policies of the company did produce quite marked cleavages in the South Chicago settlements.

After a survey of immigrant participation in the 1919 steel strike, David Saposs, a labor historian who assisted John R. Commons, concluded that "in general, the immigrant strikers' own priests and clansmen leaders, as well as their newspapers, did not support the strike." Saposs points out that unlike the Jews and Finns, who brought proletarian traditions to this country which had been developed in the industrial and commercial centers of Russia, the southern European immigrants had no such traditions. The organizers of their ethnic associations were highly susceptible to pressures from American commercial leaders whom they respected, and to whom they were often materially indebted. In consequence of this, when the immigrant steelworkers began supporting militant labor organizations, serious divisions between the new labor leaders and older ethnic leaders were opened in the mill neighborhoods. These cleavages often figure prominently in the course of contemporary labor union politics in South Chicago.[6]

In summary, each of the major corporations in South Chicago was active in the pre-union decades of the century with the Americanization of its workers. Each also elaborated specific labor policies, especially with regard to unionism, which help explain differences in how these local unions operate as community-forming institutions. The Wisconsin Steel Corporation, the United States Steel Corporation, and the Republic Steel Corporation, all had mills in South Chicago where cleavages among laboring groups and the policies of the company combined to produce an emphasis in union politics on ethnic succession. To varying degrees the companies helped instill anti-union ideals of Americanism in the mill neighborhoods. Today these ideals are a constant barrier to the introduction of progressive social welfare policies in local union politics.

International Harvester and
Independent Unionism

Policies which the International Harvester Company applied at their Wisconsin Steel Works produced traditions of independent unionism in the Irondale and Slag Valley neighborhoods which persist today. The workers in the Wisconsin mills are represented by the Progressive Steelworkers Union of Wisconsin Steel, by far the largest independent union in America's basic steel industry. Perhaps nowhere is the neighborhood history of an industrial union better exemplified than in the competition between the CIO and the "company union" at Wisconsin Steel. This competition reached its climax in April 1945, when the plant's workers voted to retain their independent union rather than join with the United Steelworkers of America, CIO.

Until 1937, the employees at Wisconsin Steel were represented by a Works Council, a joint committee of elected rank-and-filers and appointed plant executives. All the McCormick family plants had operated with this form of employee representation since 1919, when it was instituted to fight the AFL's organizing drive in Harvester operations. The Works Council at Wisconsin Steel was one of the best organized and most carefully nurtured of the councils, for it was used with immediate effect to combat striking workers in the 1919 steel strike. This paternalistic form of rank-and-file representation was, Ozanne found, very effective.

Throughout 1920, a year of inflation, there was not one request at Wisconsin Steel for a wage increase. Instead the council busied itself with such activities as running contests for vegetable gardens and home yard beautification, elaborate prizes going to the winners, with cutting living costs by getting the company to buy and resell to employees jams, potatoes, and 25,000 men's suits made in England; running an inter-departmental baseball league; recruiting citizenship classes among Harvester's many foreign-born workers; and helping management explain, particularly to the foreign-born, the 1920 version of Harvester's profit sharing plan, known as the "extra compensation plan."[7]

Older steelworkers in Irondale and Slag Valley, many of them now retired, have vivid memories of this era of company unionism. They remember purchasing coke and food offered by the Works Council, but they also remember that when they were out of work in the 1930s they had to steal heating fuel from the company. My Irondale neighbors were quick to point out that the acquiescence of the Works Council could hardly be blamed on their immigrant fathers. At International Harvester all noncitizens were excluded from member-ship in the council and this tended to increase the bitterness between the second-generation northern Europeans and the newer Serbian, Italian, and Mexican residents of the neighborhoods. Here was Ameri-canization in practice; the theory being that only Americans, whether workers or managers, could be trusted to guide the course of labor relations in the mills. Of course there were limits on the extent to which even Americans could be trusted to see their common interests, and the company retained the right to veto decisions of the Wisconsin Works Council.

Exclusion from an organization in which their neighborhood rivals were gaining some status tended to make the newcomers in Irondale and Slag Valley responsive to the mill's CIO organizing drive. When the Wagner Act (1937) outlawed Employee Representation Plans such as the Harvester Company had pioneered, the Wisconsin Works Council became the Progressive Steelworkers Union, under the leader-ship of an Irish-American from Irondale. Almost simultaneously the CIO's Steel Workers Organizing Committee (SWOC) began a recruit-ing drive in the mill. For the first time in its history, the Irish and northern European dominance of the plant's rank and file was seriously challenged. During the next eight years there were two unions in the plant, both with headquarters in Irondale, and the competion divided families and ethnic groups outside the mill.

Table 7			CIO Membership, Wisconsin Steel, 1945, by Ethnicity, Place of Residence, and Occupation (Percent)		
	N.E.	Polish	Ethnicity		
			S. Slav	Italian	Mexican	Black
Residence:						
Other Chicago						
neighborhoods	18.0	20.4	39.0	35.1	30.4	73.3
Irondale	5.5	13.7	48.0	33.3	34.3	. . .
Occupation:						
No. 3 mill hands	6.5	7.9	7.1	11.1	20.0	47.1
Loading	38.0	42.0	72.0	50.4	19.4	. . .
(N)	(436)	(236)	(223)	(91)	(272)	(101)

The data in table 7 are tabulated from the CIO membership rolls prior to the representational election which ended the struggle between the rival unions in 1945. They demonstrate the overriding importance of ethnic and residential ties, as well as occupational solidarities, in what might otherwise have been thought of as a struggle between competing philosophies and practices of labor representation. The leadership of the Progressive Steelworkers was largely recruited from the Irish residents of Irondale, while the CIO leaders were South Slavs and Italians from the same neighborhood.[8]

The CIO usually had its greatest success among middle and lower status occupations, and among lower status ethnic groups in the plants it organized. This generalization is clearly supported in table 7. The comparison between workers living in Irondale and those outside the immediate mill neighborhood also indicates that the election was perceived as a struggle for dominance in the neighborhood. In Irondale only 5.5 percent of the Irish and northern European workers supported the CIO, as against the 48 percent CIO membership for the neighborhood's Serbians and Croatians. On the other hand, while CIO membership was higher among the South Slavs than in any other local ethnic group, even here the CIO did not command a majority. Obviously there was considerable difference of opinion among the South Slavs in Irondale, for many who were not CIO members could be expected to vote for the Progressive Steelworkers.

The data show that occupational solidarities could exert an influence over union participation which altered the normal participation of an ethnic or racial group. Thus, for black workers, all of whom had only recently broken the color barrier in the plant, CIO membership was a natural outgrowth of their tenuous position in the mill's occupational community. Where blacks had managed to join work groups on the rolling mills, their CIO membership remained relatively high but was much lower than the overall black CIO membership. For other ethnic groups the comparisons between loaders and mill hands are quite striking. As described earlier, the loaders and mill hands have about the same status in the plant, but the organization of their work and their relations with the company are quite different. The hierarchical arrangement of mill work brought the newcomers under the influence of northern European rollers and heaters who tended to identify their interests in the steelmaking process with those of company officials. The loading crews often develop their solidarity in opposition to company officials, and, as expected, they would be partisans of the more militant CIO.

When the CIO lost the representational election, as the data suggest they would, the greater class militancy of the CIO was discredited in favor of the ideals of Americanism established in the days of the Works Council. In Irondale and Slag Valley the tradition of independent unionism was firmly established; the union would remain entirely in the hands of the Wisconsin workers, but control of the union's leadership would be a neighborhood affair. Thus, today, politics in the union hinges on competition among leaders of neighborhood primary groups. Control of the union continues to symbolize an ethnic group's dominance in the mill neighborhoods around the plant, but the maintenance of that control rests on success in recruiting leaders from the diverse primary groups that form in the plant and in the mill neighborhoods.

*Republic Steel: Class Violence in
a Neighborhood of Second
Settlement*

On the East Side, the Republic Steel Corporation pursued a policy of militant anti-unionism which culminated in the 1937 Memorial Day Massacre in that neighborhood. Here is a case of a local union whose formation was marked by severe community conflict and tragic violence. In the aftermath of that conflict the union was devalued as a community institution, and residents of the East Side have never attached as much significance to control over the union's leadership as do residents of Irondale and Slag Valley. The Republic Steel Corporation had never developed traditions of company unionism in its East

Side plant, but when faced with a CIO organizing drive in its mill, it used every possible means to exacerbate ethnic cleavage in the neighborhood surrounding the plant.

The ecology of the East Side was quite different from the situation of ethnic heterogeneity which characterized Irondale and Slag Valley in the 1930s. On the East Side, the northern Europeans, particularly second-generation German, Scandinavian, and Irish families, had established a neighborhood of second settlement on the vacant flatlands north of the Republic plant. Representatives of the second wave of immigration, South Slavs, Italians, and some Poles, were beginning to pressure the earlier settlers on their northern boundary. The new arrivals encountered considerable hostility as they attempted to move south; the southern Europeans were treated as unwelcome invaders, just as they had been treated in earlier decades in the older mill neighborhoods. In addition, the location of the Republic mill inhibited the growth of occupational tavern groups which could relieve territorial animosities between the northern and southern segments of the neighborhood. The mill was separated from the neighborhood by large open prairies, and in consequence there was little commercial development at the mill gates.[9]

The Republic Steel CIO local in 1937 had been hastily organized under the leadership of southern European unionists from the north end of the neighborhood. They had been aided by organizers from the United Mine Workers who had been assigned to the plant by the SWOC. On 26 May 1937, in conjunction with a nationwide strike against the "little steel" companies which were refusing to recognize the CIO, steelworkers at Republic's East Side plant walked out of the mill to join the strike. But the walkout was not unanimous, for at least two hundred out of the twenty-five hundred steelworkers remained on the job. Men active in the union at the time agree that those who refused to strike were generally from the northern European segment of the neighborhood—if they were from the local area at all. The perception of company officials supports this view from another perspective. In his analysis of the events on the East Side, Tom Girdler, Republic's founder and president wrote:

The few who actually went on strike that day were chippers. Chippers are employed in steel mills to "chip" surface defects out of steel billets, defects such as seams and scales. The "chipping hammer" they use is the same type of pneumatic tool used by riveters, except that in the business end of a chipping hammer there is set a chisel-like blade.

Suddenly there was a great clatter in the billet mill as these fellows, responding to some signal, threw down their tools and began to chant, "strike, strike, strike." For the most part these were young fellows who bore Italian names. After they had rallied a band numbering between 100 and 150 they trooped through successive buildings of the plant. Everywhere they appeared they tried to hustle men away from their jobs. There was scuffling wherever workers resisted.[10]

Shortly before the strike began, in anticipation of the possibility of mass picketing, the local police commander moved almost two hundred Chicago patrolmen into the plant, where a temporary headquarters was established. In addition, the company had been openly stocking gas and automatic weapons in the plant, and people who participated in the strike have described to me the location of machine gun emplacements on railroad cars along the plant gates. The following testimony of the local union president reveals something of the emotional intensity which gripped the East Side as the strike began.

Mr. Yuratevac. And just as the men was going out of the gate the men would cheer them and shake hands with them, and they was moving back and forth and lots of them was standing there. There was police officers outside. They was talking to the police officers, and guys wanted to get inside the plant and they could not get through because there was too big a crowd, and they told the men not to go inside, they told them the men was on strike, and they went back. A lot of them asked if they was allowed to go in there, and they said they was allowed to but it would not be right because of us fellows being on strike, and they turned about and about 9 o'clock that night the police officers chased us away.[11]

Harassment of pickets and incidents of clashes between strikers and the police continued into the next day as tension increased on the East Side. The police prevented CIO organizers from talking to men remaining in the plant, a policy which gave rise to speculation that some men were being held against their will inside the mill. At the same time the East Side plant became something of a focal point for national opinion because of the number of men who remained in the mill and the increasing level of community conflict the strike was generating. In this regard, an SWOC memo of 29 May 1937 issued by Philip Murray shows that, of nineteen Republic plants struck by the CIO, only the East Side plant was attempting to maintain a semblance of production.[12] A widely accepted opinion among older steelworkers on the East Side is that some of the men who remained in the plant were burning tarpaper in the furnaces to give the impression that the mills were continuing to make steel.

The Massacre and
Adjustment to Tragedy

With the help of favorable press from the local community paper and
the *Chicago Tribune*, the company kept rumors circulating on the East
Side that families of men remaining in the mill had been threatened by
union representatives. On Thursday night, the day after the strike
began, twenty-one men were arrested in a fight between pickets and
police. Rather than provoke further incidents, the union organizers
eased pressure on the picket lines and called a mass meeting for
Memorial Day, Sunday, at Sam's Place, an empty tavern near the mill
which was the temporary union headquarters.

The Memorial Day meeting that Sunday was followed by a march to
the plant gates for a session of "mass picketing." When police blocked
the path of the strikers to the mill gates, tempers raged. Someone in the
crowd apparently threw a stick in the direction of advancing police
lines. The police immediately opened fire on the crowd, killing ten
persons and seriously wounding almost a hundred others with their
clubs.

In the aftermath of the massacre, events quickly bypassed the East
Side. A mass funeral ceremony for the dead workers was held in South
Chicago and drew forty thousand participants from the entire Chicago
metropolitan area.[13] Chicago liberals took up the cause of the striking
workers and instituted an investigating committee led by University of
Chicago faculty and Hyde Park activists, among them Paul Douglas
and Leon Despres, both liberal leaders in the University of Chicago-
Hyde Park community. At the national level, the labor investigating
committee under Senator Robert La Follette of Wisconsin devoted a
series of its hearings on violations of free speech and rights of labor to
events at Republic's East Side plant. This investigation documented the
collusion between company and police officials and indirectly discredited the police version of the massacre.

The La Follette investigation revealed that in the minds of the police,
as well as of the *Chicago Tribune* and company officials, there was no
question that communist organizers had incited the volatile passions of
foreigners throughout the course of events leading up to the massacre.
In this regard the testimony of Sergeant Lyons is typical of the attitude
toward the strikers as expressed by police and company officials:

Mr. Lyons. The class of people that live and work in these mills—
except, I will say, the minority are probably American born—I will say
the majority of people working in the mills are of foreign extraction—

I mean are foreigners to this country, or are of foreign extraction,
where they have talked a foreign language in their homes for years and
probably haven't got as much respect for the American flag as I have.[14]

Interested outsiders to the East Side, both in Chicago and at the
national level, viewed the events of the Memorial Day violence in terms
of class confict, the working-class steelworkers versus corporate officials acting through the agency of city police and the conservative press.
But for the people involved in the events, the police as well as East
Siders from both ends of the neighborhood, it was impossible to
separate the objective origins of the tragedy from ethnic and residential
ties of the men involved. Records of arrests and injuries show clearly
that southern Europeans and outsiders to the East Side, or at least to its
south end, played a predominant role on the side of the strikers. The
forces of "law and order," on the other hand, were overwhelmingly of
Irish background. There were at least five police officers at the mill
gates on Memorial Day who either lived on the East Side or who had
relatives there. Thus in many instances the men who were involved in
the massacre on both sides had personal knowledge of each other, as
the following description from one of my interviews indicates.

(V., East Side Steelworker, 61)
  I was standing over a woman who had been hit. I was trying to help
her up when I see this cop pointing his gun at me. I'm shouting at him
not to shoot when I hear a click. His gun was empty. I know I'm alive
today because of that. The rest of the day I spent taking people to the
hospital, mostly in South Chicago, and I ruined a pretty new car. But
the most amazing thing is that guys saw their neighbors shooting at
them. N—— [a longtime resident of the East Side] swears he was shot in
the belly by a cop who lived down the block from him.[15]

Events such as the Memorial Day Massacre mobilize the energies of
concerned citizens and activists from outside the community for a
relatively short period after the actual conflict. But people in the local
community adjust to a tragedy of major proportions in more personal
ways and over long periods of time. It is clear that on the East Side,
where industrial conflict heightened the tensions of ethnic territorial
succession, the local union was discredited as an organization which
could provide community leadership beyond the mill polity. Until the
1950s, the local union leadership at Republic was essentially the same
as it had been in the union's formative years. A number of the unionists
who had led the strike went on to important positions in the heirarchy
of the United Steelworkers of America, but on the East Side itself

union leaders have never had the prestige associated with similar positions in other South Chicago neighborhoods. Rather than increase class solidarity on the East Side, the severe community conflict associated with the birth of local unionism further reinforced the marginal position of union leaders in the mill neighborhood.

As the Italians and South Slavs who had been the most militant activists in the Republic local in the forties gained acceptance in East Side parishes, they predictably began to espouse the more conservative values of second- and third-generation neighborhood solidarity. Although this is a general phenomenon throughout the South Chicago area, it has been particularly true of the East Side because this is an insular neighborhood of second settlement. The intense polarization which accompanied unionism on the East Side left the leadership of the local union in the hands of dedicated unionists who for many years had little opposition from ethnic or neighborhood leaders. But this was an empty victory, for it came at the expense of the union's symbolic position in the East Side. Until 1969 the union's headquarters were in another neighborhood, and the affairs of the union tended to rouse little interest in the local neighborhood.

United States Steel: Competition
between Unionist and Ethnic
Leaders

The long history of labor organization at the South Works of United States Steel created a relatively large group of experienced and committed unionists in the Bush, Millgate, and Bessemer Park, the neighborhoods which surround the plant. In the period from 1919 to 1945 this group had a definite left-political orientation, but company recognition of the union was not accompanied by tragic violence as it was on the East Side. First, the ecology of the mill and its surrounding neighborhoods was similar to the situation in Irondale and Slag Valley. There was a well-developed network of affiliations based on occupational ties which cut across ethnic bonds and created the basis for collective action in the formation of the union. Second, the United States Steel Corporation in 1936 abandoned its militant anti-unionism, under pressure from the federal government, and adopted a policy of concession and cooperation with the unions.

The 1919 steel strike had marked a significant change in the course of nativism at South Works. Largely through the influence of left-wing leaders such as W. Z. Foster, the AFL steel unions reversed Gompers's policy of excluding the immigrant from union membership. Although

Foster had little hope of instituting industrial unionism in the steel industry in 1919, the admission of immigrants was a major step toward the industrial unionism of the CIO era because it brought the unions masses of receptive and generally poorly skilled workers. In neighborhoods around the South Works, therefore, despite the growth of the large Polish immigrant enclave and status differences between Poles and more established northern European segments of the population, the development of unionist traditions in the 1919 strike paved the way for greater neighborhood solidarity in support of the union than was the case in Irondale or the East Side.[16]

Unionism suffered a severe setback in the 1919 defeat of the AFL, but in the 1930s depression pro-union sentiment at South Works flourished once again. Through depression layoffs and periods of mass unemployment, the Amalgamated Iron and Steel Workers, AFL, and craft unions such as the United Roll Turners continued to grow at the South Works. The latter union was organized at South Works by George Patterson, a blacksmith and roll turner from Bessemer Park. A man of firm socialist convictions, Patterson became the leader of CIO-SWOC organization in the plant, and the first president of the South Works local union after 1937.

In 1934, U.S. Steel made a belated attempt to institute company unionism in its numerous plants. All the unions operating in the South Works were incorporated into the company-led Employee Representation Plan. The ERPs which were established throughout the U.S. Steel empire came about through the urging of Arthur Young, a vice-president in the Carnegie-Illinois division. Young had come to the corporation from International Harvester, where he had been successful in using the Works Council to fight independent unionism. In fact, from 1919 to 1945, Young had directed the Works Council at Wisconsin Steel in combatting pro-union sentiment in Irondale and Slag Valley.

At South Works during the mid-thirties, despite the nominal incorporation of craft unions in the company union, George Patterson and his co-organizers were having great success in organizing internal opposition to the plant's ERP. During 1935 and 1936, when the Steel Workers Organizing Committee of the CIO was created, the South Works employees organized their own independent union, the Associated Employees. In 1936, the year before it merged with the SWOC, membership in the independent union increased from approximately fourteen hundred to over three thousand.[17]

Faced with the possibility of a major strike which would pit them against the CIO at a time when labor had the sympathies of public opinion and the national administration, the corporation adopted a policy of concession and cooperation. It abandoned its attempts at organizing company unions and recognized the CIO locals in its plants. In so doing the company averted a strike and opted for future cooperation with a "responsible" union. Obviously Arthur Young had not succeeded in building in three years what had grown slowly, over more than thirty years, in the Harvester plant, and there was little possibility that South Works could have followed the pattern set at Wisconsin Steel, where the company-sponsored union defeated the CIO. On the other hand, since U.S. Steel recognized the union without seriously polarizing the South Chicago community, as could have been the case had there been a major strike, the birth of the union was not marked by the kind of animosities which turned East Side residents away from the Republic local.

In consequence of the shift in corporate policy which led to union recognition without community conflict, plus the tradition of unionism which cut across ethnic cleavages in the mill neighborhoods, the unionists at South Works continued in control until after World War II. But early recognition by the company also increased the prestige of the union outside the mill, and union leadership became an attractive position from which to gain an ethnic following. This was particularly true for lower status ethnic groups in the mill such as the Poles.

During the organizing drive, Patterson and his staff had recruited a nucleus of respected Polish unionists. Generally, the CIO organizers were well attuned to the attitudes of immigrant groups in the mills, and invariably recruited rank-and-file organizers who could appeal to the worker's ethnic solidarity as well as to his unionist principles. With recognition, however, the first-generation organizer found himself without the skills required to fill the local labor leader's changing role. Unable to express himself well in English, for example, he could not follow the complicated procedures required in the grievance process. Given this shortcoming, the immigrant organizer could not realistically expect to run for grievanceman, the first step toward local union leadership. In consequence of this, most immigrant unionists in the South Works returned to the rank and file after 1937 without ever holding union offices.[18]

By the end of World War II, over 50 percent of the South Works labor force was of first- and second-generation Slavic origin. Politics in the local increasingly came to reflect competition between ethnic and unionist leaders. The former were successful in capturing the leadership of the local in the late forties, when a Polish second-generation bloc won control of the local. The leader of this slate was a good example of the ethnic leader in union politics. His reputation was based almost entirely on family prestige; his brothers were prominent professional men who had built their careers on service to the Polish community of South Chicago. This leader appealed to ethnic solidarity and the ambition of Poles and other Slavic minorities to dominate the union. The unionists tended to stress improvements in the activities of the local and the national union, and they were concerned with the inclusion of newer ethnic groups in the mill polity. Despite their losses from 1945 to 1957, the unionists undertook the political socialization of a new generation of rank-and-file men who would win control in the next decade.

The proportion of Slavic ethnic groups at South Works began to decline rapidly in the late 1950s, as blacks and Mexicans entered the mill in large numbers to fill vacancies created by the occupational and residential mobility of the older groups. The hegemony of ethnic leaders was obviously threatened by this change. At South Works the challenge to Polish dominance in the plant was led by aspiring unionists from the Polish group itself, new young leaders who could appeal to the Poles and other nationality groups on the basis of unionist and ethnic principles. These were men who had come into contact with the first-generation rank-and-file unionists and had applied their lessons to the contemporary ethnic composition of the mill.

Unions and the Community,
1950–70

Since the 1950s, professionals in local welfare service agencies and intellectuals outside the area have expressed disappointment in the local unions' record of involvement in the community. They point to the unions' general apathy in combatting air pollution, in sponsoring new education and health care programs, or in leading the workers to demand greater power to determine the conditions of work in the mills. Here, as at the national level, the unions are criticized for having become satisfied with piecemeal gains in wages and benefits and for having abandoned the progressive political role they played during the years of struggle for recognition. While there is much justification in these criticisms, even professionals who had worked in South Chicago for many years were largely ignorant of the day-to-day activities of the local unions. They had little appreciation of the community-forming processes which mark the politics of these rank-and-file institutions.

Each grievance which originates in a section of the mill involves the workers, their union representatives, and managerial officials in a system of morality and ethics. For example, the case of a worker fired for drinking on the job raises a series of questions which have wider significance than the grievance itself. Should other rank-and-file men, who may also be his neighbors outside the mill, come to his support despite the common danger that his behavior entailed? Is the grievanceman being active enough in seeking justice for the man, or is he over-identifying with the demands of management? Will the workers and their grievanceman be able to "hold their heads up" outside the mill when the facts of their involvement in this case become widely known? To the outsider the grievance system is a means of adjudicating industrial conflict, but to the workers the system reveals much about a man's character. The outcomes may have important meaning for one's reputation in the network of peer relations outside the mill.

Every three years the local unions discussed here, and all the smaller ones in the area, hold elections for union office. For the individual candidates the vote tally is a measure of success in building a reputation as a labor leader or as a leader of an ethnic faction, or both. For the coalitions of ethnic, occupational, and neighborhood primary groups which back a slate of candidates, the results may be the final test of years of negotiation to overcome the barriers which once divided their allegiances. Thus the politics of ethnic or racial succession to union office should not be viewed, as it often is, as an impediment to more "issue oriented" politics. The history of union politics in South Chicago demonstrates the impossibility of separating issues of class interest from politics of succession in the mills and their surrounding neighborhoods.

It is true that most of the steel locals in South Chicago never developed very deep roots in the more radical traditions of the American labor movement. In the 1950s many of the progressive unionists were purged from CIO staffs, and those who returned to the mills and the neighborhoods found it difficult to organize opposition to the rampant Americanism of the McCarthy period. Nevertheless, progressive traditions in the rank and file persist in varying degrees in the contemporary politics of South Chicago's local unions. The old CIO organizers have played an important role in socializing new generations of labor activists. George Patterson retired recently from the union, but his teaching and example remain important for the younger South

Works leaders. A frequent speaker at union affairs, Patterson never misses the opportunity to remind his racially mixed audience, "We were the Black Panthers of our day. The things those fellows are trying for today, we were after then. And we got the same treatment."

Union activists who openly raise progressive issues continue to encounter the same difficulties that plagued them in the organizing years. Certainly company involvement in union affairs is much less direct than it was in the 1930s, but the anti-union themes of Americanism can be raked over by local actors who support company interests. For example, a man who had been a radical unionist in the 1930s recently forged a coalition of progressive whites, Mexicans, and young blacks in the Republic Steel local union. It appeared this coalition would win the union election in 1970. Two days before the election, the local newspaper, which regularly prints public relations material for the company, ran a banner headline accusing the leader of this coalition of having been a communist in the 1930s. Plant foremen posted the headline in the mills, and the coalition was defeated in a close vote. Thus when local unionists worry about introducing progressive planks in their election platforms, it is not without reason based on years of bitter experience.

The issues which outsiders would like to see raised in local union politics are increasingly important to the coalitions which seek to win recognition in the locals. Young union leaders in South Chicago are actively seeking ways to educate the rank and file on issues of housing, education, and control over the flow of work. But the underlying issues of their campaigns continue to center upon the succession to union leadership by various ethnic and racial groups. Indeed, these are perhaps the most fundamental issues the union can deal with, for the eventual adaptation of blacks, Mexicans, and other new factions in the community will depend in great part on the conditions of their succession in local union politics.

5

The Dynamics of Union Succession

A union election at one of the three large mills in South Chicago is a major event for the steelworkers of the community. Weeks before election day the telephone poles around the union halls are plastered with campaign posters announcing the various slates of candidates and their slogans. In taverns at the mill gates talk runs to the coming election; opinions on the probable outcomes are often the source of quite heated debate. Some taverns become informal campaign head-quarters for a given slate of candidates, while other taverns, whose owners attempt to remain neutral, are visited by the candidates on the campaign trail. Usually on a payday when he can count on a big crowd, the candidate will buy drinks for the house in return for the opportunity to stand on a chair for a short campaign speech. And of course the excitement of the campaign reaches inside the mill as well. Although formal campaigning at work is prohibited, campaign slogans are chalked on walls and on machinery, and talk at breaks is usually about the coming election.

Election day itself in a mill election may involve the active participation of two hundred or more men. The candidates and their primary group supporters will take the day off in order to be at the polls from early morning until the closing at night. In the eddying crowd of candidates, supporters, voters, and spectators, there is always a great deal of shouting, mainly of encouragement to candidates and voters as they enter the union hall, but there is also no lack of veiled insults to the opposition in the form of joking innuendos and loud asides. After the polls close the various factions usually continue to circulate between the taverns and the union hall where the votes are being counted. Often, when the results are announced, tempers may rage. A man may vent his feelings of injustice and betrayal, or an entire losing faction may rail at their opposition's tactics one last time before retreating to sad post-mortems at their tavern headquarters. For the victors, on the other hand, particularly if their entire slate or the majority of it has carried the election, the news of victory is a signal for a triumphant entry into the union hall and celebration lasting far into the night.

Observations such as these are based on the climactic moments in union politics.[1] The fact remains that voter turnout in South Chicago union elections, as in local unions in general, is relatively low. Usually the range in turnout is from 40 to 50 percent of the eligible voters. Thus it is clear that large segments of the mill's labor force are not touched by the issues and personalities involved. One reason for this failure is the inability of local union officers to influence company wage and benefit policies. Local union politicians claim that the settlement of contracts at the national level is a cause of local apathy. The problem of voter apathy is greatest among young workers whose commitment to careers in the mill is weak, and turnouts also tend to be low among workers who live outside the mill communities. For the latter the aspect of community conflict usually present in steel mill elections is lost. Involvement in the union's politics is greatest for men whose primary groups draw them into competition for prestige in the mill and the mill neighborhoods. Throughout South Chicago there are groups of workers whose participation in union politics has served as the basis for primary group formation. In each ethnic generation the reconstruction of primary attachments around common participation in union politics is a first step toward the ethnic group's eventual participation in other community institutions.

Reputations on the Line: Personal Mobility through Union Politics

Many more men will enhance their personal prestige through union politics than will ever be apparent from lists of candidates or attendance at local union meetings. When a South Chicago steelworker runs for union office as part of a slate of candidates (the most common arrangement in steel locals), his candidacy is openly supported or opposed by many men who themselves would never dream of running for union office. Often these are men who are either too old, too foreign, or too uneducated to present themselves as public figures. They may be tough older brothers of the candidates whose reputations as former street gang leaders mark them as "heavies"; they may be immigrant milieu; or they may be "old-timers" in the mill who never made a bid for office themselves but are the leaders of important work groups.

These are the men an aspiring labor leader needs to have in his camp; their open support is the currency of local union campaigns. Such support represents a commitment of honor which rarely goes unnoticed in the mills or in the mill neighborhoods.

Workers use the phrase "putting it on the line" in reference to the risk in prestige taken not only by the candidates but by their supporters as well. A man puts his reputation "on the line" when he speaks out for a candidate or a slate in his work group or in his tavern. Should his candidate lose the election, his reputation as a behind-the-scenes leader suffers an incremental decline. On the other hand, failure to commit himself may also cause a man to lose prestige in his peer groups at work and in the neighborhood. A man who fails to commit himself to a candidate when such leadership is expected of him is said to have "shit in his blood." It is interesting to note that both these expressions are used in adolescent youth groups in talking about courage in fights. As any number of writers have observed, leadership in the adolescent peer group may serve as a step toward adult political careers. But the achievement of leadership in community political institutions such as the local union requires more than the limited reputation which the leader of a corner group can normally build. In particular, the fortunes of any individual leader are intimately linked to the types of participation in union politics which characterize his ethnic and residential groups. An extreme example of this would be the black street gang leader whose reputation in his neighborhood would be unknown in a South Chicago steel mill since outside the mills the blacks are scattered throughout the South Side's black metropolis.

For the candidates themselves the rewards which accompany union politics are obvious. Election to union office, even if not to one of the three full-time positions in the local, takes a man out of the mill for union business. Salaries for union office are not usually higher than what a man would make in the mill, but the work is thought to be more varied and interesting despite the longer hours it entails. Beyond the material inducements is the prestige which a man who successfully wages a campaign for local office gains. Generally, this gain is greatest to the extent that the man's candidacy involves the aspirations of his ethnic and residential groups. A local candidate from one of the important ethnic groups in South Chicago gains more overall prestige than does a man from outside the community, since the former's reputation extends outside the mill itself and involves the aspirations of an ethnic or residential segment in South Chicago.

Ethnic and Racial Mobility through Union Politics

Poles, Serbians, Italians, and Mexicans, the groups with important settlements in South Chicago neighborhoods, view success in union politics as a source of the group's prestige in the mill community in general. Thus leaders of well-established groups such as the Poles and Serbians strive to maintain their group's control over top union positions. In general, the mills are still said to "belong" to the ethnic group which controls union leadership over a number of elections. As table 8 indicates, the idea in South Chicago of which ethnic group controls a mill is based more on possession of top leadership positions than on either the numerical proportion of the group in the mill's labor force, or recent developments in the union polity.

Table 8   Ethnic Groups and Union Leadership in Three Plants, 1960s

Mill	Ethnic Group Said to Control Union	Ethnicity of Union Presidents in 1960s	Approx. percentage of Labor Force	Insurgent Groups in the Mill*
South Works ...	Polish	Polish	30	Black, Mexican
Wisconsin	Serbian	Serbian	15	Mexican
Republic	Italian	Italian	10	Black, southern, white, Mexican

SOURCE: Interviews with rank-and-file members of each local union.
*Refers to groups which have most frequently challenged incumbent leaders in the previous decade, or whose support of incumbents maintains their office.

For new ethnic groups in South Chicago, or segments of older ones such as the Mexicans and the DP Serbians, victory in a local union election is a signal to politicians and other activists in the community that the group is achieving enough unity and leadership skill to compete outside the confines of its own ethnic institutions. Thus, succession to local union offices has almost invariably preceded capture of leadership positions in other communal institutions. In the early phases of building ethnic unity union politicians play a central role in uniting the competing segments of their ethnic settlements.

Ethnic or racial groups which compete for leadership positions in the union, but which are not represented in the mill neighborhoods, do not stand to gain much prestige in their residential communities as a result of gains in influence in the local union. Black steelworkers in the South Chicago mills best exemplify this situation. Aside from the small and extremely depressed black enclave in Millgate, blacks are not a local group in the mill neighborhoods. In consequence of this, victory in a union election does not elevate the prestige of any identifiable black residential segment, and the communal inducements to competition for union leadership are missing among the black steelworkers. Lack of a territorial base in the mill neighborhoods does not necessarily decrease the motivation of black steelworkers to seek union office, but it presents conditions which increase the difficulty of blacks' establishing unity in the mills.

Despite their lack of a territorial base in South Chicago's mill neighborhoods, black workers compete vigorously for leadership positions in the local unions.[2] In the spring of 1970, for example, a coalition ticket headed by a veteran black unionist defeated its opposition at the South Works local of the United Steelworkers. This campaign was important in the politics of Chicago labor unions for a number of reasons. First, no black worker had ever held the presidency of this largest steel mill local in Chicago. Second, the results were a victory for a coalition of blacks, Mexicans from South Chicago, and progressive white unionists of second- and third-generation Slavic ethnicity. For the black unionists who led this coalition ticket, the victory marked the culmination of years of political organization and negotiation in the mill. It was particularly welcome in that it came through a coalition with segments of the mill's white ethnic groups rather than through a complete racial polarization of the mill polity.

In summary, an ethnic group which has a territorial base in the mill neighborhoods stands to increase or at least maintain its prestige in the community through competition for union office. An ethnic or racial group which does not reside in the mill neighborhoods stands only to enhance its prestige inside the mills. Regardless of this important distinction, competition through union politics presents opportunities for status mobility for a much larger number of men than will ever appear as candidates on the ballot. Viewed from this perspective, union politics involves the formation and maintenance of personal reputations. At the group level, the formation of leadership reputations which overlap and bind the various segments of an ethnic group is a prerequisite to unity in other areas of community politics. Two broad ecological situations are of concern here, one in which a group is represented in the mill neighborhoods, the other in which the group is found only in the work setting. These situations present different obstacles to the formation of unionist reputations within a group and thus to the eventual establishment of ethnic unity in politics.

Ecological Obstacles
to Ethnic Unity

Two sources of cleavage in the ethnic or racial groups represented in South Chicago's steel mills are segmentation arising out of the division of labor, and territorial and generational segmentation of the group in the mill neighborhoods.[3] The first applies with least ambiguity to the situation of black steelworkers in South Chicago's mills. Territorial segmentation presents the greatest problems for the Mexicans of South Chicago, and segmentation by generations is a problem particularly for the Serbians.

Obstacles to Black Unity

The major obstacle to black unity in the mills arises out of the division of labor itself. If a leader is to become known throughout the entire steel plant, his reputation must extend across the various departments, from the ore docks to the finishing end of the plant. Within a department he must be known to men on each of the three turns, and within a turn he must have contacts at the level of the extremely diverse work groups which constitute the basic units in the functional division of labor. Lacking access to networks of affiliations outside the mill, the black union politician at South Works or Wisconsin Steel must build his reputation inside the workplace. He must first gain a following among his nearest workmates and in his mill department, and gradually he may extend his sphere of acquaintances throughout the occupational community of the plant. The only rank-and-file institution in the workplace to link the diverse segments of the mill is the plant's grievance system. Thus it is through the union itself, by participation at its lowest levels of organization, that the aspiring black leader in South Chicago steel mills gains the reputation necessary to forge the unity of his group in the mill polity.

Obstacles to Mexican Unity

Mexican steelworkers in South Chicago are not disadvantaged by lack of territorial ties in the mill neighborhoods. On the other hand, territorial segmentation between the Irondale and Millgate Mexican enclaves presents serious obstacles to unity in union politics. As previously detailed, the Mexicans of South Chicago remain relatively segregated in these two enclaves. Among Mexican adolescent groups, the major source of opposition and conflict stems from disputes between boys from opposing territorial segments of the group. This animosity carries into the adult years and becomes manifest in disputes between aspiring political leaders from the two Mexican neighborhoods.

The fact that the Mexicans do live in the local community allows work relationships between men from the different territorial segments to be continued outside the mill in the network of neighborhood tavern affiliations. The division of labor in the mills creates an ecology of affiliations among Mexicans in the mill neighborhoods which crosses boundaries of territorial segmentation. It is this network, as it appears outside the mills, which must be exploited and strengthened by the aspiring Mexican union leader.

Obstacles to Serbian Unity

Serbian union politicians face problems in maintaining an influence in local union politics owing to their declining numbers in the mills. The arrival of first-generation Serbian and Croatian immigrants since World War II has strengthened the potential base of support for Serbian union activists. At the same time, conflict between immigrant and second-generation Serbians presents a problem for the second-generation Serbian labor leaders. They must attract the immigrant Serbians without sacrificing their prestige in the second- and third-generation Serbian group. Nevertheless, if the Serbian labor leaders are to maintain their influence, they must generalize their reputations beyond the ethnic group itself.

Where they have assumed union leadership, the fortunes of Serbian unionists come to be associated with the fortunes of other ethnic groups, such as the Poles and Italians, groups at the same stage of ethnic dispersion in South Chicago's neighborhoods. In other words, where they compete for leadership of a local union, Serbian labor leaders attempt to represent the aspirations of all the white ethnic groups at the same stage in the natural history of ethnic adaptation in the community. Therefore, Serbian labor leaders often appeal to neighborhood rather than ethnic solidarities. In the face of declining numbers, unity is a less serious problem for an ethnic politician than is the need to reconstruct a following of people who share neighborhood histories.

Table 9 summarizes the various ecological barriers which confront the Serbians, Mexicans, and blacks. As in any political system, succession to union office involves a sequence of steps which include the emergence of leadership without factions, coalition formation at

Table 9   Obstacles to Ethnic Unity in Three
                                                  Unionist Groups

Ethnic Group	Ecological Distribution	Source of Cleavage	Basis for Political Following
Serbians	Dispersed, declining numbers	Generations	Neighborhood solidarities
Mexicans	Territorially segmented	Territorial	Occupational ties extended outside mills
Blacks	Excluded from mill neighborhoods	Occupational	Grievance system in mills

nominations, the campaigns, and finally the vote itself. Success at each of these stages will depend on the activities of primary groups of men who engage in a three-year cycle of competition for union leadership. Despite the pressures they will exert upon one another's allegiances, these groups meet continually in face-to-face situations in the mills, the union halls, and the neighborhood taverns. Thus, even groups which may be locked in bitter competition must strive to maintain civil, adult relationships.

Formation and Maintenance of
Unionist Groups

Unionist leadership styles and tactics in South Chicago vary in large measure with the cleavages that divide a particular ethnic faction. But a common prerequisite to leadership is seniority in the mill. Only in unusual circumstances can a man expect to run for even the lowest union office before he has accumulated from five to ten years' seniority, and the average age of incumbent full-time officials in the South Chicago unions was forty-eight. Therefore, as the various strategies which leaders of the three groups invoke in forging political unity in their factions are described, one should keep in mind that local unions in South Chicago are political institutions dominated by men who are in the prime of their adult careers, both as the heads of families and as steelworkers.[4]

Serbian Union Leadership:
Neighborhood Primary Groups

Primary group formation. Serbian labor leaders maintain their influence in South Chicago unions (particularly at Wisconsin Steel) through the formation of heterogeneous neighborhood primary groups. Generally, men of southern and eastern European ethnicity have retained their hold over union leadership through the activities of groups which base their solidarity on residential rather than on ethnic attachments. Thus, the core of Serbian leadership at Wisconsin Steel operates in a group of second-generation men of varying ethnicity. This group is composed of ten to fifteen men who grew up in Irondale. Earlier in their lives, as adolescents and young men, they fought each other as members of ethnically homogeneous street corner groups. As football players, baseball players, and boxers, they wore uniforms paid for by the ethnic parish and tavern. Now, as respected neighborhood and mill activists they compete vigorously in union and ward politics.

The leadership group of second-generation Serbian and Italian unionists at Wisconsin Steel functions in the South Chicago neighborhoods, particularly in Irondale, as an identifiable clique of labor politicians. The group appears at innumerable affairs sponsored by neighborhood organizations, including church dinners, football banquets, Republican and Democratic committee affairs, aldermen's golf outings, American Legion banquets, and important functions sponsored by the neighborhood improvement associations. In all these the leadership group from Wisconsin Steel can be counted upon to buy a block of tickets as well as a page in the ubiquitous ad books. Attendance at such neighborhood affairs is an important feature of the group's political style. Such functions are an invaluable source of information on the intentions of possible opponents, of complaints which can be ironed out if necessary, and for general renewal of contacts with respected leaders in the mills. As a union election approaches, the Serbian and Italian leadership group will call in their debts from leaders of the neighborhood organizations; they will expect to hear that the latter are "putting in the good word" for their candidacy.

Managing ethnicity. Although they form unionist primary groups on the basis of neighborhood rather than ethnic attachments, the Serbian labor leaders must also negotiate with other ethnic leaders in order to retain the Serbian vote that does remain in the mills. The unionists manage their own second-generation ethnicity in such a way as to overcome the tensions which divide South Chicago's Serbians. Second-generation Serbians who lead the church and mutual benefit organizations expect the Serbian labor leaders to side with them in their disputes with the immigrant Serbians. If they did this, however, the Serbian labor leaders would lose votes among the immigrants. As the following case demonstrates, the labor leaders manage their ethnic attachments in such as way as to become intermediaries between the competing generational segments of the Serbian populations.

Steve is a second-generation Serbian leader of the neighborhood primary group which runs the local union at Wisconsin Steel. In the 1970 union election he is faced with a serious challenge from a coalition of Mexicans, and some blacks, and a dissident group of Slavic workers. This opposition is led by a Serbian candidate who is not very well known in the neighborhoods outside the mill, but could potentially split Steve's traditional Slavic and southern European support in the rank and file. As we discussed his election strategy, Steve summed up his perception of the situation:

"You know, Will, I think we're in pretty good shape. The blacks are split both ways, we've been working pretty hard on that. I'm getting it from the Mexicans here in Irondale, but we've got them in a corner because they didn't go against me direct. Now the DPs are going to go with us because I've stuck by them in the past."

Steve's support of the DPs is a matter of some controversy among second-generation Serbians in South Chicago. The immigrants left the old Serbian parish in 1964 and began building their own social center and church. Bitter quarrels and court fights have marked relations between ethnic leaders in the two groups ever since. Steve tries to stress that he is a labor leader and not a church man; therefore he must attempt to support his friends on both sides of the dispute. His primary group of unionists at Wisconsin Steel have supported any DP fund-raising campaigns, and now, during his campaign to retain control of the Wisconsin union, Steve must get the support of the DPs in the plant.

Steve's ally in the DP group is a man often referred to as "King Peter." Peter is a steelworker at Republic who has been a leader in organizing the immigrants to build their own ethnic institutions. An older man, he has considerable seniority at Republic and acts as an informal job counselor for the immigrant Serbians in all the local mills. Shortly before the election in Steve's plant, Peter invites him and his group of neighborhood men to the inaugural festivities at the newly opened immigrant Serbian church on the East Side. King Peter makes sure that Steve is seated on the dais, the only second-generation Serbian to be given that honor, and in the course of the afternoon, Peter reminds the large crowd how much Steve has done for them and how they may return his favors by remembering that there is an important election coming up at the Wisconsin plant.

Serbian patrimonial leadership. The maintenance of their leadership in the local union through the activities of a neighborhood primary group produces a form of patrimonialism in the conduct of union affairs. Since the Wisconsin local is an independent union which retains rather close working relations with the company, it is possible for union leaders to dispense favors to friends and allies in Irondale and other mill neighborhoods. Also, because they do not have to share their funds with other levels of a union hierarchy, the neighborhood leaders at Wisconsin Steel are in a position to help other neighborhood leaders to a greater degree than is found in any of the unions affiliated with the United Steelworkers of America. Leadership of the local union is almost entirely a matter of personal allegiances, backed up by the dispensation of favors and gratuities. Judgment of a leader's ability in this union is based on his ability to call upon a neighborhood following and to hold that following through the maintenance of personal attachments. Whenever it appears that a member of the unionist leadership group is losing his following, the group will do everything possible to provide him with the material potential to shore up his support. Failing in that, the group must exclude such a person and attempt to replace him by someone with more developed allegiances in the mill and the neighborhood. Thus, even among members of the leadership group who share common ethnic backgrounds, the perceived source of solidarity is not ethnicity as much as it is the personal reciprocities that have been accumulated among the men over years of association.

Mexican Union Politics:
Ethnic Primary Groups

Primary group formation. In contrast to the Serbian and Italian strategy of building reputations as leaders of the white population in the mill neighborhoods, the Mexicans of South Chicago and Irondale are in an earlier phase of their political development. Before they can hope to extend their influence outside the ethnic group itself, they must first settle the problem of who shall represent them in union politics.

A combination of extensive kin ties and achieved status tends to be prerequisite for a Mexican steelworker's initial entry into union politics. The most successful union politician in South Chicago to date, for example, could count on six brothers in various departments who could act as campaign managers in those segments of the labor force. In addition to this advantage, he had graduated from high school and had completed a number of years of college before and during his career in the mill. In contrast to the first-generation Mexicans who provided the majority of his supporters, the second-generation Mexican labor leader had little trace of Spanish accent and could act and dress the role of the union politician without necessarily calling attention to his ethnicity. Despite outward appearances, however, the Mexican union politicians usually have formed few attachments outside their ethnic group before entering union politics. This fact partially explains their preoccupation with establishment of ethnic solidarity among Mexican rank-and-file workers. This must be done before their leaders can extend their influence outside the immediate bounds of the ethnic group.

Mexican union politicians overcome the territorial animosities which divide their population by forming primary groups in which occupational attachments, along with ethnicity, are the main criteria for recruitment. These primary groups are formed by Mexican men who work in the same mill but often come from opposing Mexican neighborhoods in South Chicago. Four taverns, two in Irondale and two in South Chicago, are the gathering places for men who are active in union and ward politics. These taverns are also the headquarters of adult Mexican men in the two opposing neighborhoods. As indicated earlier, the boundaries betwen these often competing enclaves are not taken lightly, and it is only on the basis of shared experience in the mills that Mexican men from Millgate come to patronize the gathering place of Mexican political leaders in Irondale. Thus, a Mexican union activist from Millgate who works at Wisconsin Steel in Irondale will often boast that he knows the men at Juan and Tina's Tavern or at the J & M Corner Club, and that he frequently spends time with them. When the need arises for bargaining between the two groups, as for example when the Irondale Mexicans need the support of the South Chicago men in a union election, men who belong to the occupational groups which cross territorial boundaries perform the vital function of maintaining communications between the two groups of Mexican unionists.

Managing ethnicity. Union activists from the two territorial segments of the Mexican population agree that control of Mexican union politics at Wisconsin Steel should belong to the Irondale men and that control of Mexican union politics at South Works should remain with the Millgate Mexicans. Despite this understanding, there is often considerable conflict between Mexican union activists in the two neighborhoods. For example, in a recent union election at Wisconsin Steel, the Mexican vice-president of the local chose not to challenge the incumbent Serbian president but rather to support another Serbian for the presidency. The Irondale Mexicans hoped that support of the latter would make him more responsive to the demands of the Mexican unionists and pave the way for increased Mexican influence in the local. The Millgate Mexicans in the Wisconsin local felt that the Irondale contingent should have taken the risk of directly challenging the incumbent. Since the Irondale men chose not to do so, the Millgate men argued that they could support both the Irondale Mexican for the vice-presidency and the incumbent Serbian for the presidency. Their motives for supporting the incumbent Serbian were complex. First, they saw the opportunity to gain recognition in the white ethnic groups of Irondale and the East Side. Second, they did not believe that the Serbian challenger for the presidency had a chance to win even with their support. With some finesse they could satisfy the competing demands of their Mexican counterparts in Irondale and the Slavic union leaders as well. Thus for a period of two months before and after the election in Wisconsin Steel, relations between the Mexican unionists in the two territorial enclaves were exceedingly strained. The Irondale contingent considered their right to lead the Mexican labor force at Wisconsin Steel to have been violated. For their part the South Chicago Mexican unionists maintained that the Irondale Mexican candidate had been shown to have "shit in his blood" when he failed to challenge the incumbent directly. They argued that this had warranted their independent action. Generally such disputes occur frequently and are settled over time through the same channels in which they occurred, that is, through the network of occupational ties as they extend into the Mexican neighborhoods.

Mexican equalitarian leadership. Leadership in the primary groups of Mexican unionists is based on a combination of family attachments, occupational ties, and mutual respect among equals. Since they deal mainly with other Mexican men, and because they have not yet assumed control of all the machinery in any of the union locals, the Mexican unionists have little patronage to distribute in building their networks of allegiances. This results in more emphasis on the personal qualities of leaders and on the maintenance of allegiances which rest on men's honor, as explained by the most prominent Mexican unionist in South Chicago.

We only have about 10 percent of the vote here at South Works, but if we can keep it in line it can be the swing vote in a close campaign. We always knew this but up to a few years ago we couldn't get any unity in our people. When I first ran for financial secretary of the local I fixed it so that we wouldn't have to worry about our people getting split into more than one group. I had my brothers and guys from the neighborhood that I've known all my life put out the word that when it came to the nomination meeting, we would all sit together and vote the same way. Well, when we came to the meeting there were a few guys, Chicanos, who thought they would go on their own and support the other ticket. When the meeting began and we all sat together, they were ashamed and we teased them so much that they didn't have the heart to put themselves up on the other ticket. So that was the first time we hung together and it made all the difference.

Once a man, such as the speaker above, is elected to union leadership, his status in the Mexican unionist groups is confirmed, but in each succeeding election the call for solidarity is based on appeals to peer group solidarity. In their deliberations the Mexican unionists attempt to bring as many men into the discussions as possible, and the role of the leader is that of first among equals.

Black Union Politics:
Occupational Primary Groups

Occupational groups. Given the dispersion of black steelworkers throughout Chicago's South Side, there is only one route whereby black workers in South Chicago's mills can gain the reputations necessary to forge unity in their ranks. The aspiring black labor leader begins his career by competing for recognition in his work group and his mill department. He must make his name at work, inside the mills, at the lowest levels of the division of labor. Where they exist, black caucuses in the mill polity may approximate the outside networks of affiliations which facilitate reputation building among the white ethnic groups of South Chicago. The caucus can provide the locus for competition between aspiring black leaders from which eventually will come a set of leaders who can establish unity and discipline in the black segment of the mill. But how do leaders emerge in an ethnic or racial caucus where there is no differentiation based on ascribed criteria? Obviously race and ethnicity do not confer status in such caucuses, nor does kinship or neighborhood reputation, since the men here are strangers before entry into the mills.

In other industrial unions, age and degree of militancy may be important variables in explaining the emergence of leadership in minority caucuses. In unions which have had traditions of racially integrated leadership, but in which blacks have gained only limited power—a situation common in Detroit area UAW locals—the leadership of black caucuses tends to be young and militant. Ability to articulate militant themes and to organize alienated young workers become criteria for leadership roles. This situation is accentuated in the auto industry by the relative preponderance of unskilled assembly-line workers. There the work situation is highly atomized, but at the same time it permits rather high visibility to militant actors.[5]

Large concentrations of unskilled, young, dissatisfied workers are not common in the steel industry. The young black workers in South Chicago steel mills are probably no less dissatisfied as a group than their counterparts in the auto plants, but such men are dispersed throughout the mills in small groups, where they work on laboring tasks and interact with older and more experienced black workers. The latter form the moral core of black society in the steel mills, a subject discussed in more detail in an earlier chapter. In consequence of this, black caucuses in South Chicago steel unions are dominated by men who have ten or more years seniority and who have already begun to establish their reputations in the mill's occupational community.[6] A quite typical case of the emergence of black leadership in South Chicago steel mills is found in the election at South Works which, for the first time, saw black unionists win the presidency of that largest mill in the city.

Managing racial unity. The group of black unionists who captured leadership of the South Works local in June 1970 had been organizing the black segment of the mill's labor force for a period of almost ten years prior to that climactic election. In 1960 only one black union politician managed to capture a grievanceman's position (out of the ten such positions available), despite the fact that in a number of divisions blacks were the largest single group, if not the majority. Generally, aspiring black unionists lacked experience in union politics and were unable to exploit potential conflict among white and Mexican steelworkers.

The degree of unity in an ethnic or racial group which will ensure that an opposition group cannot divide its loyalties is itself the result of political competition within the group. An indication of the lack of unity and leadership among black steelworkers at South Works in 1960 is the fact that the only black who did win a grievanceman's position was opposed in his department by two other black candidates as well as the white incumbent. By defeating two other black candidates in the grievanceman's race, the winner, Bob Hatch, became the undisputed leader of his department. In the decade to come no black man would ever challenge his leadership. With a safe constituency in his department, Hatch could extend his influence in the union polity through a series of negotiations with aspiring white politicians.

As other successful black unionists began to emerge in their mill departments throughout the 1960s, Hatch led this growing group of skilled black union politicians in the formation of a racial caucus. During the decade the influence of this group of fifteen to twenty black unionists increased in proportion to the increase of blacks in the mill's labor force.

The rise to prominence of the black unionists was not due to sponsorship or any form of white benevolence. Nor was it directly due to the increasing numerical strength which blacks were gaining in the mill. The important fact was that in a number of departments black unionists had achieved a degree of unity which made it impossible for competing unionists to find blacks to challenge the current black leadership in those sections of the mill. An indication of this is the fact that in the elections of 1964 and 1967, Hatch and two or three other black unionists were sought by all of the white factions in the union polity, even those most associated with traditional Polish dominance of the mill.

In the 1964 election, Hatch and the other black unionists contributed to the upset of a coalition of conservative Polish unionists who had dominated the South Works local throughout the 1950s. By helping negotiate an aggregation of progressive Polish and Mexican unionists, the blacks demonstrated that no slate could win an election at South Works without their support. Thus in the following election the conservative opposition found it impossible to divide the loyalties of the black unionists and was forced to endorse Hatch and two other blacks in the hope of gaining black votes. By 1970 conditions were opportune for Hatch and the black union activists to make their bid for the union's presidency: the progressive Polish president they had supported had joined the union's staff, and the proportion of blacks in the mill had reached almost 50 percent.

The black unionists under Hatch assumed leadership of the progressive coalition of blacks, Mexicans, and Polish liberals in the 1970 union election. This progressive slate would be opposed by remnants of the older and more conservative white unionists who had led the union throughout the fifties. Under normal circumstances Hatch and his coalition could have expected an easy victory. But the situation was vastly complicated when the small left-wing faction (Trotskyist) in the plant nominated a dissident black unionist to oppose Hatch on the grounds that he was too moderate. Given the normally lower turnout among young black workers, a maverick black candidate could split enough votes away from Hatch to make him lose the election. This would be most likely if almost all the white voters refused to support a black president at South Works.

The gloomy projections in table 10[7] were drawn up at one point during the union's election campaign when Hatch and his allies began to feel that racial polarization in Chicago since the riots following Dr. King's assassination could stimulate a large white turnout and prevent the black candidates from gaining enough white votes to offset the normally lower turnout among young black workers. In fact the

Table 10   Estimated Turnout and Vote for
                                               Union President, South Works Local
                                               65, USWA, 1970

South Works Labor Force		Estimated Turnout		Estimated Vote		
				Hatch	White Opponent	Black Opponent
Black.........3,300	(45%)	1,650	(50%)	1,300	50	300
Mexican...... 700	(9%)	350	(50%)	300	50	...
White........3,500	(46%)	2,100	(60%)	200	1,800	100
Total 7,500		4,000		1,800	1,900	400

election did generate a tangible increase in racial tension around the
mill. During the election day vigil at the polls, Hatch, who is an
extremely large and powerful man, as are most of the other black
unionists, suffered a number of insults from white steelworkers.

At one point during the day he said, "Bill, this is really a bitch ain't it?
I've had a few of these old SOBs pass me at the door here and say, 'How
you doing boy?' If I wasn't the candidate, I'd have belted 'em one, but
here I am giving all these guys the glad hand."

   The projections of the progressive coalition strategists proved to be
overly pessimistic, as the final results show. With the election of a black
president who undoubtedly received at least 15 percent of the white
vote, the black unionists successfully climaxed ten years of political
organization. They elected a black union president and a number of
black officers, while maintaining a strong interracial and inter-ethnic
coalition, similar to the ones they had participated in when they had to
be satisfied with the scraps of power in the union's leadership. Of all
the votes cast (3,508), Hatch received 1,721, his white opponent 1,496,
and his black opponent 291.
   Black bureaucratic leadership. The residential separation of black
workers from the mill neighborhoods requires them to build their
unionist leadership groups inside the mills, largely by proving their
competence in the grievance system of the local union. Of course the
black unionists must possess individual qualities which mark them as
worthy of respect among their fellow black workers, but if they are to
gain a political following among non-blacks as well, they must
demonstrate their competence in mastering the intricacies of the
plant's grievance machinery. This may be the case for white workers
also, but it is particularly true of the blacks who do not have recourse to
ethnic and neighborhood networks among steelworking families
outside the plant. Success as a grievanceman is measured by a man's

ability to carry cases which arise in his mill department through the plant's advocacy system. Cases which cannot be settled at any of the more informal bargaining steps in the grievance procedure may ultimately go to arbitration before an impartial panel. In these instances the grievanceman must cooperate with union staff members to prepare briefs, call witnesses, and determine if appeals to higher levels of the process are warranted.

Most of the unionists who are successful in the grievance system are self-taught. They spend long hours of study at home, at occasional union seminars, and in conference with more experienced staff officials of the union. The more dependent a unionist is upon success in this system, the more legal expertise he must develop, and the more likely it is that he will become a specialist in the politics of the grievance bureaucracy. Such specialization may lead to eventual careers as professionals in the union hierarchy. As a union politician begins to spend increasing amounts of time operating in the grievance system, his political following in the rank and file may decline for lack of contact, and this will increase his dependency upon the administrative hierarchy of the union. Since black unionists in the South Chicago mills have difficulty converting their political following in the plant to a political following in the outside community, they are especially likely to follow administrative career paths within the union. Thus, the problem of retaining political leadership in the rank and file while mastering the legal advocacy system of the industry is especially acute for the blacks. Once they achieve positions in the union, their opportunities for association with mill workers are more limited than is the case for white and Mexican unionists who live in the mill neighborhoods.

Conclusion: Aggregation and Succession in the Unions

With varying degrees of success, steelworkers' unions in South Chicago perform the traditional role of organized labor in local communities. As Tannenbaum stated it,

> In terms of the individual, the union returns to the worker his "society." It gives him a fellowship, a part in the drama that he can understand, and life takes on meaning ... because he shares a value system common to others. . . . Trade unionism is ... a social and ethical system, not merely an economic one. It is concerned with the whole man. Its ends are the "good life."[8]

It is particularly for groups of political activists that the union provides a peer group fellowship. Out of the ten thousand workers at the large South Works plant, for example, there are about one hundred and fifty men who participate regularly in the yearly cycle of union meetings and social events, although many more men and their families will come to one or two social events held at the union hall during the year. But the unionist groups which are regular participants in the yearly cycle of union events also play a critical role in the overall communal life of the South Chicago area. These are the people who negotiate aggregations of workers in the mills and in the mill neighborhoods. These aggregations of union leaders are themselves negotiated in the process of union politics. In a working-class community the unionists are agents of ethnic adaptation, for the union is not a closed society of workers but one which bridges the barriers of local segmentation and in various ways channels the participation of ethnic and racial groups in other community institutions.

The patterns of ethnic and racial succession which mark the three major steel unions in South Chicago were established earlier in the century when the unions were organized, and when they were among the first communal alternatives to the segmented neighborhood and ethnic associations of the area. Since at least the 1930s, succession by a racial or ethnic group to leadership positions in the local unions has been perhaps the primary focus of union politics in the area. At each of the three mills the significance attached to succession, and the degree to which unionist themes are mixed with ethnic politics, has depended on the neighborhood history of the local union. But in each steel mill the negotiation of leadership groups among the main ethnic and racial segments of the labor force has been the mainstay of union political processes. The succession of groups such as Serbians, Mexicans, and blacks to the leadership of a local union is rarely the simple matter of one group's establishing its hegemony based on numerical strength in the rank and file. In the process of winning power in the union, the cleavages which divide a group are overcome, attachments among group leaders are reconstructed, and alliances are formed with outsiders.

The Serbian unionists at Wisconsin Steel manage to subordinate their ethnic attachments to the neighborhood ties they share with Italians and other long-time residents of Irondale and Slag Valley. Thus when people in other South Chicago neighborhoods perceive the leadership at the Wisconsin plant to be Serbian, or "Hunky," this is not entirely accurate. The Serbians there manage to retain what ethnic vote remains for them in the mill, and this involves gaining trust among the immigrant Serbians. But their control of the union depends more upon their success at leading heterogeneous primary groups which are formed in the neighborhoods and which associate in neighborhood institutions.

By the time Mexican unionists succeed in winning leadership positions in local mills, their group has also undergone some important internal adaptations. Primary groups of Mexican unionists negotiate agreements between the competing territorial segments of their group. Each gains a sphere of influence over its neighborhood steel mill, but there is recognition of the need to establish precedents for cooperation and leadership which cut across territorial cleavages and create unity where none existed before. The Mexican unionists who establish these precedents for collective action can then turn their energies to other community institutions. They work to enlist others of their group for competition in ward politics, or for competition in the welfare agencies of the larger community.

Among the three groups, the blacks are in a unique position because, as I have observed before, their exclusion from the mill neighborhoods forces them to depend most heavily on the negotiation of black leadership inside the workplace. Contrary to what white workers may believe, the black workers are not automatically united in their racial solidarity. They too must select leaders and unify behind them; they too are divided and their leaders must bridge divisions within their ranks. Indeed their exclusion from the mill neighborhood deprives the black workers of a base within which they can negotiate their unity outside the plant. Inside the plant they are segmented by the division of labor, and it is only within the union itself that black leaders may emerge who can unify a black caucus and whose skill in the grievance system can win support among white workers and white unionists. Thus when black steelworkers finally succeeded in winning leadership at the South Works, their victory was not a "black takeover" as much as it was an indication that the blacks have managed to become leaders in the negotiation of aggregations of workers from a variety of ethnic and neighborhood backgrounds.

Succession in local union politics will establish the conditions of a group's entry into other community institutions, and particularly into the party organizations of the ward. The primary groups which are formed by an ethnic or racial segment in union politics may be enlisted in ward politics or may negotiate aggregations of participants in opposition to ward political leaders. Also the leadership strategies developed by an ethnic group in union politics may be applied elsewhere in political life. The patrimonial leadership of Serbian unionists is a mirror image of the traditional leadership of ward party organizations; the egalitarian group leadership of the Mexicans continues as they become active in ward politics; and the bureaucratic leadership patterns which evolve among black steelworkers, and tend to channel them toward careers within the union, make it difficult to aggregate black unionists in ward politics. In general, therefore, a group's experience in the politics of union succession provides the first precedents in the management of ethnicity for participation in other community political processes.

Part 3

Ward Organization and Ethnic Succession

Urban politics at the local level is too often viewed as a mere derivation of the economic and cultural characteristics of the citizens in a political territory. Thus, geopolitical units such as wards are often classified according to indexes of traditional versus modern political behavior; urban politics becomes a matter of working-class provincials versus middle-class cosmopolitans, or "river wards" versus "newspaper wards." Students of urban politics at the local level have tended to apply two models of political behavior: first, a provincial, ethnically segmented population supports a form of traditional or personal rule embodied in the ward machine and its boss; in the other model, cosmopolitan voters whose needs are not suited to the capabilities and resources of traditional ward politicians heed the appeal of candidates who base their claims on reasoned argument and persuasion.

The chief shortcoming of these models is their failure to consider the dynamics of political change. Local political institutions are seen as powerless to adapt to improvement in the economic and educational backgrounds of local populations. Political institutions are thought to play little role in the transition from patrimonial to issue-oriented politics. Where ward political organizations are successful in recruiting the educated and economically secure residents of new neighborhoods, such success is viewed as anomalous. It is explained as a carry-over from political traditions formed in the central city's river wards, or it is a function, as in Chicago, of creative political maneuvering by the most powerful figures in the urban machine.

Political leaders in South Chicago's Tenth Ward have had considerable success in adapting their techniques of political mobilization across a wide variety of neighborhoods. This suggests the need for an alternative orientation to local urban politics. A distinctive feature of local level politics is that competition and conflict occur within the context of personal relationships. For example, when the alderman and the Democratic committeeman struggle for control of the Tenth Ward Democratic Organization, both leaders will attempt to build organizations of neighborhood primary group leaders. Thus when voters choose between one or the other set of contending ward leaders, they are also choosing among entire groups of ward residents, many of whom they know personally from their own and adjacent neighborhoods. Viewed from this perspective, local ward politics is a matter of recruiting the loyalties of citizens who command the friendship and trust of families living in a three-block area of the city. As the basis which established this trust changes, so must the political organization modify its appeals for precinct leadership and mass support. Ward political leaders attempt to fit the backgrounds of their precinct organizers to the political styles of the various territorial segments of the ward. Through the continual recruitment of new leaders, the ward political organization adapts to the changing ecology of the community. In turn, the party organization becomes perhaps the most important locus for ethnic adaptation and ethnic succession.

6   The Political Ecology of an Industrial Ward

Ward politics in South Chicago's Tenth Ward is at once the arena of fierce competition between locality groups and the biggest, most lively social game one can play. No institution does more to bring the various ethnic and territorial segments of the area together for communal action. Some of the most important dates in the yearly calendar of South Chicago social events are sponsored by the party organizations. Hundreds of families in the Tenth Ward owe their social mobility to success in the precincts and to the rewards of patronage. Many hundreds more are inevitably drawn into the politics of the ward by appeals to their ethnic, personal, or civic commitments. The leaders of the ward party organizations are the elite of the community; the ward "boss" and his lieutenants are the core of the area's upper middle class, but with few exceptions they trace their power and their leadership to a base of kinship and ethnic attachments in the steel mills and the mill neighborhoods.

In contrast to the more narrow focus of steel union politics, the ward organizations involve the activities of all strata in South Chicago's population. First, the party organizations are not exclusively male political associations as are the unions. Women play increasingly important roles in organizing the social events of the ward and in mobilizing neighborhood precincts. Therefore, as new ethnic groups attempt to gain power in the ward organizations, they must also develop the political leadership of women in their groups. Second, the ward organizations are not limited to the blue collar work groups of the area. The unionist and other blue collar groups who enter ward politics are joined by middle-class merchants and professionals, as well as a diverse group of patronage workers, gamblers, former fighters, college students, and leaders of church and civic voluntary associations. Thus, in union politics the typical social event is a dance or a beer and hot dog rally, while the ward organization sponsors fashion shows, golf outings, and dinner parties at the more fashionable restaurants of the area.

During my years in South Chicago, the Tenth Ward Democratic Organization went through a series of intense political battles to establish a successor to the ward boss who had died shortly before I came to the area. It is true that like other working-class wards in the city of Chicago, the Tenth is a "machine" ward. The local Democratic committee distributes upwards of three hundred patronage jobs to its workers, and it regularly returns handsome majorities for local, state, and national Democratic candidates. But between 1967 and 1970 the Tenth Ward became embroiled in a series of bitter campaigns to establish the new set of primary groups which would run ward affairs in the years to come. In this period of political "civil wars" in the ward, all the negotiations which aggregate political activists were made visible. Competing factions of the ward attempted to recruit leaders from the various ethnic groups and residential neighborhoods. In each precinct it was necessary to recruit leaders who would respond to different appeals depending on the nature of solidarity and conflict in their neighborhoods.[1]

Neighborhood Solidarity and Political Mobilization

To build an effective ward organization of precinct level workers, the leaders of a local party organization must have answers to two important questions about the area's neighborhoods. First, they must understand as much as possible about the nature of solidarity and conflict in each neighborhood. Are the residents divided according to long-standing ethnic cleavages, or are they all relative newcomers to the area for whom ethnic solidarity is not an issue? If the latter is true, if the residents are not divided according to ethnic affiliations, then what is it they need or seek in their political leaders? If they are poor, the answer may be found in the traditional favors and friendship of the patronage worker. If they are residents of an economically secure neighborhood of second settlement, they may respond more to personal loyalties and to appeals to their sense of morality in local issues.[2]

Assuming they understand the conditions of neighborhood solidarity in these neighborhoods, the ward leaders must still succeed in recruiting the most effective precinct leaders they can possibly find. In the newer neighborhoods of the ward, these precinct leaders must command the respect of a heterogeneous group of neighbors. In the

older mill neighborhoods, the precinct leaders are most likely to be men
and women who have had success in organizing the political ambitions
of their ethnic segment in the neighborhood and in the steel mills. Of
course many other backgrounds are possible and often necessary, but
in each case the precinct captain's leadership style, and the captain's
relationship to higher ward leaders, is an outgrowth of ethnic and
neighborhood solidarity itself.[3]

Neighborhood Political
Mobilization

In South Chicago the distinction between neighborhoods of first and
second settlement is clear. The former are the old tenement neighborhoods such as Millgate, Slag Valley, and Irondale. As their names
suggest, these are the mill neighborhoods, located at the entrances to
the major steel mills of the ward. Neighborhoods of second settlement
are the newer bungalow tracts on the East Side and in the Manors.
They have had their largest growth since the 1940s. In general, the
neighborhoods of first settlement continue to receive first-generation
newcomers and are likely to show rather high degrees of ethnic
segregation. Here first-generation blacks, Mexicans, or immigrant
Slavs are replacing second-generation Slavs, Poles, and Italians. In the
more heterogeneous neighborhoods of second settlement, the common
ecological pattern is for Italians, Poles, South Slavs, and middle-class
blacks to be replacing northern Europeans of quite diverse ethnicity.
These trends are summarized in table 11.

Table 11

Ethnicity of Voters in Precincts of
First and Second Settlement Neigh-
borhoods, 1969 (1932 in parentheses)
(Percent)

	No. of pre-cincts	N.E.	Polish	S. Slav	Italian	Mex-ican	Black	Other	Total
First settlement:									
Millgate	3	1.7	1.8	2.0	0.0	22.9	65.0	6.6	100
		(76.0)	(1.9)	(16.6)	(1.1)	(1.0)	(00.0)		
Irondale	4	23.7	7.5	21.0	16.4	26.3	1.0	4.1	100
		(55.0)	(0.7)	(22.8)	(20.3)	(00.0)	(00.0)		
Slag Valley	6	22.1	12.0	43.0	8.6	7.4	00.0	7.9	100
		(49.4)	(3.0)	(30.2)	(6.4)	(00.0)	(00.0)		
Second settlement:									
East Side	11	46.4	9.1	19.2	13.0	0.8	00.0	11.5	100
		(75.5)	(1.9)	(10.7)	(8.7)	(0.0)	(00.0)		

Every ward political organization will count among its precincts
some unmobilized ones in which leaders must be found to organize the

political behavior of the residents, and others which are politically mobilized and whose politics are relatively predictable. The techniques used for mobilizing precincts will differ in neighborhoods of first and second settlement. A mobilized precinct in ward politics is one in which residents are more or less unified behind a set of precinct leaders. Acting through their precinct leaders, the residents of politically mobilized precincts take the initiative in pressing demands for representation or better services from the ward political organization. In neighborhoods of first settlement political mobilization is usually an outgrowth of the aspirations of a given ethnic segment. In neighborhoods of second settlement, political mobilization is manifested in a greater variety of negotiations within the precincts. On the East Side, for example, groups of neighbors continually press their precinct leaders to force the ward political organizations to deliver services or to take positions on issues such as school busing, sex education, and air pollution—issues which are of immediate concern to voters in these precincts. But East Siders also require that their precinct leaders be members of local primary groups whose solidarity is based on more personal attachments.

The unmobilized precincts in Millgate are those in which new immigrant groups, or severely disadvantaged ones, have not become organized to form a unified majority in the precinct which will support precinct leaders. Unmobilized precincts in neighborhoods of second settlement, such as those in the Manors, are usually in blocks constructed since World War II which are not part of the internal ecology of residential shifts in the ward. These precincts are located in the western section of the ward and tend to be composed of middle-class Jewish families and newly arrived black home owners. Quite typically they are part of larger residential sections which were gerrymandered into the ward during the 1960s in an attempt to weaken the power of independent Jewish and black politicians from the wards to the north and west of the Tenth. For this reason, the residents of these unmobilized precincts are strangers to South Chicago in a way which second- and third-generation Polish families moving from South Chicago to the East Side are not.

Precinct Captains: Professional, Ethnic, and Amateur

As they review precinct assignments in preparation for political battles in the Tenth Ward, ward leaders make two basic types of assignments. A neighborhood either has arrived at a group of leaders who may function as precinct captains or it has not. In the case where an unmobilized neighborhood presents no obvious candidates for precinct captain, committeemen must appoint someone from within the organization to "handle" or "work" the precinct. The men and women who accept such assignments are professional captains. Normally their occupational careers bind them to the organization and they do the bidding of its leaders.

Where local neighborhoods in the ward have sorted out their own leadership, the committeeman's time-honored aim is to select neighborhood leaders who can bring out the largest vote for his candidates at the least cost to the organization. Here is the situation in which the political organization must recruit the loyalties of men and women who represent the aspirations of people in a three face-block area. In neighborhoods of first settlement, such leaders most often emerge from the process of negotiated aggregation among segments of local ethnic groups. People who organize the political activity of voters in relatively segregated ethnic precincts may be termed ethnic captains.

In blue collar neighborhoods of second settlement, the ward organization most often selects men and women who may be termed "amateur captains." Although this term is now commonly associated with reform movements in American cities, the continuing success of local political organizations in Chicago is based in part on their ability to compete with reform factions for the services of precinct leaders who are neither professionals nor ethnic leaders.[4] The amateur captains recruited into the Tenth Ward political organizations are men and women who have come to represent both the personal and civic aspirations of their neighbors. Table 12 provides a summary of the types of captains in Tenth Ward politics in relation to the precincts which they organize.

Table 12	Number and Type of Precinct Leadership by Degree of Mobilization and Neighborhood Type, Tenth Ward, 1970	
	Neighborhood Type	
Degree of Political Mobilization	First Settlement	Second Settlement
Low	Professional 5	Professional 11
High	Ethnic 24	Amateur 32

SOURCE: Interviews with South Chicago political activists.

*Professional Captains and
Their Territories*

Professional precinct captains in Tenth Ward political organizations (both Republican and Democrat) have made their occupational careers and local reputations within the party organizations themselves. Regardless of their skill as political strategists and organizers, these are men whose fortunes depend on the party organizations they serve. In general they are known by their contribution to the ward party organization rather than by reputations made within specific ethnic or residential segments of the ward. Early in their careers they accepted patronage jobs, and in so doing they shifted their primary allegiances from territorial segments in the ward to the party organizations.

Among the professional precinct captains in the Tenth Ward Democratic Organization are men and women whose ethnicity and neighborhood origins do not suit them for assignment to traditional South Chicago precincts. This applies, for example, to Irish career politicians who have worked faithfully in patronage jobs and whose primary allegiance is to the Cook County Democratic Organization. Although the Irish no longer have distinct settlements in the ward and have not been in command of Tenth Ward politics for over twenty years, there is a nucleus of men and women of Irish descent in the Tenth Ward Democratic Organization. These are people who are professional politicians as the term is defined here, and it is this group which tends to carry out assignments in the politically unmobilized precincts in the ward's western section.

A second group of professional captains are the young men who share ethnic ties with the ward leaders. Patronage workers between the age of twenty-five and forty, of second- or third-generation Polish, South Slav, or Italian ethnicity, are frequently not in a position to work the precincts in their own neighborhoods. Leadership of the Slavic and southern European precincts remains in the hands of older ethnic leaders, and the younger patronage workers must discharge their obligations to the ward organization by accepting assignments to precincts outside their own neighborhoods. Here they will attempt to organize voters to whom they may be total strangers. Eventually these younger professionals may take over the precincts in their own neighborhoods; in the meantime they serve the important function of mobilizing precincts in transitional sections of the ward.

Professional Assignments:
Gerrymandered Sections and
Slum Enclaves

Gerrymandered sections. The five precincts in the northwestern corner of the Tenth Ward are political no-man's-lands. First, they are often shifted around among the Seventh, Eighth, and Tenth wards. Second, they are in neighborhoods of second settlement, almost all of which were constructed in the last thirty years. Finally, since 1965 they have undergone a transition from Jewish to black residency. Since the combination of these factors has prevented the emergence of political leadership in these precincts, the ward political organizations must assign captains there in order to bring out the vote in important elections. If properly worked, the rather unorganized precincts in this western frontier of the community could deliver almost one thousand unanswered votes to the Tenth Ward Democratic Organization.

Slum precincts. A second assignment commonly made to professional captains involves organizing the slum precincts of the ward. The fifty-third precinct in Millgate, directly at the gates of the South Works, is such a precinct. The black population of Millgate presents the traditional pattern of a highly dependent population whose first-generation leaders are willing to cooperate with the white political leaders in the ward. As was once the case for all the first-generation ethnic enclaves in South Chicago, the black leaders in Millgate are clergymen and grocers. They do not define their role in the neighborhood as involving ethnic political mobilization, but their influence among neighborhood people makes their allegiance essential to the organization which seeks to win Millgate's votes. It is the job of the professional captains who "work" Millgate to insure that these local leaders will "bring their people to the polls on election day."

Even in a primary election, the fifty-third can deliver on the order of three hundred votes for the Tenth Ward Democratic Organization to ten or fifteen for its opponents. Of course such precincts are precious to ward political organizations. An aldermanic challenger, for example, would need to win six precincts by a margin of fifty votes in order to offset the influence of one precinct such as Millgate's fifty-third. Although the vote count may cost the Tenth Ward Democratic Organization from $300 to $400, the return on the investment justifies the expense. But money is by no means the only investment which goes into winning large margins in slum precincts of a ward such as the Tenth. Through countless small favors, offered without condescension or bureaucratic mystification, the professional captain builds a fund of trust between himself and first-generation face-block leaders in the precinct. Over years of political campaigns the professional captain learns which intermediaries can be counted upon. As a veteran captain in the Millgate area expressed it:

You can pour all the cash you have in the 53d, and it wouldn't do any good unless it goes through the right people. A hundred to C——, the grocer who's got to have ten times that much in debts out in the precinct, will do a lot more than giving the money to bottle gangs in the taverns. Maybe those guys'll vote, but maybe a lot of them won't make it to the polls. C——, though, he'll give out chickens before the election to the dependable families, houses with a lot of voters.

In the last five years, however, as the black and Mexican populations in Millgate have become more conscious of their need for ethnic mobilization, the overt role of professional captains in these precincts has declined. It has become increasingly necessary for the ward political organization to recruit leaders in the Millgate precincts who represent the aspirations of their ethnic segments. When leaders of an ethnic or racial segment begin to mobilize the political aspirations of their neighbors, the professional captain's final contribution to the precinct comes in his efforts to coopt these emerging ethnic politicians into the ward political organization.

Ethnic Captains and Their Neighborhoods

Ethnic precinct captains are generally not appointed by the ward political organizations to fill gaps in the organization. Instead they are men and women who have begun to organize the political solidarity of their ethnic segment in the ward. They organize in an attempt to gain more representation and a greater share of honor for their group in local political organizations. The progression in South Chicago's ethnic enclaves from first-generation ethnic leaders, who are treated as intermediaries by professional precinct captains, to the emergence of second-generation ethnic politicians has remained quite stable over this century. The same features of political development as experienced by Polish and South Slav precinct leaders appear now among Mexicans, the newest working-class ethnic group in the Tenth Ward. A natural history of the emergence of second-generation ethnic captains in Tenth Ward neighborhoods generally includes the following stages:

1. The precinct captain is a second-generation man who represents the older ethnic group in the precinct.
2. As a new immigrant group moves into the precinct, the captain

cooperates with first-generation leaders in the new group. The latter are usually tavern owners, clergymen, and grocers.

3. As the density of the immigrant group increases from one block to the next, and as a second generation comes of age, the new group begins to resent its political subservience to the now weakened older group. The old captain thus attempts to recruit one or more assistant captains from the young second-generation group.

4. The second-generation assistants are leaders of male primary groups in the neighborhood. Their activities are centered in one or more second-generation ethnic taverns. The most successful of these assistants will be men who have also begun to gain prestige in the parental generation. In these steelworkers' neighborhoods such prestige stems from a man's reputation in the mills, as well as family ties. The most successful assistants hold good jobs in the mills and are often active in union politics as well.

5. The old captain enlists the services of second-generation assistants by offering them the opportunity to increase their prestige in the tavern-based primary groups. He also offers social contacts beyond the ethnic segment. *The old captain does not offer patronage jobs unless pressed since most commonly he has used his quota of jobs in his own group.*

6. With the departure of the old captain, leadership of the precinct will go to the most influential and energetic of the second-generation assistants. He will officially represent the precinct in the ward organization, but in organizing the precinct he will enlist the help of large numbers of his peers.

7. Since the new precinct captain will already have established considerable seniority in the mill before taking over the precinct, it is unlikely that he will take a patronage job himself. Whatever patronage he commands will go to younger men in the precinct, often his kin or God relations. These young men will eventually become professional captains and will serve where assigned by the ward committeeman.

Although this natural history is quite similar to models of ethnic recruitment in machine politics described elsewhere, it differs with them in regard to the role of patronage.[5] In a ward such as the Tenth, where the influence of mill employment has served to decrease the importance of material inducements to political activism, the role of patronage in ethnic politics is diminished. Thus, of the sixteen Mexican precinct captains in Irondale and South Chicago who entered ward politics in the late 1950s, only one holds a job "with the city." All the others have high seniority jobs in the mills or own small businesses such as taverns or insurance agencies. A similar pattern was characteristic of the Polish and South Slavic precinct captains whom the Mexicans have replaced in the old mill neighborhoods.

Symbols of Succession: Ethnic
Leadership in Irondale Precincts

The fortieth precinct in Irondale is typical of precincts in neighborhoods of first settlement which are manned by ethnic precinct
captains. Although this precinct is among those organized by Mexican
captains, the situation here is not qualitatively different from one new
ethnic group to another. Perhaps the best way to understand differences in political activity between unmobilized precincts of second
settlement, and the fortieth in Irondale, is by observing an election in
the precincts.

Precincts in the unmobilized neighborhoods in the Tenth Ward are
quiet places on election day. The professional captain hires one or two
checkers to sit in the polling place to mark off the voters' names as they
enter the polling place. Often the captain will have canvassed more
than one precinct in the neighborhood in the common case where a
number of precincts vote in the same school or church. At periodic
intervals during the day the captain walks through the precinct to place
reminder notes on the doors of voters he knows intend to vote for his
candidates. When the polls close the captain assists the judges in
reading the automatic counters and in closing the voting machines.
This task accomplished, he will bring the results of his day's work to
the ward headquarters where the precinct results are tallied.

The scene at Bright School, where the voters of the fortieth cast their
ballots, is markedly more animated on election day. If the weather is
good, the day has a distinct holiday spirit. Within legal distance from
the polls the captains will have mounted campaign posters, and a great
effort is made to give each entering voter a slip with the candidates'
names and machine position for use in the voting booth. This is a day
when the adults of the precinct will see each other at the polls before or
after work. After they vote, groups of neighbors often congregate
outside to gossip and discuss the political situation in the ward or
the precinct.

If the election is of any importance to the Mexican precinct leaders
in the fortieth, tavern primary groups in the precinct will be mobilized
to bring out the vote. The captain and one or two of his close friends
lose a day's pay in the mill in order to stand at the entrance to Bright
School and greet the voters. Less committed friends spend time at the
polls before or after work to assist the captain in going through the
precinct. The high point of the day's activities, aside from learning the
results on the machines, is the visit to the precinct by the ward

committeeman and his candidates. It is hoped that the full complement of precinct workers will be on hand to greet these notables, and that the latter will be impressed with the amount of activity the captain has generated in the precinct.

The ethnicity of the precinct workers in the fortieth is the most important symbol of ethnic succession that can be claimed in the precinct. It is a public statement that the ward leaders perceive the precinct as "belonging" to the Mexicans. Through their efforts in the precinct the Mexican captain and his peers will continue to project the image that theirs is the only "organized" ethnic group in the precinct. Thus the Mexican tavern which serves as the clubhouse for Mexican political activists and mill work groups becomes a political headquarters during campaigns. Taverns in the fortieth which are owned and patronized by Serbian and Italian men are dull by comparison. Serbian steelworkers at Joko's or Eli's continue to perceive ward political events largely in terms of the honor of their group, but when they wish to know about political events in Irondale, they must gossip with the Mexican steelworkers with whom they stop for a beer after work.

Ethnic Precincts and
Negotiated Aggregations

The symbolic importance of precinct leadership for new ethnic groups also suggests the limits of precinct leadership in neighborhoods such as Irondale. It would be a mistake to assume that the symbolic value which precinct leadership carries necessarily implies that the Mexican captains are considered leaders by other ethnic groups remaining in the precincts.

Succession to precinct leadership, as table 13 indicates, may occur well before a group comprises the majority of voters in the precinct. And the fact that the fortieth precinct is led by a Mexican captain does

Table 13   Ethnicity of Registered Voters in Precincts Where Mexican Captains Replaced Polish or Serbian Captains, 1965–70 (Percent)

Neighborhood & Precinct	Mexican	Polish	Serbian	N.E.
Irondale, 40	40.0	3.1	24.9	21.4
Irondale, 52	29.8	5.9	18.6	21.4
Millgate, 16	49.2	31.0	....	13.7
Millgate, 17	64.8	11.6	4.1	11.3
Millgate, 18	34.6	17.2	5.0	27.4

not mean that an alert ward leadership will fail to make appeals to the Serbians and Italians who remain there. As mentioned earlier, Mexicans are the overt leaders, visible outside the polling place, but men who hold patronage positions from the precinct are members of older ethnic groups. Leaders of these older ethnic segments will participate directly in ward elections, but their contribution to the party's effort will not be as visible as that of the Mexican captains.

Although they have relinquished the symbolic leadership of the precinct, the Mexican captains and the ward committeeman will approach the older Serbian and Italian precinct leaders to make sure that their constituents vote properly on election day. Since the older ethnic captains continue to obtain material rewards, particularly in jobs for their relatives, they must share in the responsibility for the precinct's voting behavior. Without the aid of these influential neighbors from the older ethnic groups, the younger Mexican captains could not mobilize political action outside their own group. Once inside the ward clubhouse, the symbolic leadership of the Mexicans in the precinct is less important to them than their association, as equals, with the older ethnic leaders in the neighborhood. After the polls close, the entire group of precinct activists, Mexicans, Italians, and Serbians, will meet at the ward headquarters to present their vote tally proudly and to watch the results from other precincts. Around a table of drinks they will visit with other groups of precinct activists and boast how "we delivered our precinct by two to one."

Such a group is truly a negotiated aggregation. Brought together by their common participation in the precinct and the ward party organization and selected for the respect they command in their ethnic neighborhood and for their skill at mobilizing neighborhood primary groups, they will be sought after by all factions of the party in times of conflict within the organization. Over the years the people in this aggregation of neighborhood ethnic leaders may develop deeper personal attachments arising out of their common experience in ward political campaigns. Alternatively, ethnic competition in labor union politics, or enticements offered to their groups from other factions in the party, may lead these ethnic leaders to renegotiate their precinct affiliations.

Amateur Captains and
Neighborhood Mobilization

Precincts on the East Side, the area of the Tenth Ward which has traditionally received blue collar migrants from the older ethnic neighborhoods of South Chicago, are mobilized by appeals to residential solidarities and civic virtue. The concern of East Side residents for the status and stability of their neighborhoods is translated into demands that the ward political organization improve its services, or that ward leaders take positions on issues such as racial busing, urban renewal, air pollution, and sex education. The East Side was initially settled by northern European immigrants and their children, and in consequence the area has retained much of the anti-machine sentiment common in Scandinavian and German populations. Finally, as seen earlier, the influence of Republic Steel's anti-union policies on the East Side served to limit the role of local unionists as political leaders. Indeed, the company continues to sponsor Americanism seminars for East Side residents at its plant headquarters. These seminars tend to aggregate the area's most insecure political segments, namely, its small core of John Birch Society activists, its Wallace–American Independent party organizers, and the leaders of neighborhood improvement associations. The majority of these activists are women, often of second- or third-generation Slavic or southern European ethnicity. In general, they are relative newcomers to organized politics. As they gain recognition on the East Side by raising issues of public morality and neighborhood safety, the leaders of the ward party organizations will attempt to recruit them into the cadre of amateur precinct captains on the East Side.

Throughout the history of the Tenth Ward, East Side residents have nominated "favorite son" candidates for alderman and for the state legislature. Invariably these are men who have appealed to the East Sider's sense of local solidarity and concern for public morality but who have not had a wide following in other neighborhoods. Therefore, newer settlers in the area, South Slavs, Poles, and Italians, have had to adapt to a political style more influenced by public issues than was true in their ethnic neighborhoods of first settlement. Activists in the ward's Democratic Organization and working-class reformers who support East Side favorite sons must campaign in the local press and in the numerous public forums which East Side civic associations provide during political campaigns. It is not unusual, for example, to find more than two hundred and fifty East Side residents crowding the Illiana American Legion Post for a debate between aldermanic candidates, and local elections often generate rancorous conflict in East Side precincts.

The East Side political style may best be characterized as "white, working-class populism," the set of attitudes and political behavior which expresses distrust both of big business and of government insulated from the popular will, plus a fear of foreign ideologies and peoples. One may begin to understand this political disposition as it appears in ward politics through letters written to the local newspaper by East Side residents. These letters all represent public statements by East Side citizens during a bitterly contested aldermanic campaign in the Tenth Ward. This campaign pitted the incumbent alderman, an East Side favorite son, against the incumbent Democratic committeeman, Edward Vrdolyak.

The writer of the following letter refers to a deal which the incumbent alderman allegedly made with the Republic Steel Corporation to sell an unpaved city street to the company at a considerable bargain.[6]

To Ald. John Buchannan (10th):
I have been made aware that you did in fact make deals with big corporations (i.e. the Republic Steel land grab), the biggest steal since the Louisiana Purchase. I have been made aware that you have in fact given an additional year extension on air and water controls to the detriment of the citizens of this and adjoining ward to U. S. Steel, Wisconsin and Republic Steel.
I have been made aware that you did in fact make and are continuing to make, hand in glove agreements with syndicate and known communists; deals which make our Ward the garbage pit of America.

In the same election, supporters of the alderman attempted to capitalize on indictments against a number of the committeeman's allies, including his brother. These charges stemmed from a series of stag smokers which the Tenth Ward Democratic Club had unofficially sponsored, and in which a prostitute and a hotel room were the raffle prize. The following letter is quite typical of the East Side emphasis on respectability and public morality as it related to this incident during the campaign.

Mr. Vrdolyak is very much like a Hollywood prima-donna, always wanting his name in the news even if he has to buy a $20 trophy just so he can make the news print.
Today ... the 10th Ward is an eye sore with so many political posters, signs on every barn, fence, lawn and lamp poles. People who take pride in their neighborhoods have every reason to resent this infringement because they feel this kind of cheap political advertising deteriorates the values of the fine surroundings in which they built their homes.
When I attend Mass every Sunday, I note that Alderman Buchannan

serves as an usher while you and I know . . . that Mr. Vrdolyak's Club members with his knowledge were indicted for promoting stags across the state line which is a federal violation. This also includes his brother.

Your dear friend told you about Mr. Buchannan. But did he also tell you all about Mr. Vrdolyak? You see . . . decent people want upright leaders with clean and decent morals to represent them. Vrdolyak states that he is a Catholic and is a Fourth Degree in the Knights of Columbus. On this stag deal he is unworthy of belonging to either group that certainly frown on his doings.

As political conflict polarizes East Side voters, even seemingly trivial services performed by the alderman's office or by the Democratic Organization become emotionally charged issues. The following exchange between East Side residents typifies this situation.

And why are they taking garbage cans they know Alderman Buchannan has given to the people and putting E.R.V. [his opponent's initials] on them and passing them out to the residents.

What a low-down trick to be doing. His sickening sign says he will "serve the people."

Wake up people, do you think you are going to get free services if you elect him? Don't kid yourself. You will pay dearly for anything you want done.

Like Alderman Buchannan says, "Stop and think" for the good of the 10th Ward and the people that live here.

I am a democratic booster for good government.

B——

To The Daily Calumet:

As the service director who picks up all donated or purchased garbage cans and delivers them to those 10th Ward residents who need them, I would like to set the record clear for B——, and for the many readers of the Daily Calumet.

All our cans are donated or purchased from companies throughout the city. I have supervised the collection of these cans; many of us use our own personal time to cut the tops and make them presentable for our residents. We ourselves stencil the cans we deliver. . . .

Where did B—— get the information that I and my helpers are stealing Buchannan cans? Stop shouting lies and calling names. Buchannan should prove what he can do for the 10th Ward if he wants to be their representative and should stop trying to feed his hate to the people in the 10th Ward.

These letters begin to capture the paradoxical nature of politics on the East Side. Here is a large area of blue collar second settlement, comprising at least eighteen precincts, in which the perceived importance of local politics has increased with improvement in the material condition of the population. While it is true that "there is no Democratic or Republican way to collect garbage," on the East Side seemingly trivial issues such as the provision of garbage cans may become inflamed issues. But these issues are simply outward signs of underlying competition for rectitude and status. The East Siders' sense of civic virtue cannot be separated from the strain which political competition places on the personal attachments of political activists and their precinct neighbors. When political campaigns are perceived as moral crusades, and when such campaigns are waged among people who meet in daily face-to-face encounters in their immediate neighborhoods, the risks to one's personal reputation, and to the reputation of one's neighborhood primary group are far greater than they are in a national election. This aspect of local level politics is most clearly visible in patterns of recruitment for precinct leadership on the East Side.

Amateur Captains and the East Side Politics

Contested elections on the East Side, such as that between the Democratic committeeman and the East Side alderman, produce serious tension and anger in that neighborhood's precincts, as well as in its community forums. Conflict becomes rancorous and tempers explode as groups of neighbors compete with each other for support in their precincts. The East Side becomes a politically "burnt-over district" as garbage collection, contributions to parish churches, and the zeal with which a candidate pressed the anti-busing issue to higher political levels are discussed in the door-to-door campaigns waged within its precincts.

The often fierce competition between East Side residents for recognition and rectitude is a continuation of patterns established during the period of ecological invasion in the 1930s. Today the competition between new and old residents is blurred, but competition continues between institutions such as the local churches. The two main Catholic parishes in the East Side sponsor a series of social events and organized activities, and in so doing, the activists in these organizations compete with each other over which events are better organized. This competition often overlaps with political competition on the East Side, as various factions in ward politics attempt to outdo each other in donations to the neighborhood organizations. For example, both churches sponsor primary school level football teams which each involve upwards of thirty boys, their families, and coaching staffs. The teams practice regularly, they outfit the boys in expensive uniforms, and their rivalry often provokes near riots between the parents on opposing sides of the field. Other teams are organized by parents with children in the public schools, but none can compete with the two major teams, and none involves adults in as many fights and disputes as does competition between the parish teams.

Ward politics on the East Side involves precinct activists in similar competition for respectability. The sample reported in table 14 represents not only precinct captains on the East Side but the large majority of precinct activists in general. This includes election judges, precinct workers, and campaign volunteers who normally participate in aldermanic elections and ward primaries. The sample is taken from the rosters of a political combination in the ward which took over ward leadership in the mid-1960s and is representative of both the supporters of East Side favorite-son candidates and of the Tenth Ward Democratic Organization. The relatively large number of precinct activists available is an index of the high degree of political mobilization in East Side precincts. The group reported in table 14 represents an average of approximately twenty workers per precinct, and even if only half were to participate in a particular election, there would be at least ten workers in each precinct on election day. In fact, it is not

Table 14   Ethnicity of East Side Precinct Ac-
                                                  tivists, Aldermanic Elections, All Fac-
                                                  tions, 1960–70
                                                  (Percent)

	N.E.	Polish	S. Slav	Italian	Other	Total
Precinct activists ...	46.2	13.8	20.0	13.9	3.8	100
(N)	(209)	(60)	(86)	(59)	(16)	(430)
Registered voters ...	46.4	9.1	19.2	13.0	11.5	100

unusual to find relatively large groups of men and women actively at work organizing voters during East Side political campaigns. Of course the election must be contested, and must involve candidates or their supporters who are well known to East Side residents.

The small groups of neighbors who organize East Side precincts are recruited during periods of turmoil in the ward when factions organize for succession to ward leadership. Leaders of the competing factions go down the lists of East Side residents who have had political experience and attempt to find the most respected residents to take responsibilities in the precinct. Often material inducements are suggested; some need summer jobs for their children, or help with legal matters, or advice and aid in dealing with building inspectors. More likely, however, such activists are recruited by appeals to their neighborhood status. The call to organize a precinct is recognition that one is a person to be respected and trusted. Invariably such people are long-term residents of the precinct who are reputed to "know everybody there." Also it is quite likely that the captains recruited for East Side precincts will have jobs which command respect, or they will be the wives of men with substantial jobs in the mills or the railroads.

As the campaign begins, the precinct captain makes the rounds of the precinct in an attempt to locate support and to recruit a group of about ten activists who can help organize the precinct. Usually these will be the family's best friends in the immediate neighborhood, but often such aides are newer residents who wish the chance to become known and respected themselves. For such people the behavior of the precinct captain provides a model, and one continually hears gossip about East Side captains emphasizing their selflessness and devotion to the campaign and the candidates. The following conversation between two election judges who were recruited by different East Side captains is typical of the East Siders' stress on personal sacrifice in local politics.

A——: We only carried our precinct by twenty votes but it would have been much worse if it hadn't been for Nick P. You know he's a roller at Wisconsin, and he has a lot of trouble with his feet, but you should have seen him out in the rain, every day, in and out of every house in the neighborhood. And on election day he was walking the precinct all day, and then he goes to work that night on the eleven o'clock.

Y——: Well, Ralph in our precinct is the same way. He gets himself all worked up over the election, doing our precinct and seeing over two others. This time he ended up in South Chicago hospital for two weeks for his ulcer, but he got out in time to work the precinct for a week before the election.

The fact that these are contested precincts places East Side captains under considerable pressure. During political campaigns the captains are asked to give estimates of the results in their precincts, but more than in any other type of precinct it is difficult to predict the vote in East Side precincts. At the same time, success in precinct organizing carries greater personal reward to the East Side captains than it does in those organized by professional or ethnic captains because local campaigns take on the aspect of moral crusades. Although the material spoils of victory have less importance on the East Side than they do elsewhere, the slack is more than taken up by the rectitude and status which victory in his precinct confers on the East Side captain.

As the campaign proceeds, climactic events occur which increase the solidarity of precinct primary groups. A scandal revealed will bring forth shows of solidarity in the precincts; a rally or a parade to be organized calls for long hours of preparation in which people come to know each others' personalities better. For example, during a bitter aldermanic campaign in the Tenth Ward in 1967, the city had the worst snowstorm in its history. The ward committeeman, who was involved in one side of the campaign described his perception of this event as follows:

S——— (former Tenth Ward committeeman). We had planned a big rally and torch parade for the night when the snow started. I went with the family to the rally and it was snowing so bad we didn't think anybody would be there. But you know hundreds of people showed up. They could hardly keep the torches lit. They talk about what a dirty business Ward politics is, but when I saw my people out in the snow that night, I cried right there in front of everybody.

The morning after this rally Chicago was buried under several feet of drifted snow. On the East Side a frantic "Battle of the Shovels" began as opposing groups of precinct activists competed with each other to dig out their neighbors' cars and walks, and thus demonstrate which faction could provide better service. The friendships and animosities formed during three days of snow removal contributed to the feeling that the vote results would be a judgment of the moral standing of the precinct primary groups. Inevitably such judgments provoke greater insecurity among the political actors on the East Side than among ethnic captains who know they can count on a bloc of votes once their ethnic segment in the precinct is mobilized.

Attenuation of Ethnic
Attachments on the East Side

Political appeals on the East Side are made to the voters' feelings of morality and their desire for recognition in their neighborhoods. If they are to carry elections in East Side precincts, Tenth Ward Democratic leaders must compete for the services of precinct leaders who operate in neighborhoods where ethnic attachments are attenuated. The ethnicity of captains recruited by competing factions in the ward corresponds closely to the general distribution of ethnic groups on the East Side (table 14), and direct appeals for an ethnic vote are rarely made. Nevertheless, local politicians are not in agreement about the extent to which various ethnic groups dispersed in East Side neighborhoods may be mobilized by an appeal to ethnic solidarity.

In general, supporters of East Side favorite sons are more likely to be of northern European ethnicity, while supporters of the Democratic Organization candidates are more likely to be representatives of the second wave of immigrants, the Poles, South Slavs, and Italians. But the outlines of ethnic alliances are never clear. Personal loyalties in the precincts and appeals to civic virtue always align members of the same ethnic groups on opposing aggregations in the precincts. Ethnicity is important, however, in the initial recruitment of precinct activists on the East Side. A Polish committeeman is likely to have greatest success in recruiting Polish campaign workers; a Croatian will have most contacts and personal attachments among the South Slavic groups on the East Side. The greater the dispersion of an ethnic group in neighborhoods of second settlement such as the East Side, the more ethnicity becomes a form of personal attachment rather than a shared sense of descent and solidarity. Politicians may recruit the allegiances of precinct leaders on the strength of these personal ties, but they can never be sure that they will get an "ethnic vote" in such areas, nor does the ecological dispersion of their group allow them to measure with any certainty if such a vote exists. Elsewhere in the ward, politicians are quite open in their attempts to mobilize an ethnic vote and, in fact, these attempts may revive notions of ethnic solidarity even in areas where ecological dispersion is quite advanced. In general, however, in neighborhoods such as the East Side, ethnic attachments are one means for enlisting the support of precinct level primary groups which are formed by appeals to personal attachments and notions of civic responsibility. Overt appeals to ethnic solidarity must be abandoned.

Turnout and Mobilization
in Tenth Ward Precincts

Political mobilization in a precinct should be related to voter turnout in ward elections. It is reasonable to expect the rate of voting in precincts worked by professionals to be lower than rates in precincts led by either ethnic or amateur captains because the professionals only encourage voting by people they know will vote properly. Table 15 shows this to be the case; turnouts in ward elections are heaviest in the precincts of second settlement led by amateur captains, while those led by professionals have the lowest turnout rates.

Table 15   Mean Voting Turnout (percentage of
registered voters) in Precincts Organ-
ized by Professional, Ethnic, and
Amateur Captains, 1963–70

Precinct Leadership	No. of Precincts	Democratic Primaries	Aldermanic Elections
Professional	3	46.4	43.1
Ethnic	3	64.6	51.5
Amateur (East Side)	3	59.2	68.4

Voting turnouts are highest on the East Side, in precincts which are
organized by "amateur" captains. Table 15 indicates, however, that
voting rates in ward Democratic primaries, in which the Tenth Ward
Democratic committeeman is elected, are highest in ethnic precincts.
These figures reflect the fact that the German and Scandinavian
populations which originally settled the East Side have maintained
traditions of Republican and independent voting which have persisted
into the 1970s. In all the aldermanic elections held in the Tenth Ward
during the 1960s, East Side political activists divided their loyalties
between candidates from the East Side and those who represented the
Democratic Organization in the ward. Voting rates are high on the East
Side because aldermanic elections there are bitterly fought contests
where competing primary groups in the precincts attempt to bring out
as many voters as possible.

Ethnic, Personal, and
Civic Politics

South Chicago machine politics in the 1970s is a much more complex
system than it was in earlier decades of the century. The steel mills still
keep local residents firmly tied to their local neighborhoods. In
consequence, they place greater emphasis on local politics as a path to
social mobility and as a moral system than is usually the case in
middle-class communities. On the other hand, different residential
segments of the community make conflicting demands on the political
institutions of the ward. In older neighborhoods, ethnic groups demand
power in the ward organizations. They seek the enhancement of their
group's prestige by organizing precinct level leadership. Elsewhere,
particularly in the areas of second settlement, ward leaders must deal
with the conflicting demands of working-class populists, progressive
unionists, middle-class reformers, Birch Society activists, and primary
groups of neighbors. The ward leaders operate in a political ecology
which has all the dimensions of national politics but in which political

affiliations cannot be separated from the networks of personal attach-ments among ward politicians and their neighbors. Thus, if a ward leader intends to develop support among the newer black residents of the area, he must also ease the racial insecurity of white voters in other neighborhoods where he has strong ethnic and personal ties. The ward leaders can make rational political calculations: support for one group's demands will cost support in another quarter of the ward. On the other hand, these choices are often more agonizing than they are at higher level political systems because as ward politicians say, "These are people we have to live with."

The politics of ethnic neighborhoods involve leaders in a host of negotiations which will alter the basis of ethnic solidarity in their groups. Mexicans may lead groups of Mexican activists in Irondale, but to do so throughout the ward, they must develop affiliations among their members which bridge the cleavages in their ranks. They must also negotiate aggregations of political activists which include other ethnic leaders in their neighborhoods. Among themselves the Mexicans, or the Poles, or the South Slavs may say, "We are in this for us. We've got to get our share." But ethnic solidarities are continually redefined in the process. The Serbians and the Croatians learn to view themselves as "Hunkies" and to see their common cause; the Mexicans must make peace between the competing territorial segments of their group in the ward. Precedents and reputations which facilitate these changes were established in union politics, but they will continue to develop in ward political institutions. Gradually, ethnic solidarity will become less self-conscious, less a matter of a group attempting to win ethnic power, and ethnicity will come to be one among many dimensions of personal attachments which may be used in the aggrega-tion of organization activists.

This does not mean that ethnicity "disappears" as a basis of solidarity in politics. On the contrary, the resources and institutions of South Chicago ethnic groups provide essential support even for third-generation ward politicians. The ethnic subcultures of this blue collar community continue to specialize and thrive. They are continually rejuvenated by the arrival of new immigrants, and the invasion of other ethnic and racial groups in the area. Activists in ethnic institutions express pride when one of their members succeeds in local politics, and they attempt to mobilize an ethnic vote even when the politicians themselves are reluctant to do so openly. For their part, the politicians increasingly circulate in a world of people from different ethnic backgrounds, a world in which personal attachments may be based on ethnicity but are equally likely to have grown out of years of neighborhood association, or to have developed out of common competition in the political institutions themselves.

The most important civic issues which ward politicians must handle are those arising out of ecological change in the community. Respectability in the blue collar areas of second settlement is established within neighborhood primary groups which compete in local institutions. The civic issues which often mobilize these groups, issues such as concern over Americanism, dissatisfaction with ward services, or fear of racial invasion, are outgrowths of the fierce competition for respectability in these transitional areas. But the aggregation of locality groups in ward politics is not merely derivative of ecological change. In fact, further analysis of ethnic politics in South Chicago will show that succession in ward party institutions is often a prerequisite to ecological succession.

7

Mexican Succession in Ward Politics

Political power in urban wards rarely comes easily to a new ethnic group. If power is to be won at all, it must be gained over a generation of struggle, wasted savings, small victories, and frustration. During the decade of the 1960s the second-generation Mexican leaders in Irondale and Millgate enjoyed a few brief moments at the center of political attention in the ward. Through skillful organization they overcame the divisive influence of territorial competition, and when the opportunity presented itself, they ran their first candidate for public office. At the end of the decade Mexican political fortunes were turned back through fiat at higher levels of city politics. After ward redistricting, South Chicago's Mexican population entered the decade of the 1970s with almost as little formal influence in ward politics as they had before the 1960s. Nevertheless, the South Chicago Mexicans had learned a series of valuable political lessons: they made progress in unifying the territorial segments of their group; they chose a set of leaders who could command respect not only among Mexicans but in other segments of the community as well; they began to develop the leadership potential of Mexican women; and they tested the limits of precinct primary groups and negotiated coalitions. Although they were frustrated in their attempts to win power, Mexican ethnicity in South Chicago in 1970 was much better adapted to the realities of political competition than it had been in the previous decade.

*Territorial Segmentation and
Symbolic Competition*

Territorial segmentation, the concentration of the Tenth Ward Mexican population into two neighborhood areas, Irondale and Millgate, is the major obstacle to political unity for this relatively new ethnic group. Adult Mexican men in both neighborhoods once fought with each other as members of adolescent street corner groups, and such conflict continues among adolescent boys' groups today. The gravity of this conflict varies as a function of distance between Mexican segments. Thus the worst incidents of violence involving Mexican boys have occurred between groups from South Chicago and from the larger Mexican settlement in Chicago's 18th Street area. The death of a South Chicago boy during one such incident in 1968 has made cooperation between these distant Mexican settlements almost impossible. Within South Chicago, conflict between Irondale and Millgate Mexican boys is routine, but the controlling influence of Mexican adults and street workers has served to check the most violent opposition.

Among Mexican heads of families, territorial loyalties no longer produce violent confrontations, but old rivalries are not easily forgotton. Since attachments formed at work bridge neighborhood boundaries, adult men of the second generation may circulate freely between the two neighborhoods. Nevertheless, competition between the two neighborhoods continues throughout the adult life cycle. Most commonly this competition takes symbolic form, as tavern-based primary groups in Irondale and Millgate attempt to demonstrate influence in their own neighborhoods. In both Millgate and Irondale, the Mexicans share their neighborhoods with older ethnic groups. Thus the degree to which either Mexican segment proves its influence in its own neighborhood is also a symbolic victory in the competition between Mexican leaders in the two neighborhoods. A good example of this symbolic competition is found in the Mexican Independence Day celebrations held in both Irondale and Millgate on 15 September of every year.

Mexican Independence Day
in South Chicago

Although Irondale and Millgate are separated only by the Slag Valley neighborhood, Mexicans in both neighborhoods organize separate Mexican Independence Day celebrations. There is almost no cooperation between the two neighborhoods in the organization of this event. In Irondale the streets around Trumbull Park are roped off to accommodate taco stands and strolling families. Bleachers are erected in the park itself and a scaffolding is constructed for the piñata. In Millgate the streets around Our Lady of Guadalupe are roped off for a parade which will include a troop of Mexican horsemen as well as a large mariachi ensemble. All these events require a good deal of organization and sizable cash outlays. The cost of a mariachi ensemble, for example, varies between $400 and $600, and when other expenses are included, it is impossible to stage a neighborhood fiesta for less than $1,500. This expense may be partially defrayed by the dances held in both neighborhoods, but the celebration invariably runs organizations in both neighborhoods into the red.

The fiestas are a day of pride for members of "la Raza" in Irondale and Millgate. Unlike the Fourth of July celebrations, which are normally organized by non-Mexican groups, on Mexican Independence Day, the neighborhoods "belong" to the Mexicans. Their "huero" (white) neighbors are guests at the fiesta. Also, the fiestas represent a show of organizing ability and neighborhood prestige for Mexican leaders. Millgate families who visit relatives in Irondale, for example, report on the quality of the latter's celebration and often criticize the roles of various leaders. These judgments invariably influence the reputations of the men and women who organize the fiestas.

Given the political overtones of the celebrations, it is not surprising that those who take the most active roles in the celebrations are second-generation Mexican precinct activists. Upon this group falls the task of unifying the two neighborhoods for political action outside the ethnic group itself. Although it is a difficult process, unification is built by those who share attachments formed at work and in union politics.

Internal Cleavage and
Ethnic Political Organization

During the decade of the 1960s, the Tenth Ward Democratic Organization passed through the severe crisis of succession mentioned earlier. In this period of transition in ward politics, as leaders representing various ethnic and residential segments in South Chicago struggled for control over the party organization, the Mexican unionists of Irondale and Millgate began taking an extremely active part in these negotiations. In general, they remained loyal to the incumbent group of South Chicago politicians who first introduced them to ward politics as assistant precinct captains in the 1950s. In return for this loyalty the Mexican leaders not only became full-fledged precinct captains in the early 1960s, but they were able to place a number of their young precinct activists in patronage positions. Despite gains made during this period, however, the Mexican precinct captains did not operate as a unified interest group within the Democratic party organization. Even within the ward's party organization, territorial rivalries between the Irondale and Millgate Mexican factions remained apparent. Both sides tended to compete, for example, on election days to demonstrate the greatest influence over voters in their precincts. By the mid-1960s, however, as morale in the Tenth Ward Democratic Organization declined, Mexican leaders began to negotiate a new basis for unity between their neighborhoods in an effort to improve rapidly the bargaining strength of the ethnic group as a whole.[1]

The Tenth Ward
Spanish Speaking Democratic
Organization

Unification of Mexican ward leadership began with creation of the Tenth Ward Spanish Speaking Democratic Organization in 1966. To those outside the ethnic group, the new organization represented a claim by the Mexicans to political autonomy in their neighborhoods. The existence of an ethnic political organization within the Tenth Ward Democratic Organization could be seen as a public statement that the Mexican precinct politicians had achieved sufficient stature in ward politics to command their own political organization within the parent association. In the Mexican group itself the internal arrangements which led to the new organization were even more important. Creation of the new organization required nothing less than the unification of the two competing Mexican leadership groups.

John Chico, a prominent Chicano unionist and leader of the Millgate Mexican precinct captains, described the process of unity formation as follows:

We all knew that we should have the organization, but it wasn't easy for us to get together with the Irondale guys. Of course most of us knew each other from growing up in South Chicago and from the mills, but we weren't used to working together. It took a lot of doing to bring us close and it still takes a lot to keep us going.

I took the South Chicago guys one night over to Irondale, to the J & M Club, and we sat down with the Irondale guys and drank with them all evening. There was me, Mel, Paul, and Cesar [his brothers], Shadow, Fat, and Gil, almost all the South Chicago captains. They had their guys there and we just spent the night drinking and talking about how much we could do if we could only get together.

I think it was important that the South Chicago guys went over to Irondale first. We have more precincts than they do. The South Chicago Mexican group is bigger than Irondale and they get sensitive about that.

We met this way over about a month, sometimes in Irondale at the

J & M and sometimes in South Chicago at my brother Mel's tavern. Every time we would get stiff together we would hit it off better, and after a while we were going pretty well. This is how we started the organization really, by coming together and drinking a little and getting to trust each other that way. When we formed the organization, it was agreed that I would be the president and that Ed Hernandez [an Irondale leader] would be the vice-president.

As the preceding remarks indicate, organizing the Spanish speaking Democrats depended on the development of trust between two adult primary groups, rather than upon arrangements between leaders in a formal hierarchy. While negotiation of the new Tenth Ward Spanish Speaking Democratic Organization forged a bond between the two Mexican segments of the ward, problems arising from competition between the two neighborhoods continued to plague Mexican leaders as they organized the political strength of their group in ward politics. Immediately after the formation of their organization, however, the Mexican unionists were faced with disunity within their group from sources other than territorial competition.

Additional Dimensions of
Cleavage in Mexican Leadership

The Tenth Ward Spanish Speaking Democratic Organization was aligned with the incumbent faction in Tenth Ward politics. This forced the ward's opposition faction to negotiate with an alternative Mexican group in order to win at least some of the Mexican vote. The background of the Mexican men whom this challenging faction brought together reveals additional dimensions of cleavage within the leadership of ethnic segments in urban communities in general.

Immigrant brokers. The challenging faction in Tenth Ward politics during the 1960s was successful in recruiting Mexican precinct activists from two sources. First, some immigrant and older second-generation Mexican ethnic leaders were attracted to the challenging faction. Generally, this group was composed of ethnic leaders whose political careers centered on the internal organization of ethnic institutions in Millgate and Irondale, rather than on the mobilization of Mexican precincts for competion in ward or union politics. These Mexican leaders see their role as that of brokers between ward party organizations and their neighbors in the precincts. Generally they are small businessmen and church leaders, with second-generation families.

The unionist leaders regard this group as conservative "Tio Tacos," a translation of the familiar term "Uncle Tom." Second-generation unionists, such as John Chico and the other Mexican labor leaders in Irondale and Millgate, attempt to combine practical ward politics with the symbols of Mexican nationalism. They openly identify with the Chicano movement, and given their labor backgrounds, they are likely to associate themselves with the United Farm Workers movement in Chicago. More than any other Mexican leaders, they are able to draw upon the appeal which the UFW and Cesar Chavez have in Mexican neighborhoods. The first-generation ethnic leaders have claim to little of this ethnic pride. Their influence is found in personal obligations which extend into the precincts and which constitute the traditional relationship between ethnic brokers and their constituents. This pattern of neighborhood political leadership was described earlier in connection with the black precincts in Millgate. It would apply equally to the Mexican precincts had the younger Mexican unionists not managed to usurp the influence of first-generation ethnic brokers. Again, this was made possible by the unionists' success in labor politics, and their virtual monopoly over symbols of Mexican cultural pride.

"Heavies." A second group of neighborhood influentials which joined the opposing Tenth Ward faction was a small group of superannuated Mexican street fighters. Men with nicknames such as "the Rat" and "the Hawk," and with reputations in the Mexican precincts to match their names, were not part of the unionist leadership group. Criteria for leadership change as a generation matures in South Chicago. As some men begin to demonstrate their ability to organize a vote in a union election, or to mobilize a precinct for a ward primary, the reputation of former street fighters pales in comparison. But a new aggregation in ward politics will have need of just such men as these. Lacking a complete precinct organization, new leaders in ward politics will often be short of lower status men who can recruit labor to perform the hundreds of manual tasks needed for competition in local politics. Even seemingly minor tasks such as painting signs and posting them on buildings and lamp posts for a ward election are quite difficult to organize without the personnel such as former street fighters can supply to do the heavy work. And when a campaign becomes heated, as is often the case in Tenth Ward politics, a challenging faction may see fit to call upon its "heavies" for various strategies of intimidation, including the systematic removal of the opposition's street signs and lamp posters. In consequence of this, the small group of Mexican street fighters, whose status was on the decline in their own ethnic group, could find their services in great demand in the opposing Tenth Ward political faction.

In summary, since they were not encouraged to participate in the Mexican unionist group, both the first-generation ethnic brokers and second-generation street fighters were available for recruitment by the opposing faction in Tenth Ward politics during the 1960s. In fact, this recruitment pattern is quite typical of the political arrangements which newly established ethnic groups form in ward political organizations. Mexicans entered this faction as lower status participants, men incapable of delivering the vote in their home precincts, and thus possessing less bargaining power than was the case for the Mexican unionists on their side of the factional schism in the ward. On the other hand, events in Tenth Ward politics in the late 1960s would prove that this lower status Mexican group had formed the more fortunate alignments outside their ethnic group. As the incumbent faction increasingly lost strength in the ward, the Mexican unionists would face a series of crises in which their loyalty to the ethnic political organization would conflict with the demands of new ward leaders.

Ethnic Autonomy versus Organizational Loyalty

In ward politics, as in electoral politics at any level, an ethnic faction may find that its struggle of many years to achieve unity and to gain recognition in the larger community is badly set back in one day at the polls. When such setbacks occur, as happened to the Tenth Ward Spanish Speaking Democrats in 1968, the loyalties of the group will be severely tested. The leaders of ethnic organizations in ward politics will have to decide either to sacrifice the hard-won autonomy of their organization or to endanger the future of their ethnic group in the new aggregation of ward leaders. The more progress ethnic leaders have made in creating autonomous ethnic political organizations, and the more they have based their leadership on symbols of ethnic cultural pride, the more likely they will be to maintain their opposition to the ward leadership even in the face of increasing individual and group deprivation.[2]

In the Democratic primary election of 1968, the incumbent faction in Tenth Ward politics, the faction which had the active support of the Mexican unionist group, finally lost the leadership of the ward's party apparatus. The opposing faction, led by Edward Vrdolyak, a young attorney of second-generation Croatian ethnicity, carried the ward by a narrow margin despite the best efforts of the Mexican captains in their precincts. As the new faction took control of the party organization, the Mexican precinct activists were the first victims of an inevitable purge.

As a veteran precinct captain in the Tenth Ward Spanish Speaking Democratic Organization observed,

One of the first things Vrdolyak [the new Democratic committeeman] did was take away the few jobs we had. Even Bob N., who is crippled and couldn't work in most jobs, lost the little job he had. This is the kind of stuff we have to put up with. We are loyal Democrats. We came up through the Pasini Organization [the recently deceased committeeman] and like lots of others, we went down with the organization. Now we are the ones who are being made examples of. You don't see him firing any of the Hunkies, or Italians, or Pollakos. Them he's going to try and line up in the organization, but we get the ax.

Indeed, the new ward Democratic committeeman reacted harshly against the Mexican unionists. In part this was due to the fact that as the newest ethnic group in the ward, they were the most expendable. Also, the Spanish Speaking Democratic Organization and its leadership represented a threat to the political hegemony of the Tenth Ward Democratic Organization. But after the flush of victory began to fade, and the new committeeman was faced with further political crises in the ward, he began to adopt a somewhat more conciliatory position with regard to his former Mexican adversaries. In fact, the committeeman's more compromising position would exert far greater pressure upon the Mexican precinct activists than had his open hostility.

From the new committeeman's position in the ward, the existence of an autonomous ethnic political organization in Tenth Ward Democratic politics was an embarrassment at best. Since the Spanish Speaking Democrats represented a competing Democratic political organization, all political logic demanded it be weakened by forcing it to surrender its autonomy to the party. On the other hand, the precinct captains who organized the Tenth Ward Spanish Speaking Democrats could control a large segment of votes in South Chicago and Irondale. A few months after his victory in the committeeman's election, the new leader of the party began feuding with the ward's alderman. Since the latter had brought the new committeeman another large segment of votes in East Side precincts, loss of the alderman's support would need to be offset by an almost equally large number of precincts. Thus as the rift widened between himself and the alderman, the new committeeman made tentative overtures to the Mexican unionist group.

The Mexican captains were not willing to be brought into the newly aligned Tenth Ward Democratic Organization at anything less than the level of influence they had attained in the waning years of the old regime. Although one or two of their members would "go over to Vrdolyak," the majority of the Mexican captains stood firm in their refusal to consider the committeeman's suggestion that the Mexicans join his reorganized party apparatus. John Chico explained his position on the question as follows:

Vrdolyak said he'd make me president of the Tenth Ward Democratic Organization if I would agree to disband the Spanish Speaking Democrats. We could have something like it, he said, but it would have to be competely inside the regular organization.

There was no way we could go for that deal. Here he fires our guys, a few lousy jobs, nothing big like Ward superintendent or stationary engineer, you know, and he expects us to turn around and join his organization like that. We couldn't have looked our people in the eye. I had to tell him we weren't ready for that.

Throughout the waning years of the decade, the Tenth Ward Spanish Speaking Democratic Organization remained a center of opposition to the committeeman's consolidation of ward political groups. John Chico and the Mexican unionists capitalized on any opportunity to register voters in their precincts and to organize additional precinct level leaders in their organization. In 1969, two years after their setback in the committeeman's election, the Mexican unionists had a chance to take the initiative in their competition for power in Tenth Ward politics. In a special Illinois election to elect representatives to a Constitutional Convention, the Spanish Speaking Democrats took their first step into electoral politics by sponsoring a Mexican candidate for public office.

The Lessons of a First Candidacy

The traditional model of machine politics neglects the fact that while it may be extremely difficult to unseat powerful ward politicians, there is almost always one or more factions in a ward which is willing to try if given any but the longest odds.[3] For this reason, special elections such as the 1969 Constitutional Convention delegates election are extremely unwelcome to established ward politicians. Special elections do not particularly motivate regular Democratic precinct captains because such elections are usually not of obvious importance to the fortunes of the party organization in the ward. Funds for campaign expenses are usually scarce, and the professional precinct captains are likely to relax in their precinct mobilization. These conditions present an ideal opportunity for ambitious factions to test their strength against the ward political organizations. John Chico's candidacy in the 1969 Constitutional Convention election is a case in point: defeated in the committeeman's election (indirectly) and now outside the ward's Democratic organization, the Constitutional Convention election gave the Tenth Ward Spanish Speaking Democratic Organization a chance to sponsor its own candidate and thereby to negotiate political influence outside the Mexican precincts.

John Chico's candidacy represented another unusual turn of events in Tenth Ward politics. As financial secretary of the largest steel-worker's local union in Chicago (U. S. Steel, South Works), Chico ran against the regular party candidates as a labor candidate. Throughout his campaign he had the active support of local steelworkers' unions from the South Chicago area. In brief, many of the local union politicians in the area were disappointed that the new committeeman had not chosen a recognized labor candidate as one of the party's two candidates. Taking an unprecedented action, therefore, local unions in South Chicago voted to field a candidate to run in the primary election. Normally labor unions in Chicago do not oppose the Democratic party at any level of city politics, but as John Chico explained the situation which led to his candidacy,

When Vrdolyak chose his two men and wouldn't go for a steelworker, enough guys in the locals were ready to put up a candidate so that I could see that I could have it if I wanted it. That's the bitch about this business, Willie, nobody dumps anything in your lap, you have to hustle for it, and if you have shit in your blood, you're lost. This chance is what we needed to have a Mexican candidate in the ward. I could get Local 65 to put me up for it because no one else was ready to push for it except me.

Thus the first public candidacy for a Mexican in the Tenth Ward (and in the entire city) was aided by the desire of local labor leaders to demonstrate their political influence in the area as well.

During the four-month campaign, from August to November 1969, South Chicago's Mexicans were able to draw upon the finances, physical facilities, and political organization of local unions in the South Chicago area. Without these resources available to them throughout the campaign, the Mexicans could never have presented a public candidate at this time. On the other hand, when John Chico was finally defeated at the polls, after winning a place on the final ballot in the primary election, his loss was interpreted by local labor leaders as another instance of labor's inability to compete directly with urban political organizations. For the Mexicans, one of the most important lessons gained from Chico's campaign was the knowledge that their labor affiliations would be an insufficient base from which to challenge the more entrenched ethnic groups in the ward.

Lesson I: Unionist Reputations
Are of Limited Value in
Ward Politics

Convergence between unionist and ward political roles is uncommon in older South Chicago ethnic groups. For example, although Serbian unionists continue to play a prominent role in ward politics, the majority of Serbian precinct captains and ward political activists are either professional politicians or white collar employees of various types. There is a marked differentiation between union activists and the younger Serbian politicians in business or governmental occupations. This is even more true of the South Chicago Poles. Polish unionists are generally not active in ward politics, and the prominent Polish politicians in the ward are local businessmen and white collar employees. In the Mexican case, steelworkers who have received much of their practical training in politics inside the mills are most likely to lead their group into ward politics.

Mexican union politicians are the first group to form attachments outside the Mexican neighborhoods. Since they join coalitions with union activists from other ethnic groups, and other neighborhoods of the community, they have contacts over a much wider territory than do the older ethnic leaders in the Mexican neighborhoods. But these contacts and attachments are limited to men who are active inside the mills and in the union halls. Since unionists from the older ethnic groups are not the same men as those Poles, Italians, and Serbians in ward politics, occupational attachments are of limited value when the Mexican unionists attempt to negotiate aggregations in ward politics. This situation came clearly to the fore when John Chico attempted to build support for his candidacy outside the Mexican neighborhoods of the Tenth Ward, as the following excerpted field notes will indicate.

Thursday night, September 1969: Jack D. (a well-known Polish precinct captain from the East Side) took me and four of the Spanish Speaking Democrats, including Chico, to Palozzo's Tavern in the old Italian section of the East Side. Jack had to coax the four Mexicans to come with him by explaining that Palozzo is in a position to swing a lot of support their way in the November election. Like many of the Italian neighborhood leaders, Palozzo has not yet made his peace with the new committeeman and is supporting the alderman in the feud. In return, the committeeman has resorted to various harassment strategies which include putting heat on the bookmaking operation which uses the tavern as a base.

None of the Mexican men had ever been in this tavern and all were visibly uncomfortable. Although we sat at tables, Jack managed ,to introduce us to Palozzo. The latter was working behind the bar, but he stopped to meet Chico and wish him luck in his campaign. Aside from this brief exchange, there was no serious political talk with Palozzo.

Despite the fact that they are all experienced precinct captains and successful union politicians, the Mexicans have few contacts with the Italian community in South Chicago. The Millgate Mexicans owe their political careers largely to activity in the South Works local. Since few Italians work at South Works, compared to the number employed at the Republic Steel and Wisconsin Steel plants, there are few Italian activists in union politics at the South Works plant. Thus it is not unusual that the Mexicans are strangers to Palozzo's neighborhood. Although it is directly across the 95th Street bridge from their own blocks, the Mexicans have had little opportunity to form acquaintances there.

Jack D. left us as we departed from Palozzo's Tavern and the rest of us continued on to South Chicago, where we stopped for a beer. John Chico was disappointed that he and Palozzo had not discussed politics. He felt that Jack D. was simply using the Mexicans to show off his influence to some well-known neighborhood politicians. John was quite pessimistic about his chances for winning any substantial support among the ward's Italian voters. On the other hand, John believes that the Irondale Mexicans will bring in some Italians because they share their neighborhood with many Italian families. The Italians are quite active in the Wisconsin Steel local union where many Irondale Mexicans also work. Despite this fact, however, John is sure that the Irondale Mexicans would have only indirect contacts with the Italians in Palozzo's East Side neighborhood. He doubted that the Irondale Mexicans would have been any more comfortable in Palozzo's Tavern than his group was this evening.

After leaving John and the Mexican group, I went to Lolich's Place outside the Wisconsin Steel plant. Jack told me he would stop there before going home, and I knew I would find him there. The two of us helped Mike Lolich close his tavern and accompanied him for a late snack. Jack complained that the Mexicans are too inexperienced and stubborn to hope to win anything in the ward now. Indicative of this he feels is their reluctance to meet in anything smaller than groups of four or five. Jack feels that real bargaining must take place between leaders themselves. Had Chico come with Jack alone to talk to Palozzo, they could have done some business. Accustomed to dealing with established ward politicians, Jack has little understanding of Mexican primary group politics.

Prominence in union politics does not assure the Mexican leaders of support from other ethnic leaders even when the latter are antagonistic to established ward leaders. Nevertheless, success in union politics does merit the respect and attention of prominent neighborhood political figures. Thus an Italian neighborhood leader such as Palozzo is more likely to respect and to consider supporting a Mexican unionist leader than he would someone whose reputation is based on activity within the Mexican neighborhoods alone. Unionist reputations may serve to initiate contact between neighborhood leaders, but the trust necessary to negotiate working coalitions at the precinct level must be built over longer periods of contact across territorial boundaries. As the preceding field notes demonstrate, the Mexican unionists were also hindered in their negotiations by the egalitarian, primary group style of their political organization. In this regard, the political lessons which they gained from the campaign forced changes in the most characteristic features of Mexican political life.

Lesson II: Primary Groups
Cannot Operate outside
Territorial Boundaries

Control over voting behavior in the fourteen to twenty precincts in which the Mexicans have their influence is a far cry from ability to organize a precinct-level campaign in a 72-precinct ward. And in the election in question, the voting territory included 120 precincts, since sections of other wards were included in the voting district. Thus, as they met with political activists outside their neighborhoods, the South Chicago Mexicans began to understand for the first time the extent to which entry into public politics requires alteration of their group's political style and mode of organization.

First, it became clear that if they were to come even close to manning all the precincts in the ward, they would have to place their own people—Mexicans from Irondale and Millgate—into precincts outside their neighborhoods. But precinct politics in ethnic neighborhoods such as Irondale and Millgate traditionally involves the participation of male primary groups. It is almost impossible to induce men who are only beginning to overcome the territorial animosities which divide their own ethnic group to leave the security of their tavern primary groups to canvass voters in strange neighborhoods. Only exceptional persons would consider such assignments: younger, more educated people would do so but they are in short supply in a relatively new ethnic group. The ward political organization, on the other hand, can easily field ten or fifteen professional precinct captains who will canvass strange precincts at the request of the committeeman.

In attempting to induce some of their men to canvass strange precincts, the leaders of the Tenth Ward Spanish Speaking Democratic Organization encountered no little frustration. Within their neighborhoods, the tavern-based primary groups routinely mobilize five to ten men in each precinct, mainly for work shortly before the election. But rarely would any of these men agree to go outside their immediate neighborhood to canvass voters. Non-Mexican unionist leaders affiliated with the Chico campaign encountered similar difficulties. A labor leader such as Robert Hatch might have up to fifteen black steelworkers willing to take precinct assignments in the ward, but almost none of these men would be able to bring himself actually to canvass a strange precinct. Quite commonly unionist politicians from the mills will even be reluctant to canvass precincts in their own neighborhoods. This is a difficult lesson of local politics which both Mexican leaders and the younger South Chicago unionist leaders gained from the Chico candidacy. Fortunately, there were precinct workers available, both in the Mexican neighborhoods and outside, who could take assignments in strange precincts. In a number of instances Mexican women came forward to perform in this capacity, a trend which has far-reaching implications for the future of Mexican ethnicity.

Lesson III: Women Must Play
Active Roles in Ward Politics

At the level of tavern-based primary groups, politics is a man's activity. In newer ethnic groups women are rarely included in the decision-making process. Rather, they are expected to assist men in organizing fund-raising activities by taking "feminine" roles at ticket counters, in kitchens, and on decoration committees. In the campaign offices women perform secretarial tasks, and on election day the majority of judges and checkers inside the polling places are women. Generally this is true of all politically active ethnic groups in the Tenth Ward, and it is particularly so for the Mexicans. Throughout the Tenth Ward, men stand in front of the polls on election day to greet arriving voters, and men take the credit or blame for precinct results even though in many cases it is the wives and daughters of these captains who do much of the canvassing prior to election day.

Mexican political activists retain a degree of the "machismo" ethic which often results in situations where the entry of a woman in public politics is perceived as threatening to a husband's status as political leader in his immediate neighborhood. Thus during the Chico campaign a number of cases arose in which Mexican women who were actively involved in canvassing precincts outside their neighborhoods asked the candidate's campaign staff to refrain from public recognition of this activity. Nevertheless, as the campaign progressed and it became obvious that few Mexican men would go beyond their neighborhoods to canvass voters, a group of women in the Mexican precincts began taking increasingly active roles as precinct organizers. By their action an additional eight to ten precincts were "covered" during the campaign. Also, in addition to their entry into street level politics, wives and daughters of the Spanish Speaking Democrats appropriated greater responsibility for the organization of public events associated with the campaign. Through this activity the Mexican women were responsible for the largest portion of funds raised during the campaign.

It would be difficult to exaggerate the importance of this first experience in electoral politics for South Chicago's Mexican women. By the end of the campaign a number of women were attending the Mexican organization's strategy sessions, and the male leadership group readily acknowledged that the active and public participation of Mexican women would become an essential feature of future politics in their group. Indeed, in the months following Chico's defeat at the polls, as the male leaders assessed the lessons of the campaign, it was their wives and daughters who took the first new political initiatives. The women affiliated with the Tenth Ward Spanish Speaking Democrats organized an appeal to the City Council to change the name of Bessemer Park in South Chicago to Latin American Memorial Park. Although this issue would soon be appropriated by the male leaders of the Spanish Speaking Democrats, the fact that women had taken the initiative in this matter indicates the degree to which politically active women were changing their role in the group's political life.[4]

John Chico lost the election in November 1969 to a candidate sponsored by the regular party organization in the ward. Although he polled enough votes in the mill neighborhoods of the Tenth Ward to win the election there, he failed to attract enough votes in the more middle-class sections of the ward, or in middle-class neighborhoods outside the ward. Since the Mexicans and their unionist allies had made a number of strategic attempts to gain votes in the white collar neighborhoods, their failure to win middle-class votes came as one of the most painful lessons of the campaign.

Lesson IV: Reform Politicians
Cannot Deliver Their Precincts
to Working-Class Candidates

During the 1969 campaign, the Mexicans formed a coalition with a liberal attorney from South Shore. This candidate could potentially win support for the Mexicans in the middle-class neighborhoods of the district in return for votes in the mill precincts where the Mexicans had their strength. Running as a reform candidate, the attorney had the backing of the Independent Voters of Illinois (IVI), as well as the services of professional campaign organizers attached to Chicago's reform congressman Abner Mikva. Since the voters were to choose two delegates, and would have a choice between the two regular Democratic party candidates or the two independent candidates (or any combination of two candidates), it was possible for Chico and the other independent candidate to present themselves as a coalition. For their part the regular party precinct captains were urging voters to vote for the two party candidates. Although it received little attention in the metropolitan press, the independent coalition represented a potential turning point in the politics of Chicago's South Side. Here were IVI "amateur Democrats" and South Shore black precinct leaders, allied with Mexican and white ethnic unionists from the steel mill communities to the south. If it could hold together and gain strength, such a coalition could overturn the regular Democratic party organization in two major South Side wards in the near future.

Although they may generate a good deal of enthusiasm in reform political circles, coalitions between middle class, liberal faction, and working class, ethnic factions are extremely difficult to maintain over more than one election. The primary cause of their instability is the fact that the rewards to be gained from such alliances go disproportionately to the middle-class leaders. The fate of the present coalition serves as a typical example.

With the coalition in effect, the Mexican and other unionist precinct captains were urging voters to vote for both members of the coalition, and the South Shore captains were doing likewise in their precincts. The results did not reflect the same reciprocity. In the middle-class precincts organized by the reform candidate, Chico gained more votes than either the party candidates or his independent partner. On the other hand, votes from the Mexican and other working-class precincts gave the reform candidate enough votes to defeat one of the regular party candidates. Lack of votes from the middle-class precincts cost Chico the election.

The Mexicans and their unionist allies were deeply hurt by the results of the election, and especially by what many in their group perceived to be the failure of the reform politicians to make good their end of the bargain. All the precinct organizers in the Chico campaign saw the results in class terms: "The working stiff got it in the neck as usual. We gave them our votes but they didn't come across for us." And many of the group believed that the South Shore reform politicians, both black and white, had deliberately failed to try to get votes for the Mexican candidate. More sophisticated politicians in the group were able to distinguish between the actions of the reform precinct workers and the behavior of voters in their middle-class precincts. Thus John Chico explained,

I don't think they [the South Shore reform captains] did as much for us as they could, but it's not only that. They just can't deliver their precincts for anybody the way we can. We tell our people how to vote and they do it for us because they trust us. It's not that way for them. Their voters have to be sold on a candidate and they're not the kind of people to go for a Chicano steelworker.

One implication of this analysis is that the future of Mexican politics in South Chicago would remain tied to political developments in the working-class neighborhoods of South Chicago instead of depending upon the formation of coalitions across community and class boundaries. This was not only due to the Mexicans' disappointment in this campaign. Following the election the necessity arose once again of turning attention to the problem of territorial segmentation within the Mexican ethnic group.[5]

Lesson V: Territorial Cleavage
Persists Despite Collective Action

Shortly following their exhausting initiation in ward electoral politics, the Tenth Ward Mexicans were faced with the choice of which candidates to support in a Democratic primary for legislative candidates. In making this choice, they would reveal to themselves and to political activists in the community at large the direction which Mexican politics would take in the future. At least three alternatives were available:

1. Support the committeeman's candidate and thus come to terms with the new incumbent faction in the ward;

2. Support a weaker Tenth Ward candidate who had the alderman's
   backing and thus continue to oppose the committeeman's faction in
   the ward; or
3. Support a black candidate from South Shore, thereby maintaining
   their own coalition and improving the possibility of further
   weakening the committeeman's power in the Tenth Ward.

These alternatives were debated in the tavern headquarters of the
Irondale and South Chicago Mexican groups, as well as in meetings of
the entire leadership group. In the lengthy discussions over these issues,
a split threatened once again to divide the two territorial segments of
the Mexican community. In general, the Irondale precinct captains
believed the Spanish Speaking Democrats should back the Tenth Ward
candidate since he and the alderman had supported the Mexicans in
their recent campaign. Support of a Tenth Ward candidate would aid
the alderman in his coming confrontation with the new committeeman.
The Irondale Mexican captains held firmly to the position that the
Mexicans should make good on their political debts within the Tenth
Ward even if the alderman's candidate stood little chance of winning.

The South Chicago Mexicans were less certain of the proper strategy
and debated the question at great length. First, they had to overcome
their disappointment with the South Shore liberal politicians, both
white and black. They saw that although their candidate had been
defeated, their coalition with the South Shore reformers had seriously
hindered the new committeeman's acquisition of power in the Tenth
Ward. Defeat of even one of his candidates had "put the committeeman on bad paper up on the Third Floor." (The mayor had seen the
committeeman's weakness and was punishing him by taking control of
some key patronage positions in the ward. Such positions are dispensed
from a small office on the third floor of city hall.) Another defeat, some
of the South Chicago Mexicans reasoned, would even more seriously
erode the committeeman's power in the ward. A loss for him in a
regular Democratic primary would lay the way open in the Tenth Ward
for a new alignment of groups in which the Mexicans could assume
more prominent positions than they ever had before.

This reasoning clearly pointed to support of the black candidate, for
he had the best chance to defeat the committeeman's candidate.
Support for the alderman's choice would appease other opposition
factions in the Tenth Ward, but it would not defeat the committeeman
again. Such action would maintain lines of support in the ward, but it
would do little to increase the Mexicans' power there. On the basis of
ethnic group interest alone, therefore, it would seem that the black
candidate would be the best choice. On the other hand, the idea of

supporting a black candidate raised difficult questions of the Mexicans' status in the defended white neighborhoods of the Tenth Ward. This issue threatened to exacerbate Mexican territorial conflict. Here the debate centered on ideas of Mexican neighborhood status as against the acquisition of political power—although such terms were not used directly. At a meeting of the South Chicago Mexican precinct captains the issue was raised by one captain as follows:

Here in South Chicago we could go for the plieto [black]. We are the ones who are holding this place together and the Pollakos know that. If we weren't moving in it would be all black now and the Pollakos would be gone. With us here they can stay. Look at them on my block, they're fixing up their houses, they ain't going nowhere.

The Irondale guys could never go for a plieto with the way their people are there. Do you think they can go ask the Hunkies and Italians to vote for a black? Remember what they went through at the project. [Trumbull Park riots, 1954] A Pancho ain't going to get them people to go for a black, so you can forget the Irondale guys if we go for this.

These remarks drew general assent from the other Mexican precinct captains at the meeting; support of a black candidate would endanger the solidarity of their own ethnic political organization. The Irondale captains would lose face in their neighborhood if they campaigned for a black candidate. The best strategy from the point of view of the Mexicans' influence in ward politics conflicted with the role of politics in the Irondale segment's struggle for neighborhood status. Thus, in the interest of unity within their group, the Spanish Speaking Democrats chose to give half-hearted support to the weaker Tenth Ward candidate. In the primary election the black candidate did even better than had been expected. He lost to the organization candidate by a margin of votes which the Mexicans could have made up by campaigning for him in their precincts. The candidate whom the Mexicans did support polled relatively few votes. Worse still, he joined the new committeeman's faction shortly after his campaign defeat. Nevertheless, the Mexican leaders had few regrets despite these lessons from hindsight. They had acted both in the interests of group solidarity and to improve their status in the Tenth Ward mill neighborhoods. To whatever extent possible, they would build on these precedents in the future.

Gerrymander: Succession Stymied

In the fall and winter of 1970, the Mexican captains prepared to enter the aldermanic campaign in which the Tenth Ward alderman would face the new committeeman. In this genuine political showdown, the Tenth Ward Mexicans had good reason to feel optimistic. They had achieved an unprecedented degree of solidarity both within their precincts and between their neighborhood segments. They had sponsored a public candidate who could serve as spokesman for their group in ward politics. Friendships and trust between their own leaders and precinct activists outside their neighborhoods were developing rapidly. And within their political organization more women and younger, educated people were taking an active interest in political action. Although their inclination was to support the alderman against the new committeeman, they would wait upon developments in the ward before declaring their support. Most importantly, their support would come on a quid pro quo basis in which Mexicans would have more strength than ever before. Unfortunately, none of this optimism was warranted. Through fiat at higher levels of city government, the Mexicans were almost completely taken out of Tenth Ward politics.

Before the aldermanic election, in the winter of 1971, the Tenth Ward was redistricted. All the South Chicago precincts were placed in the Seventh Ward, which included most of the middle-class and black South Shore neighborhoods. With only the Irondale precincts remaining in the Tenth Ward, the Spanish Speaking Democratic Organization was effectively gerrymandered out of existence at the ward level. The Mexicans were bitterly disappointed by the gerrymandering. Many had suspected this would be their fate in the 1970s, just as the Polish population had been gerrymandered to varying degrees throughout its tenure in South Chicago. Just prior to the redistricting, the South Chicago Mexicans made the symbolic gesture of walking out of a state Democratic rally during a speech by Mayor Daley. But as a gerrymandered ethnic group in the 1970s, the Mexicans would not choose to support the Republican party, as many of the Polish political leaders had done earlier. Instead, the Mexicans would follow the black example and concentrate much of their energy on building the Chicano movement throughout the city. At the local level, however, many of the Mexican activists would make private accommodations with ward leaders.

Ethnic succession in local urban politics is often treated as a "matter of fact" process in which ethnic subleaders gradually win local offices. Robert Dahl, for example, observes that in the "first stage" of ethnic politics, "Some of these ethnic subleaders eventually receive nominations for minor offices, such as alderman, where the constituency is drawn predominantly from the subleaders' ethnic group. In this stage the group ordinarily has a high degree of political homogeneity; ethnic similarity is associated with similarity in political attitude, and there is a pronounced tendency toward voting alike."[6] Even if one focuses on the politics of a major city's largest ethnic groups, stage models of ethnic political succession tend to neglect the processes whereby ethnic leaders emerge, and whereby a group's "political homogeneity" is established. For smaller ethnic groups in the heterogeneous industrial settlements of major cities, the model is even more problematic. Without commanding majorities in their wards, small ethnic segments will never win power in local politics unless they negotiate aggregations of political leaders which include other segments of the community. And even when these negotiations are quite advanced, decisions at higher levels of metropolitan politics may dramatically alter the course of ethnic political adaptation. Frustrated in the normal process of community political succession, the South Chicago Mexicans are developing stronger minority group consciousness and elaborating local traditions of Chicano cultural nationalism. But the Chicano movement is no substitute for succession to power in the community political institutions.

Their increasing participation in the Chicano movement in Chicago, and at the national level, brings South Chicago Mexicans into ethnic interest group politics. They focus attention on the cultural bias of language programs in local schools; they lobby for Mexican delegates to national Democratic conventions; and as a recognized minority group, they assume positions in federally financed welfare agencies. But in the mill neighborhoods of South Chicago, respectability is still measured in the aggregation of precinct power and ward authority. A few judgeships and a host of Mexican employees in Model Cities agencies do not appreciably improve the delivery of vital services to Millgate and Irondale. To win power in the community political system, the Mexicans must manage their ethnicity within networks of personal attachments which they negotiate among a range of neighborhood leaders. Ward redistricting has set back the Mexicans' ability to enter such negotiations in South Chicago. Nevertheless, they will continue to compete for succession in the local unions and the ward organization.

Mexican labor leadership and the precinct influence of Mexican unionists will continue to bring Mexicans into the negotiation of community leadership aggregations. Also, the personal attachments and respect which their political leaders won before they were gerrymandered has facilitated the ecological dispersion of South Chicago Mexicans. With increasing ease and frequency they are moving into the community's neighborhoods of second settlement. In the years to come their numerical growth and dispersion will overcome the divisive influence of gerrymandering. In metropolitan and national politics the South Chicago Mexicans will identify with the Chicano subculture, and they will support self-consciously ethnic politicians at those levels. But in the local community their politics will increasingly resemble that of the Serbians, Croatians, Poles, and Italians, the groups which came before them in the history of South Chicago settlement. Like them, the Mexicans will increasingly subordinate overt appeals to ethnic solidarity and concentrate on developing their influence in the diverse networks of neighborhood primary groups.

8

Slavic Succession in Ward Politics

Second-generation precinct activists from the older ethnic groups have accumulated almost a generation of experience and status in Tenth Ward politics. Polish, Italian, Serbian, and Croatian precinct leaders already operate within local political institutions; they are insiders in the system the Mexicans are attempting to compete in. For this reason there are no Polish, Italian, Serbian, or Croatian ethnic political organizations to direct the political aspirations of those groups. Overt patterns of ethnic mobilization are more difficult to identify than in the Mexican case. In general, the degree to which ethnic ties are activated among the more established groups depends in large part on the politics of particular leadership primary groups. Typically an ambitious politician will maneuver for support in the ward by balancing ethnic, personal, and civic appeals, depending on the solidarity of specific neighborhood groups being aggregated.

Contemporary Serbian and Croatian ward leadership is characteristic of the politics of the older ethnic groups. In the Slag Valley neighborhood the Croatians and Serbians have a small ethnic territory which includes about five precincts. There the voters can be mobilized by precinct captains who appeal to ethnic attachments and attempt to play down lingering difference between Serbians and Croatians. Elsewhere in the ward, Serbians and Croatians are dispersed throughout the blue collar neighborhoods of second settlement, particularly on the East Side. South Slavic activists from those neighborhoods are members of heterogeneous precinct primary groups. Two or three Serbian precinct captains on the East Side, for example, will participate in a loosely structured primary group with five or six politically active neighbors of quite diverse ethnicity. Such groups commonly reconstruct a version of their past which deemphasizes the importance of ethnic distinctions in favor of mutual interests and shared experiences. Thus a politically active primary group will think of itself as "going way back" in the political history of the neighborhood, or the group will dwell on common experiences in the mills and the occupational taverns of the area. Although most of their communal lives are spent in such reconstructed primary groups, most people maintain prior ethnic attachments in the old neighborhoods. Thus, second- or third-generation Serbians and Croatians normally return to the ethnic associations of Slag Valley for the important ceremonies which accompany birth, marriage, and death.[1]

Serbian and Croatian precinct activists continually renew their personal ties within the ethnic groups by participating in the yearly round of ethnic social events in the old neighborhood. At the same time they are members of heterogeneous primary groups in their new neighborhoods. This means that through the farflung network of personal attachments based on ethnicity, the South Slavic politician gains access to a larger set of precinct primary groups in the new neighborhoods. On the other hand, men and women in South Chicago politics continually find themselves faced with conflicting expectations deriving from their ethnic, neighborhood, and organizational loyalties. Appeals to ethnic ties often conflict with loyalties formed in political organizations, or in heterogeneous neighborhood primary groups. At times of political turmoil in the ward, when pressures to decide between conflicting loyalties are greatest, such decisions are often justified by moral arguments and local notions of good citizenship.

If they are to win the loyalties of political activists who are torn between diverse attachments, ward leaders must imbue the old style of business and ethnic politics with appeals to public morality. This synthesis of old and new machine political styles is necessary even to negotiate support within a political leader's own ethnic group. The stakes involved in Tenth Ward politics are often extremely high. They involve activists in agonizing personal decisions which may affect not only their community status but also their material security.

Insiders in Tenth Ward Politics

The livelihood of hundreds of South Chicago families depends directly or indirectly on the leadership of the Tenth Ward Democratic Organization. Under normal circumstances the Democratic committeeman is the "ward boss." He dispenses patronage in the form of city jobs, favors and services for local residents, and introductions to other powerful actors in city politics. The political processes whereby ward bosses in South Chicago come to power have changed over the decades, but the power of ward Democratic leadership itself has hardly diminished with improvement in the level of living in South Chicago. On the one hand there remain neighborhoods of first settlement in the Bush, Millgate, and Irondale where new immigrants are crowded into rickety mill tenements. These segments of the community continue to be mobilized, in part, by the traditional material rewards of the ward heeler.[2] In the newer neighborhoods, on the other hand, the shared culture of steelworking families, independent of ethnic divisions, provides a host of opportunities for aggregating political power in the ward.

Blue Collar Culture
and Ward Power

The dependence of blue collar culture on neighborhood attachments is one of the continuing foundations of ward political power in South Chicago, and in Chicago in general. All the institutions of the neighborhoods, the churches, the taverns, and the civic voluntary associations, require the personal intervention of ward political leaders in their affairs. These institutions demand an endless series of exceptions to the formalities of middle-class legality. Many churches wish to run bingo games and to serve liquor at social functions; every neighborhood and many mill departments support small bookmaking operations, prospective tavern owners need help obtaining licenses, small building contractors need aid in dealing with building inspectors; immigrants or their relatives need help with immigration officials; the list can hardly be exhausted. As the insiders in the Tenth Ward Democratic Organization service these requests, they also establish a lucrative network of reciprocities in the neighborhoods. In South Chicago the ward committeeman holds office hours in the evenings at his political headquarters. Here he meets people with favors to ask who will be willing at some later date to return these favors even if only in the form of campaign contributions. Thus ward leadership supports a host of attorneys, insurance agents, realtors, builders, tavern owners, restaurateurs, and small bankers. The aggregation of ward leaders who control the party organization can become rich during their tenure in power, and this is another reason blue collar ward politics provokes more excitement and more deadly seriousness than the politics of middle-class wards.

Professional survival. Professional activists in Tenth Ward politics who lack a base of personal support in the neighborhoods are insecure insiders in the political system. In times of political factionalism they must struggle to preserve their careers. Should they support the losing faction they will have to "come crawling" to the winners to offer their services. Lacking a base in the ethnic neighborhoods of the ward, they must cast around for other means to win a personal following or else suffer indignities from ward politicians who have powerful local support. A case in point is the following account by a Tenth Ward precinct captain:

Al F—— (precinct captain, East Side). You know O'Hara, the ward sanitation superintendent, right? He came out on the losing side in the last committeeman's election. He figured he was going to be a loser but he had to go with the regular organization because he had one of the top jobs in the ward. Well, the night of the election, when the returns showed that the other group won, O'Hara went over to their headquarters to congratulate them. He figured they would know that he's a pro and had done what he had to do.

He got to their headquarters and there was a big crowd there. Everybody was celebrating and drinking. When the new committeeman and his boys see O'Hara walk in they go up to him and knock him down, break his glasses and start kicking him. They beat him up in front of everybody.

For a long time O'Hara was in bad trouble. He was on good paper at city hall because he's Irish and has always been a solid organization man, so he got some protection. But out here in the Tenth he was fighting for his life. Outside the organization he had nothing going for him. What he did then was to get real active in the Kiwanis and the Boys Club and all kinds of organizations. He did a lot of PR work for himself, getting his picture in the paper with these pancake breakfasts and award banquets. So people began to think he had some clout after all and he managed to survive.

Ethnic respect. The same vulnerability which troubles professionals inside the Democratic party organization in the ward also applies to ethnic segments which lose out in ward elections. As demonstrated in the previous chapter, an ethnic segment on the inside in the ward party organization can command respect in its neighborhoods and can negotiate political primary groups with other neighborhood leaders. If their leaders back a losing faction, however, an ethnic segment may not only lose the material advantages of precinct leadership but will also suffer direct assaults on their respectability. Thus the aggregation of Serbian, Croatian, and other ethnic politicians who took control of the Tenth Ward in the last years of the 1960s had recruited a group of Mexicans who were of lower status in the Mexican neighborhoods than

were the Mexican unionists. After their loss in the ward committeeman's election, the Mexican unionists were deprived of whatever
formal patronage they had, and, as these notes show, they also suffered
attacks on their respectability in the ward.

The most popular social event for South Chicago Mexicans is the
annual Cinderella Ball in which a Mexican beauty is chosen at a dance
held in the large Local 65 union hall. At this event the second-
generation unionist leaders and their allies host all segments of the
South Chicago Mexican population, as well as many of the political
leaders in the larger community. The event is a rather formal affair
which receives much publicity in the local press. Directly after their loss
in ward politics, the Mexican unionists suffered the indignity of having
the Cinderella Ball raided by local police and ward officials. The
specific complaint was that the union hall did not have an up-to-date
liquor license, but the indignity of police closing the bar at the
Cinderella Ball was a clear case of one negotiated aggregation in ward
politics using its power to attack the respectability of a competing
ethnic segment.

The succession to power in the Tenth Ward by Croatian and Serbian
politicians firmly established the respectability of these Slavic groups in
the ward, and their power permits them to influence the fate of ethnic
adaptation in newer groups such as the Mexicans. In the decade of the
1960s, the Tenth Ward underwent a transition from leadership by an
Italian Democratic committeeman-alderman to leadership by a young
Croatian ward leader. In this period of transition the various processes
whereby local power is aggregated were more clearly visible than is
usually the case in ward politics. The network of ethnic, party, and
neighborhood coalitions negotiated during the previous committeeman's tenure collapsed and was rearranged by new political leaders.
Thus it became possible to weigh the importance of ethnic ties against
other dimensions of solidarity in political groups. Since the new
committeeman is of Croatian ethnicity, he naturally began his rise to
power in large part by appealing to political activists in the Croatian
and Serbian ethnic groups. The politics of the South Slavs in the Tenth
Ward may therefore be viewed through the career of this ward leader.[3]

The Rise of a Modern Ward Boss

Edward R. Vrdolyak, the politician who became the Tenth Ward
Democratic committeeman in the late 1960s, represents a new
generation of ward leaders in communities such as South Chicago. A
graduate of the University of Chicago Law School, in his early thirties

he is the youngest of six brothers, all of whom are active in city politics either in the police department, labor unions, or ward politics itself. The senior Vrdolyak was born in Croatia and immigrated to this country in his adolescence. Through his successful tavern in South Chicago, Vrdolyak became one of the more prominent Croatian family names outside the Croatian ethnic group. In the second generation Edward is the most successful son, but one of his older brothers is active in the powerful ironworkers trade union, and another is a police commander in the West Side district. The only female sibling, Jenny Vrdolyak Simmons, is the new committeeman's administrative assistant and has become one of the most skilled campaign organizers on Chicago's South Side. Given its extensive contact in networks of ward influentials which this very brief summary suggests, it is not surprising that the Vrdolyak family itself provided the basis from which the young lawyer could begin to organize necessary support for entry into Tenth Ward politics.

In contrast to John Chico, the leader of the Tenth Ward Spanish Speaking Democrats, Vrdolyak could enter ward politics at quite a higher level of organization. Chico is one of seven brothers, most of whom have spent the greater part of their occupational careers in the steel mills. Through their contacts in the mills, and because of Chico's superior political skills, the Mexican leader was able to win prominence in local union politics. But in ward politics his influence has tended to be limited to negotiations within the Mexican neighborhoods. The same limitations do not apply to Edward Vrdolyak. Not only are the Croatian political activists better placed in South Chicago's political institutions, but the Vrdolyak family could muster considerable support for its ambitious young attorney. And on the strength of his own qualifications Vrdolyak could recruit support in more middle-class areas of the ward where Croatian attachments would normally provide little entry.

Vrdolyak's University of Chicago credentials allowed him to enter a law partnership with a number of prominent South Chicago attorneys. This partnership included professionals with extensive connections in the middle-class, Jewish neighborhoods of Jeffery Manor, South Shore Gardens, and South Shore Valley (in the Stony Island Park area). As he entered ward politics, these connections would be as important as those of his family in the blue collar mill neighborhoods of the ward. While establishing himself in this law firm, where he handled a large number of cases referred to him by his brothers and their associates in the police districts of southeast Chicago, Vrdolyak also began to move into the intense factional struggles which marked Tenth Ward politics throughout the decade of the 1960s.

Triangular Competition
for Ward Leadership

Emile Pasini, the powerful leader of the Tenth Ward during the previous decade, was weakening in the first years of the 1960s. Not only was he in ill health, but after more than a decade of his leadership as Democratic committeeman and alderman, a number of neighborhood areas in the ward were becoming restive. In the western part of the ward, the middle-class, largely Jewish population was becoming increasingly drawn into reform politics through the organizing efforts of the Independent Voters of Illinois. In the East Side, favorite-son politics was once again becoming a serious threat to ward leaders. In 1964 an East Side insurance man, John Buchannan, won a business-man's popularity contest for "Mayor of the East Side." On the strength of this favorite-son sentiment Buchannan formed an alliance with some of the liberal precinct captains in the western section of the ward, and to the surprise of most ward political activists he succeeded in defeating Pasini in the aldermanic election of that year. In that election Edward Vrdolyak worked behind the scenes to provide Buchannan with financial support and to recruit precinct-level leaders throughout the ward.

Emile Pasini's political strength had been located in the neighbor-hoods of first settlement, Millgate, Irondale, Slag Valley, and the old river precincts of the East Side. In neighborhoods of second settlement his organization could always hold its own, but these precincts were in contention during Pasini's tenure as committeeman. The size of the Polish enclave would have made it the dominant ethnic group in Tenth Ward politics. But with their neighborhoods gerrymandered between the Seventh and Tenth Wards, Polish precinct leaders could never dominate the Tenth Ward without forming coalitions with other ethnic politicians. As a member of one of the smaller ethnic groups, coalition formation had been Pasini's forte. When he died, following his defeat by Buchannan in the 1964 election, leadership of the party organization was taken over by a Polish realtor, Stanley Zima, who had served as secretary of the Tenth Ward Democratic Organization during Pasini's tenure.

Since he had inherited a weakened party organization, and one which was being attacked by energetic politicians with important precinct level connections, Pasini's Polish successor never was able to consolidate his power in the committeeman's office. Thus the succeeding five years of Tenth Ward politics would be marked by a triangular struggle between Edward Vrdolyak, Stanley Zima, and John Buchannan. This political competition reached its major climax between 1967 and 1968, when Vrdolyak and the Polish interim committeeman met in the Democratic primary election for ward committeeman.

War of the signs. The 1967 Democratic primary in the Tenth Ward was an election which will be the subject of debate and reminiscences among South Chicago political activists for many years to come. During the campaign the ward was quite visibly going through an important political struggle. Vrdolyak's workers covered every available fence and building wall with huge billboards on which the initials E.R.V. were printed in large letters. His opponent, Stanley Zima, attempted to match this massive display, and for at least four months the "war of the signs," as it was termed in the local press, helped stir Tenth Ward politicians into a frenzy of political mobilization in their precincts. Indeed the campaign took on aspects of the classic ward battles in Chicago's First Ward during Mayor "Big Bill" Thompson's administration. Fights were frequent and intimidation of opposition precinct workers was widespread. On both sides of the campaign, precinct workers complained that their car tires had been slashed or that someone had fired a shot into their campaign offices. And throughout the long campaign, politically oriented taverns in the ward were continually crowded with active participants and peripheral actors, all of whom thrived on the gossip such a campaign generates. In particular this gossip centered on the subject of shifting loyalties, as precinct workers from various ethnic and residential aggregations were approached by campaign organizers from the Vrdolyak and Zima camps.

Good citizenship and racial tension. In addition to the traditional aspects of the Vrdolyak-Zima campaign, the contest also revolved around a set of local issues. In 1966 Martin Luther King had led a group of open occupancy marchers through the East Side neighborhoods, an event which brought the fears of South Chicago white residents to the surface to an extent not witnessed since the Trumbull Park riots of 1954. In the 1967 committeeman's campaign, therefore, "school busing" and "open housing" were major issues, and both candidates attempted to establish their opposition to programs for racial integration. On the issues Vrdolyak clearly had the upper hand, for unlike his opponent he was not dependent upon directions and financial support from Mayor Daley and the Central Committee of the Democratic party. Vrdolyak could appeal to neighborhood insecurities over the issues of racial integration without fear of contradicting the Daley administration's more pragmatic position on these issues.

On environmental issues Vrdolyak also had an advantage. He could criticize his opponent for the serious problems existing in the ward's huge garbage dumps where private cartage firms were openly violating the city's waste disposal ordinances. As incumbent committeeman, Zima could offer only a weak defense of his administration's record. Finally, Vrdolyak could make a much better public presentation than his opponent. Vrdolyak's youth, his ease in public appearances, and his coterie of young political activists from various ward neighborhoods contrasted sharply with his opponent's more traditional political style. Zima had risen through the party ranks. He was skilled in the internal operations of the ward party organization but had little flair for public candidacy. In consequence, in the neighborhoods of second settlement, which during the campaign sponsored innumerable public appearances, debates, and general political meetings, he was at a significant disadvantage.

An election such as the Zima-Vrdolyak primary may not occur in Chicago ward politics more than two or three times in a generation. Here the Democratic party was split into two warring camps. As groups of precinct workers in the two campaign organizations competed for votes in their neighborhoods, the tension in the ward became quite tangible. On election day fights were common throughout the ward, especially where factions of a particular neighborhood or ethnic group were competing through the committeeman's election. Thus in the Mexican precincts there were a number of incidents of violence or threats of violence between former Mexican street fighters who supported Vrdolyak and the Mexican unionists who supported Zima. On the East Side, also, there were numerous incidents between competing precinct leadership groups. In the end, after all the speeches, street rallies, political picnics, fund-raising dinners, precinct canvassing, strategy meetings, and drinking bouts, when the polls closed and the votes were counted. Vrdolyak had won the election by the narrow margin of 140 votes out of more than 15,000 votes cast.

A margin of victory as slim as Vrdolyak's hardly qualifies one for the title of ward boss. Even after his victory, Vrdolyak would suffer setbacks in his efforts to solidify his power in the ward, as seen in the case of the Spanish Speaking Democrats. Despite all his assets as a modern political candidate, to become a ward boss in anything approaching the traditional sense of the term Vrdolyak would have to continue to appeal for support through the networks of ethnic and neighborhood attachments which constitute the moral ecology of South Chicago.

Negotiating Slavic Solidarity

Tenth Ward politicians estimate the total "Hunky" vote, which includes at least the Serbians, Croatians, and Slovenes, at between 3,000 and 4,000 votes. Since it normally requires at least 12,000 votes to win a major ward election, this ethnic vote by no means assures an ambitious Slavic politician an electoral victory. Nevertheless, if it can be mobilized, the South Slavic vote is an important base of support from which to negotiate further aggregations of neighborhood political activists. First, the existence of an ethnic territory out of which an ambitious political leader may organize his campaign is of immesurable importance to Tenth Ward politicians. Control over even a small neighborhood offers visibility and organizational resources which are lacking for candidates without an ethnic territorial base. Second, even when the ethnic solidarity of second and third generations has become attenuated over years of ecological dispersion, a politician may become a champion of latent ethnic status aspirations. In addition, it will be possible to exploit personal attachments among one's ethnic peers in order to negotiate aggregations of precinct primary groups in the neighborhoods of second settlement.

Resources of an Ethnic Neighborhood

To measure the value of an ethnic territory in local politics even if it is relatively small, one need only compare the careers of politicians who have an ethnic base to those who do not. In the Tenth Ward, the Greeks have never controlled the vote in even one precinct with any regularity, yet the Greeks are well represented among the small businessmen and local professionals of the community. When during my research period in the ward a Greek politician ran for the state legislature, he had to stress his affiliation with the Orthodox church in order to marshal even a glimmering of enthusiasm in a Tenth Ward neighborhood. He could claim that as an Orthodox Catholic he should be supported in the Serbian neighborhoods because the Serbians are also Orthodox

Christians. But aside from some passing notice of his candidacy in the church congregation, there was little ethnic support generated for him in the Serbian blocks in Slag Valley or Irondale. This politician's ties to the Greek business community would assure him the financial support necessary to attain a place on the Democratic ballot, but lacking the modest resources of an ethnic enclave, he would always be at the mercy of the ward Democratic party organization. This was not true for Edward Vrdolyak. By capitalizing on his ethnic ties in Slag Valley he could organize neighborhood ethnic resources as a first step toward wresting political power in the ward.

The remaining concentration of Serbian and Croatian voters in the Tenth Ward is located in the Memorial Park-Slag Valley section of Irondale. Here, in the four precincts surrounding the Serbian Orthodox church (St. Michael's) and the Croatian Catholic church (Sacred Heart) is the one neighborhood in the ward which is identified as "belonging" to these South Slavic groups. Nevertheless, such perceived dominance does not imply that the South Slavic voters are in the majority there, for even in these parishes there are only four precincts in which they form the majority.

The contributions which such an ethnic territory may make to the political fortunes of a young leader are not obvious from the percentage of votes the groups control in their territory. More important are the organizations and physical facilities which may become a visible base of operations for a political campaign. In the Slag Valley neighborhood Edward Vrdolyak drew upon the resources of older ethnic benevolent associations and fraternal organizations to provide the center of operations needed to mount a political campaign throughout the community. These facilities were available to him in part because the old fraternal societies could no longer generate the level of operations needed to support their continued existence.

Hrvatski Dom. Communal facilities in Slag Valley which served the needs of immigrant settlements have outlived their usefulness. Recent immigrants from Serbia and Croatia have organized new associations, and the old immigrant organizations often become financial deficits in the mill neighborhoods. At the same time, a ward politician who wishes to challenge an incumbent group must have a headquarters from which to stage the countless meetings, fund-raising affairs, and strategy sessions necessary to organize a political campaign. Thus Vrdolyak could take over the old Hrvatski Dom (Croatian Home), the large hall which had been the center of fraternal and benevolent activities for his father's generation of Croatian immigrants. In the

Hrvatski Dom, Vrdolyak found a large meeting hall in the center of his ethnic base which he could transform into a political club. Such places are not easy to come by, and their importance both as physical facilities and as symbols of political organization should not be underrated.[4]

Newer ethnic groups in Chicago, those which have become established in the city since the 1930s, no longer find it necessary to construct large communal facilities (other than churches) with their own resources. The services which such facilities offer would merely duplicate those available from local welfare institutions. In consequence of this the Mexican Tenth Ward politicians meet in taverns, in each others' homes, or in Our Lady of Guadalupe church. On some occasions they have the use of Local 65's large union hall, but this is by no means a permanent home for the Mexican political organization. In Vrdolyak's case, by contrast, the former Croatian Hall became a political club and an after-hours drinking place for politically active South Chicagoans throughout the community.

Perhaps even more important than the physical facilities available in the Hrvatski Dom was the symbolic value of its transformation into Vrdolyak's political club. Since the majority of Croatian families in South Chicago are rather well dispersed throughout the mill neighborhoods, the slow process of building trust between competing territorial segments of the group is not necessary as it is in the Mexican precincts. Drawing upon his family status, educational background, and financial resources, Vrdolyak could simply buy the primary symbol of Croatian solidarity in South Chicago. Almost overnight purchase of the Hrvatski Dom made Vrdolyak the champion of Croatian status aspirations throughout South Chicago. But capture of the symbols of Croatian leadership alone does not bring about a realignment of the ward's ethnic and neighborhood aggregation.

Ethnicity and Access
to Precinct Leaders

Lacking the entry into networks of primary attachments at the precinct level which ethnic leadership confers, an aspiring South Chicago politician would have little hope of recruiting supporters in the various Tenth Ward neighborhoods. On the other hand, command of ethnic leadership in older groups such as the Croatians and Serbians is a necessary but not sufficient basis for recruiting supporters in local neighborhoods. Men and women who are precinct activists in the party organization are not readily recruited by an aspiring politician merely by appeals to ethnic solidarity. As members of primary groups which have been reconstructed on the basis of organizational and residential ties, political activists outside ethnic enclaves must be recruited by appeals to those newer dimensions of solidarity as well.

Reconstructed primary groups are formed as second-generation men and women who have spent their adolescence and young adulthood in ethnically homogeneous primary groups also begin to participate, in their adult years, in heterogeneous primary groups. As a generation adjusts to occupational careers and establishes its families in South Chicago, old adolescent primary groups tend to disintegrate through attrition due particularly to residential mobility in and beyond the community. This does not imply, however, that ethnic ties cease to function as bonds between men and women whose adolescent friendship groups have disbanded. Rather the dispersion of corner groups over a variety of territorial segments of South Chicago creates networks of affiliation based on ethnicity which link primary groups as they are reconstructed in later life. Thus if they are to exploit their ethnic attachments in aggregating the diverse groups of precinct activists, ward politicians must understand the dimension of solidarity in these reconstructed primary groups.

Serbian Neighborhood Groups

Processes involved in the reconstruction of primary ties and in the recruitment of such groups in local politics may best be illustrated through the analysis of a typical case. The dispersion and reorganization of primary affiliations in a large Serbian corner group will serve as the case in point. The main developments in the dispersion of this group occurred between 1940 and 1970.

During the decade of the 1940s a large group of thirty to forty second-generation Serbian men participated in an interconnected set of primary groups which used Eli's Tavern in Irondale as its base of operations. By 1970 the majority of men from this group who remained in the South Chicago community had reconstructed their friendships on the basis of their participation in heterogeneous residential neighborhood work groups and political organizations. But some members of the original corner group, particularly those who established families in the small Serbian neighborhood in Slag Valley—the neighborhood surrounding the old Serbian church—continued to associate almost exclusively with other Serbian men in that ethnic enclave. A second group of men from the same 1940s tavern group established their families in Irondale. Here they had to share their neighborhood with Italian and Mexican families. Finally, a third branch of the Eli's

Tavern group is now dispersed throughout various precincts of second settlement on the East Side.

Since each of the three groups of Serbian men from the Eli's Tavern group included a number of precinct political activists, the recruitment of these men into the Vrdolyak faction was quite important for the growth of his influence among the ward's Serbians. On the other hand, the process of primary group reconstruction among Irondale and East Side Serbians required that appeals for support be tailored to the neighborhood interests of those groups. Where attachments in adult primary groups such as these were reconstructed along purely ethnic or residential dimensions it was easier for Vrdolyak to appeal to the interests of the groups. Where solidarity in adult primary groups was based on combinations of ethnic, residential, and institutional attachments it was more difficult.

"Hunky" Ethnicity in Slag Valley

The Serbian men from the 1940s tavern group who settled with their families in the neighborhood around the old Serbian church have remained most active in the maintenance of specifically Serbian institutions. One group of Serbian men and women in Slag Valley devotes its energies to the maintenance of cultural institutions, particularly those associated with the church and with the traditional Serbian culture. Largely owing to their efforts, Serbian choral and instrumental music is kept alive in South Chicago.

Earlier in the century, the immigrant generation of Serbians and Croatians in Slag Valley engaged in serious rivalries and conflict which reflected the nationalist movements in the Balkan states prior to World War II. During the interwar period it was common for Serbian and Croatian immigrants to fight with each other at ethnic picnic grounds and in the neighborhoods of first settlement as well. Among the older immigrants these old country animosities continue to smolder. They are kept alive by expatriot organizations of Chetniks and Ustasha veterans, the peasant nationalist movements which fought each other as well as the Germans and Austrians.

Among the second- and third-generation residents of Slag Valley tension between Roman Catholic Croatians and Orthodox Serbs has been attenuated. In part this is accounted for by residential propinquity. Serbians and Croatians have shared contiguous neighborhoods for over two generations, and in that time there has been substantial cultural assimilation between the two groups. Today it is not uncommon for Croatian and Serbian musicians to perform in the same taverns, for a mixed clientele. Nor is it unusual for the church choirs of the two neighborhoods to combine their efforts in local concerts and dances. In the steel mills and the communal institutions these nationality groups shared the same language and men were brought together at work despite their religious and cultural differences. At work and in union politics the fact that the South Slavs were considered "Hunkies" and could organize for political influence behind common leaders established precedents for more general political cooperation between the Slag Valley Serbians and Croatians in ward politics. The first opportunity for such cooperation was the Vrdolyak candidacy in the late 1960s. In that case the small group of ethnic precinct captains from the Serbian enclave in Slag Valley heeded Vrdolyak's appeal to "Hunky" solidarity and entered as early partisans in his Tenth Ward political faction. In other neighborhoods of the ward, where territorial boundaries denied the Croatians and Serbians a basis of solidarity founded upon territorial as well as cultural attachments, the recruitment of Serbian political activists was a more delicate matter.

Irondale Serbians and Their Italian Neighbors

Serbian men who continue to live or work in the old Irondale neighborhood are now members of heterogeneous primary groups. While earlier in the century, during their late adolescence and young adulthood, these Serbian men were part of the Eli's Tavern group, now as family heads they have reconstructed their friendships to include non-Serbians of approximately the same age range. Since the Italians are the largest group in the neighborhood with a comparable residential and occupational history, Irondale Serbians are most likely to form primary groups with their Italian neighbors and workmates in the Wisconsin Steel plant.

The negotiations which lead to primary group reconstruction along these lines are not obvious. If as adolescents and young adults the Serbs congregated in homogeneous tavern groups, as did the Italians on their side, there is little in the mere passage of time to suggest how primary groups should be reconstructed. In fact, since the Italians and Serbians attend different churches, one might expect that the conditions which led to earlier segmentation would persist throughout the life cycle of these neighborhood groups. Such might have been the case were it not for the negotiation of Irondale leadership groups in union and ward politics. In the process of winning control of the local union at

Wisconsin Steel from their northern European and Irish predecessors, and in maintaining their control of the union against challenges from their newer Mexican neighbors, the Irondale Serbians and Italians have established primary groups in which family histories and political loyalty are more important criteria of solidarity than is ethnicity. Since the union at Wisconsin Steel is independent of the United Steelworkers of America, and the resources it commands are allocated by local leaders, control over this important local political institution gives the Serbians and Italians from Irondale greater claim to influence in ward politics than simple control over their few neighborhood precincts would ever have afforded them. This, plus the fact that the former Democratic committeeman was of Italian ethnicity, allowed the Irondale activists to win prominence in the Democratic ward organization under its former leader.

Through years of political campaigns the Irondale group and leaders of the incumbent Democratic faction became enmeshed in a set of primary groups where attachments extended beyond the bonds of political fortune or ethnic and neighborhood solidarity. As an example, consider the account by a prominent Serbian union leader from Irondale of the former ward committeeman's death:

I spoke to Emile [the former committeeman] before he died. He was real sick and knew he was on his death bed. "Pete," he said, "I want you to promise me you'll take care of my family when I go, especially Billy [his son]." Then he said, and any of the guys will back me up on this, he said I should go out for his spot, that I should go for committeeman in the ward.

To have presented himself as a candidate for Democratic committeeman would have placed this Serbian unionist in contention with another member of his reconstructed primary group. This man at the time was the secretary of the ward Democratic organization, and himself a primary contender for interim committeeman. Although he is of South Chicago Polish background, this ward leader had become a member of the primary group which included the Serbian unionist as well as other Irondale political activists. A contest between the two would have seriously strained the aggregation of primary groups of which they were the leaders. More seriously, such a contest would have ended the friendship of a group of men who had worked together through years of political battles and had become intimates rather than mere political allies. The men in this political primary group, Serbians and Italians from Irondale and Poles from South Chicago are godfathers to one another's children, and rather than endanger their solidarity the Serbian unionist refrained from attempting to succeed the deceased committeeman.

The Vrdolyak faction in Tenth Ward politics would be expected to have difficulty in recruiting support among Irondale's Serbian and Italian leadership. Through his allies in the Slag Valley Serbian group, men who had been boyhood friends of the Irondale Serbian leader, the aspiring committeeman could exert pressure on the Serbian unionist, but lacking the ability to apply equal pressure on the Italians in the Irondale group, appeals to ethnic solidarity carried insufficient weight. Vrdolyak was obliged to defeat the interim committeeman, against the best efforts of the Irondale Serbians and Italians, before he could reasonably hope to recruit this neighborhood primary group into his new alignment of reconstructed primary groups in the ward. Fortunately for Vrdolyak's career in Tenth Ward politics, the East Side Serbian precinct activists were far less committed to the incumbent faction than the Irondale Serbs and their Italian neighbors were.

East Side Serbians and Neighborhood Solidarity

Serbian men from the Eli's Tavern group who later established their families in the neighborhoods of second settlement on the East Side have tended to reconstruct their primary group affiliations along lines of neighborhood solidarity. In the heterogeneous neighborhoods in this section of the community, friendship groups are formed on the basis of participation in local neighborhood activities and civic voluntary associations. Of course this is not universally true. One can point to Serbian families which have not become part of neighborhood primary groups but prefer to continue their full participation in Serbian ethnic institutions which remain in the Slag Valley neighborhood. On the other hand, Serbians from the old tavern group who take active political roles in East Side precincts must function as amateur rather than ethnic or professional leaders. Their claim to political leadership in East Side precincts rests on reputations formed in small, face-block neighborhoods. In the style of amateur precinct leaders they must maintain friendships with other political activists and leaders of local civic voluntary associations, all of whom are of quite diverse ethnicity, and whose common interests center on the preservation of neighborhood solidarity and the improvement of communal facilities.

Favorite-son politics, as described in an earlier chapter, is the mode of politics most characteristic of East Side precincts. As opposed to other segments of the ward, which tend to enter local politics through the efforts of ethnic groups leaders or professional ward politicians, the majority of East Side political activists support local politicians who champion the values of neighborhood solidarity in that section of the community. The Tenth Ward alderman during the period of Vrdolyak's rise to power was such a figure. A politician who faithfully attended the weekly round of civic-voluntary association meetings on the East Side (as well as in other neighborhood areas), the alderman's political strength tended to be limited to a network of amateur precinct-level activists on the East Side. Included in this network were Serbian activists in various East Side precincts.

As an outsider to the East Side, Edward Vrdolyak could normally have little hope of recruiting East Side captains of Serbian or any other ethnicity except Croatian. On the other hand, as he began his public drive for prominence in the ward the East Side vote was essential to his prospects. Millgate and Bessemer Park were dominated by the opposition; both the Poles and the Mexicans were opposing him there. Irondale also was in the other camp. His strength lay in Memorial Park–Slag Valley, his original ethnic base, and in the middle-class precincts in the western section of the ward. The East Side therefore was the swing area of the community, and between 1964 and 1968 Vrdolyak entered into a coalition with the alderman. In consequence he was able to use the alderman's popularity among East Side precinct-level activists in his own rise to power in the ward.

Formation of this coalition by no means assured Vrdolyak that when he ran for committeeman against his Polish rival he could automatically win the majority of East Side votes. In a large neighborhood of second settlement which tends to vote for candidates who champion values of neighborhood preservation, a new candidate from outside the neighborhood must prove publicly, through his position on local issues, that he is worthy of the East Siders' trust. In consequence of this, contemporary political issues as they are perceived in such neighborhoods become incorporated in ward political campaigns. In this manner ward politics in working-class neighborhoods becomes the arena for issues of public morality as well as for competing group loyalties.

*Ethnic Primary Group Politics
and Civic Virtue*

For older Tenth Ward ethnic groups such as the Croatians and Serbians, political succession depends on the aggregation of precinct primary groups through appeals to the varying dimensions of solidarity in those groups. Nothing irritates South Chicago political activists more than the stereotypical notion that their allegiances are to be had by the highest bidder. Certainly there are many who will be attracted to ward political aggregations by the promise of material rewards. But the large majority of political activists in South Chicago explain their political affiliations in terms of ethnic solidarity, personal loyalties, and the pursuit of local respectability. There is also nothing automatic in the mobilization of ethnic support. Ethnic solidarity must be negotiated in the process of aggregating political primary groups in the various neighborhoods of the ward. Thus Edward Vrdolyak could command the allegiances of a number of Croatian activists through appeals to kinship and common ethnic histories, but the support of other South Slavic groups, particularly the Serbians, had to depend on a variety of appeals to individual loyalties.

Negotiated Ethnicity

At the center of their ethnic territory, in Slag Valley, the opportunity for succession to leadership in the Democratic organization resulted in negotiations between Croatian and Serbian neighbors which formed the nucleus of new leadership in the ward. Serbians and Croatians in this neighborhood shared personal attachments growing out of generations of residence and similar ethnic cultural backgrounds. But even here "Hunky" solidarity had to be negotiated. Traditional animosities between Serbians and Croatians are kept alive by the immigrant generations, and when the Croatian and Serbian precinct leaders in Slag Valley combined forces they would call attention to their "Hunky" ethnicity, the shared culture and local history of South Slavic people in South Chicago, rather than any notion of modern Yugoslav nationality. In other neighborhoods, appeals to this negotiated ethnic solidarity were more problematic. Serbian or Croatian ethnicity would present a set of personal attachments which could provide access to diverse precinct primary groups, but the aggregation of these groups depended on appeals to additional dimensions of group solidarity.

In Irondale the Serbians who might normally have been recruited by appeals to "Hunky" solidarity had earlier been aggregated along with their Italian neighbors into the leadership of another faction in ward politics. Personal attachments among the Irondale Serbians and their peers in ward politics conflicted with appeals to negotiate South Slavic ethnic solidarity. Opposition between the Irondale and Slag Valley Slavic groups was quite bitter during the period of factionalism in the ward. Vrdolyak attempted indirectly to unseat the Serbian unionist leader at Wisconsin Steel, and the Irondale Serbians and Italians opposed his rise to power at every turn. It was not until he had defeated their aggregation of ward leaders in the fierce competition of ward electoral politics that a rapprochement could occur between the competing groups. Not until then would the Irondale Serbians recognize their prior attachments of common ethnicity and choose to join the Vrdolyak faction in further ward competition.

On the East Side, appeals to South Slavic ethnic attachments were even more subordinated to notions of neighborhood respectability. The South Slavic ward leaders could appeal to personal ties among the Serbians and Croatians in this neighborhood of second settlement, but precinct primary groups here have been reconstructed on attachments which are grounded upon notions of neighborhood respectability and local morality. To prove his allegiance to these local criteria of respect, Vrdolyak had to form alliances with the leaders of East Side neighborhood politics. Political activists in this area of the ward may be aggregated in ward politics through appeals to their sense of ethnic descent, through economic enticements to local businessmen (both legitimate and illegitimate), and through appeals to their desires to improve the status of neighborhood civic voluntary groups, but above all any ward leadership group must demonstrate its allegiance to the parochial values of neighborhood solidarity.

Civic Virtue, Illegality, and Racism

In private, many precinct leaders on the East Side were critical of the Vrdolyak family's reputed connections with a range of illegitimate business practices in the ward. When members of the Vrdolyak leadership aggregation were indicted for transporting prostitutes to a stag party, their political opponents on the East Side attempted to use this scandal to attack the respectability of Vrdolyak's East Side precinct groups. In response to this attack, the Vrdolyak groups had to try even harder to demonstrate their opposition to racial integration in the schools and in public housing. Over time this strategy was successful and attempts to exploit the Vrdolyaks' complicity in immoral business practices failed to gain widespread sympathy. The blue collar families on the East Side can tolerate, if not condone, unobtrusive illegal enterprise because the people who run these businesses are so often respected neighbors and ethnic kin; the small bookmaking operations, for example, are part of the blue collar culture of the community.[5] Racial integration, on the other hand, especially in the form of programs introduced by higher levels of government, is seen as threatening to the stability and respectability of neighborhoods such as the East Side.

The frequency of appeals to fears of racial invasion leads observers of blue collar politics to conclude that racial insecurity is almost a necessary component of "white ethnic" politics. In fact the opposite is true. Racial tension is most often exploited in the absence of ethnic solidarity. Ward leaders attempt to aggregate precinct support through appeals to notions of civic virtue and neighborhood insecurity when they cannot succeed through appeals to personal loyalties and ethnic solidarity alone. But any leadership group which hopes to succeed to power in South Chicago knows that exploitation of racial fears is a two-edged sword. On the one hand, it may be used to negotiate aggregations of precinct activists where the personal attachments based on ethnicity are attenuated. On the other hand, once in power, the ward leaders will have to represent the new black residents in other ward neighborhoods, and they will have to support candidates at higher levels of city, state, and national politics who take more liberal positions on racial issues. Also, there are many unionist groups in the community, groups which may include important Serbian or Croatian precinct leaders, who cannot join political aggregations which resort to overt appeals to racial insecurity. Thus once they have succeeded to power, ward leaders will attempt to negotiate further ethnic solidarities, and they will play down the racial insecurity of neighborhoods such as the East Side.

Part 4

**Blue Collar
Community and
Social Change**

9

Working-Class Society and the Nation

The National View

There are moments in the history of working-class communities when people whose lives are generally played out at the local level are suddenly brought to the attention of much larger metropolitan and national audiences. From 1890 to 1945 these climactic and revealing moments occurred most often during periods of prolonged class antagonism. The violence of South Chicago's history during the 1919 steel strike and the 1937 Memorial Day Massacre are examples. In these episodes of "labor trouble," South Chicago took its place among American working-class communities such as Homestead, Pullman, Harlan County, Flint, McKeesport, and Everett. The bitter struggles of organized labor during this period reached climaxes which forced these communities into the public consciousness of the nation. Yet underlying the local outbursts of class violence were more prolonged conflicts among the workers themselves in which they sorted out their leadership and their loyalties. As workers and citizens they brought the issues of unionism home to neighborhoods where questions of family and ethnic attachments were often as important as the right to organize for better wages and working conditions.

In the decades since World War II, status rather than class conflict has become almost the distinguishing feature of blue collar community life.[1] Thus in the public culture of the mass media, communities such as South Chicago are viewed as places where racial and ethnic tensions are most aggravated. In fact the history of community development in working-class communities lends credence to this viewpoint. During the 1950s and 1960s, South Chicago was the scene of intense conflict over the ecological succession of Mexicans and blacks in the neighborhoods of the area. The "Trumbull Park" riots in 1954, for example, brought South Chicago people into the public view once again, this time cast in the role of threatened, defensive people hoping to protect their little neighborhoods against black newcomers. This was a scenario repeated throughout the 1960s, as blacks and Mexicans fought to establish a residential and institutional base in the community. For example, in 1968, prior to the presidential election, *Life* magazine featured South Chicago as a "typical" blue collar community. The writers predicted that racial tensions in South Chicago and the other steel-producing communities of the area would lead the white working-class electorate to cast at least 30 percent of their votes for George Wallace. In fact less than 12 percent of the South Chicago voters finally voted for Wallace. Here again, neighborhood leaders in local political institutions, particularly the unions and the ward party organizations, made their influence felt in the community. South Chicago leaders did not draw their constituents away from the Wallace movement in order to maintain the coalition of working-class and liberal segments of the national Democratic party. Generally they risked their local reputations by campaigning against Wallace because they wished to maintain the balance of political coalitions in their community institutions. In the neighborhoods of South Chicago and other steel-belt communities, the leaders of the Wallace movement tended to be marginal figures who acted outside the primary groups of political activists in the party and the local unions. A heavy Wallace vote would have upset coalitions among political primary groups which were negotiated in local level political campaigns over the preceding decade.

Ethnic competition and the negotiation of political primary groups continue to play prominent roles in the contemporary politics of blue collar communities such as South Chicago. As in the past, the events which bring South Chicago people to the attention of larger audiences in the national and metropolitan society are those in which the residents compete among themselves and with outsiders for respectability and power in communal institutions. Generally this competition remains the most central nexus of community solidarity and ethnic adaptation in the area.

Throughout the 1960s social scientists and many other groups of intellectuals in the United States were rediscovering the persistence of "status groups" in industrialized societies. In some part this renewed interest in the parochial values of ethnicity, race, religion, and neighborhood affiliation was stimulated by the study of ethnic politics in the multinational states of Asia, Africa, and southern Europe.[2] In the United States, the revival of interest in primordial attachments is also a response to the apparent resurgence of self-conscious ethnic identity, not only among blacks and Latins, but among many white ethnic groups as well. On the other hand, when one looks more closely into the course of local status group negotiations in the United States it becomes clear that the seeming resurgence of primordialism in working-class communities is largely the continuation of patterns which were established in the decades of early community settlement. The widely publicized rise of the "hard hats," the "unmeltable ethnics," the "black militants," and the "Chicanos" is partially the reflection of broadly based political movements, particularly among black and Latin minorities. But these labels also reflect a failure to understand the relationship between processes of status negotiation and class mobility in blue collar communities.

*Status and Class
in Blue Collar Ethnicity*

The majority of some 1,200,000 steelworkers and their families in the United States live in neighborhoods similar to those of the South Chicago area. Similarly, miners, rubber workers, glass workers, timber workers, and many other large blue collar groups generally live in neighborhoods close to the mills and the factories. They too tend to confine their social experience to the corner taverns, the churches, and the community political institutions in gray industrial areas between slums and suburbs. Even in blue collar communities which lack South Chicago's well-defined pattern of ethnic settlement, there is still a great diversity of neighborhood types, from the older and generally poorer neighborhoods at the mill gates, to the newer, more nearly "suburban" neighborhoods within a half-hour's drive of the plants. This range of neighborhood types also reflects real differences in the relative economic success of different groups within blue collar communities.

Certainly the majority of South Chicago families desire a "decent" house in one of the newer bungalow areas of the region. Also, most parents express the hope that their children will have "better opportunities than we had when we were coming up." South Chicago people generally understand that their children's educational attainments will play a large part in their ultimate success, but they also know that few of their children will successfully compete for the "inside track" in prestigious educational institutions. Less than 20 percent of the children even from South Chicago's newer mill neighborhoods will finish college, and those who do are unlikely to settle in the community. Therefore, South Chicago parents feel that most of their children will continue to need the security of the local community and its networks of primary relations. Although they begin their occupational careers in the mills and in local businesses with better jobs than their parents started with, their mothers and fathers believe that much of what their children attain in life will depend on the personal attachments their families have established over the generations. This belief perpetuates the traditional emphasis on establishing the "decency and respect" of their families and of their local cultural groups.

South Chicago people view the progression of their ethnic groups from the dingy, tenement neighborhoods in the center of the community to the more "respectable" neighborhoods at the periphery as largely the outcome of ethnic organization, ethnic leadership, and the negotiation of coalitions among ethnic leaders in community institutions. Thus a Mexican unionist from the community expressed these sentiments on the eve of a crucial metropolitan union election in 1973:

We've been knocking at the door for so long, I just hope we have enough to make it this time. All these little elections for local union offices, aldermen, committeemen, state reps, it seems like we're always flogging our guts out in the streets and so often we've come up short. Look at all these guys like Modesto, Cesar, Juan, Carlos, Joe, Louis, and all the rest just from here in South Chicago. They've worked in elections until it's coming out of their ears and they keep coming back for the big win. I only hope we can make it this time.

This election means a lot to all of us in South Chicago, not just for the Panchos. But I naturally think most about what it could mean for the Latins here and in Indiana Harbor, and on the West Side. When you win it means you get respect and a little power. You get to have your own people calling the shots for a change. We would be able to put some people in jobs, positions in the city, and in Springfield. We need a win real bad, Willie. When you win your people can hold their heads up, they can feel confident when they go into new places.

The leaders understand, at least intuitively, that status and class mobility are often inextricably intertwined, and that both are frequently the result of political competition in communal institutions. On the other hand, this does not imply that they regard ethnic association as the mere instrumentality of class or status mobility. The persistence of ethnic identity and local ethnic organization into the third and even fourth generation of white working-class groups is not simply an indication that they have failed to become assimilated into the economic or residential "structures" of the larger society. Nor is the persistence of white ethnicity in South Chicago merely a reaction to the growing militancy and organization of blacks and Latins. As Glazer and Moynihan conclude in their revision of *Beyond the Melting Pot*, there is a compelling cultural component in ethnic identity. Even when the prejudice and discrimination which stimulated the formation of American ethnic patterns has diminished, the authors conclude that "individual choice, not law or rigid custom, determines the degree to which any person participates, if at all, in the life of an ethnic group, and assimilation and acculturation proceed at a rate determined in large measure by individuals."[3]

Voluntary versus Primordial
Ethnic Attachments

Contrasting degrees of voluntarism in blue collar ethnicity are quite apparent when one considers the local organization of groups such as the Serbians, the Poles, and the Croatians. In South Chicago, and throughout the blue collar communities of the Chicago metropolitan area, it is possible for members of all these groups to divide their affiliations between strictly ethnic association and participation in the more culturally diverse life of their neighborhoods and their community institutions. On the other hand, even though these groups have essentially the same socioeconomic standing in the area, voluntarism tends to be more advanced among the Serbians than it is for the Poles, Croatians, or the Italians. A Serbian politician and church leader from South Chicago described his perception of this situation as follows:

Our Serbian National Federation sponsors three or four sports tournaments a year in different Serbian colonies. Here in South Chicago we have had the golf and basketball tournaments in the last three or four years. It's a wonderful thing for our group here in South Chicago to organize an event for over a thousand Serbs from all over the country. We get to see our Kum who have moved elsewhere, and they bring news back about families we haven't seen in years. This way we get to know what's happening with our people in all the colonies. Also, lots of Serbs who have moved out of South Chicago to other communities in the area come to the events. Of course in our regular church ceremonies and at our picnics we draw people from all over this region. These are people who have grown up here but who moved to places like Dalton and Harvey.

There are many families here in South Chicago who devote themselves

to the group and to the church. It's their lives. You know there are
people who have businesses in our colony that depend on affairs like
these where they can see Serbs from all over the area.

It's true that the number of businesses is getting smaller, especially the
tamburitza taverns. But there is still a very big demand for Serbian
culture. We have third- and fourth-generation kids learning to play the
instruments and learning to sing the songs and do the dances. It's not
something the parents have to force them to do. They have grown up
with it, just like they have grown up with things like rock music also. I
think the kids see that unless they study the culture a little, and unless
they practice it, they won't have it when the parents are gone. Many of
the kids want this to continue. They want the church and they want
the culture.

The Serbians, like the Greeks and the Jews, are attempting to preserve
religious institutions which are separate from the dominant Protestant
or Catholic churches. There is thus a close correspondence between
their local ethnic cultures and the organization of their religious lives.
In these groups, religious institutions themselves play an active role in
maintaining the ethnic culture and in defining the moral and cultural
boundaries of ethnic association. Among Roman Catholic ethnic
groups, however, the maintenance of local ethnic neighborhoods may
assume even greater importance to the residents, since the Catholic
religious institutions themselves do not actively encourage the
persistence of ethnic cultures. In the older neighborhoods there remain
the national parishes or territorial Catholic parishes which over the
years have assumed an ethnic identity owing to the cultural preferences
of their congregants. Thus for the Poles, the Italians, and the
Croatians, the loss of an old neighborhood can mean the virtual
disappearance for the group of a local society in which the ethnic
culture may be maintained. The Serbians, like the Jews and the Greeks,
at least know that they can move elsewhere and as long as they
maintain their religious affiliations, their cultures will not be lost.
Although the move may be difficult—no adults leave the neighborhood
of their birth without suffering a great sense of loss—other blue collar
ethnic groups perceive that their loss due to ecological invasion
may be irreparable.

Despite the increasing voluntarism in blue collar ethnicity, the
kinship dimension of neighborhood and ethnic affiliation remains an
important aspect of white resistance to black or other minority
settlement. The Serbians, Croatians, Italians, Poles, and Mexicans in
South Chicago view their local ethnic networks as decent groups. They
delight in discussing the complexities of ethnic kin relations, and

second-generation parents often rationalize their sons' entry into the mills with the thought, "At least he and his family will stay in the community this way." For the many South Chicago adults who spend the bulk of their lives among their extended kin, the potential loss of their neighborhood threatens more than their status and class mobility, or the security of their participation in a yearly round of ethnic or neighborhood events. Loss of the neighborhood may also mean the end of a family organization which is the prime concern of their lives. Disruption of the close proximity between aging parents and their married children presents the threat of isolation, loneliness, and insecurity, conditions which this form of familistic neighborhood organization developed to prevent. For example, a Polish steelworker expressed this view of the matter:

This Bush neighborhood is where I grew up. It's where my own kids was raised, and most of my brothers and sisters, and my wife's brothers and sisters raised their kids here. My daughter and her family live on the next block. Most of our relatives still live in this neighborhood or fairly close. We all have been going to St. Michael's [a local Catholic church which has had an almost exclusively Polish congregation since the early 1900s] all our lives.

So now we have these Mexicans and shines moving right in the neighborhood or across 79th. I said to my wife I'd rather die than see these people coming into our church.

During my years of residence in the community, this neighborhood area was the scene of continued racial and ethnic invasion. The church mentioned was increasingly visited by black and Mexican newcomers. On the other hand, the same steelworker three years later volunteered the opinion that although the blacks and the Mexicans were slowly becoming the dominant groups in the neighborhood, his own patterns of neighborhood affiliation had not been appreciably affected. To his immense relief, the blacks seemed to prefer their own churches, and the Polish congregation was left largely unthreatened by the newcomers. He expected that many of his younger relatives would move out of the neighborhood, but his kin of an equivalent age were maintaining their houses and not making any sudden plans to leave unless "things begin to get bad for us." Most of the younger families in his Polish kinship network would probably move to newer neighborhoods of second settlement where they would be near enough to their parents to maintain the solidarity of their kinship and ethnic attachments.

The larger significance of this observation is that the continuing dependency of blue collar ethnicity on local social organization leads

South Chicago people to attempt to remain in their neighborhoods after racial integration begins. Although this is a subject which demands further research, it is clear that the provincialism in blue collar ethnicity has both positive and negative consequences for the newcomers to such areas. Once they have proved to the white residents that their settlement will not be stopped, blacks and Mexicans can expect to compete with the white residents for respectability and power in communal institutions. In this way the time-worn processes of status negotiation can continue for the newcomers as it does for the various white ethnic groups who remain in the community.

In summary, the ethnic affiliations of South Chicago residents are still grounded in their desire to establish or maintain the respectability of their families in the community. The general trend toward voluntarism in blue collar ethnicity is an outcome of the processes whereby the many ethnic and neighborhood groups choose their leaders, compete in the politics of their communal institutions, and fight to protect what remains of the ethnic and kinship basis of their local society. This appreciation of blue collar ethnicity is central to an adequate understanding of community development in industrial areas such as South Chicago, but it should not be construed as an apology for the community's history of racial exclusion.

Although it is true that all newcomers to the community have experienced at least a generation of distrust and hostility from older and more established groups, none of the white ethnic groups, and not even the Mexicans, were greeted with as much hostility as were the black families who moved into the area's neighborhoods after World War II. Motivated largely by the belief that black neighbors would diminish their own local status and increase their problems of maintaining the tenuous social order of their neighborhoods, black exclusion by white ethnic groups has perpetuated the disreputable status of black Americans. Racial exclusion has also seriously weakened the class position of blue collar Americans in general. On the other hand, South Chicago is distinguished from other urban places where the same sort of ecological invasion has occurred in that like most communities organized around huge industrial complexes, the white population can only flee to the next neighborhood rather than to an entirely different area of the metropolitan region. Similarly, the steel mills cannot easily move to another region of the country, nor is there any sizable expansion of new steel plants in the "suburbs." In one way or another the residents will have to live with each other. Thus industrial communities such as South Chicago are places where ecological invasion is a continuing process and racial and ethnic conflict is eventually channeled into competition for status and power in communal institutions. As part of the competition for power and respectability in the mills, the local unions, and the party organization, the newcomers must devote themselves to forming stable neighborhoods with their own local cultural institutions. In such neighborhood institutions as the tavern circuits, the ethnic churches, and face-block association, the newcomers begin to resolve the very parochial disputes which divide their ranks. Once their leaders compete for influence in larger communal institutions, the newly established groups begin to command respect and influence throughout the community, achievements which are prerequisite to more voluntary definitions of ethnic attachments. These processes of ethnic negotiation also produce the more general working-class culture of such communities.

For over three generations the management of ethnic and residential attachments has been almost the chief concern of South Chicago residents. It is true that status cleavages have often prevented the consolidation of class unity in the community. Nevertheless, there are processes which occur within local institutions which ease the intensity of status conflict. In the mills, the local unions, and the precinct political organizations, there are groups of friends who draw their members from the highly diverse cultural segments of the local society. Thus the conflict, the violence, and the lingering hatreds which may persist after generations of ecological invasion are only one side of the picture. The negotiations of new alliances and constituencies in which ethnic and racial cleavages are played down and blended into a more unifying working-class culture is the other side. It follows, therefore, that future patterns of ethnic negotiation in the community will depend in large part on the role which the unions and the local party organizations play in the politics of the metropolitan region and of the nation.

Community Institutions
and National Politics

Political conflict and institutional change at the national level usually result in some part from the coalition and conflict among local level leaders whose perceptions are generally more provincial than are those of national leaders. For example, the schism in the national Democratic party between the liberal–minority group wing of the party and leaders who represent largely white, working-class, and lower middle-class urban populations is mirrored in hundreds of similar schisms in local communities and metropolitan regions throughout the nation. Thus the 1972 Democratic National Convention was the scene of intense conflict between opposing factions in the Chicago delegation, conflict which clearly illustrated the correspondence between local and national level political conflict in that party. This and similar conflicts involving national labor leaders made it almost impossible for the victorious liberal wing of the party to stem the disaffection from the McGovern candidacy in the more traditional blue collar urban areas of the nation. Although it is dangerous to overgeneralize this local-national correspondence, it is clear that the resolution of these deep schisms in the Democratic party rests in large measure on negotiations among more local level leaders from the major competing segments of urban America.

If national politics often reflects local conflict and accommodations, it is also true that change in local institutions may be equally dependent upon policies and political action initiated at the national level. Perhaps nowhere is this more clearly seen than in recent changes occurring within the American labor movement. Although rank-and-file political movements occur regularly within the major unions of the nation, the pattern of oligarchical rule in the large unions has not significantly changed since scholars such as Lipset and Mills documented this situation in the 1950s. Nevertheless, the passage of the Landrum-Griffin Act, and enforcement of democratic processes in union politics by the United States Department of Labor, have made it increasingly possible for insurgent unionists to organize effective political movements in the major industrial unions. The most notable achievements in this regard were those which forced the United Mine Workers to hold a new election after the murder of Jock Yablonski in 1970, and the regulation of that election by the Department of Labor to insure that democratic processes would be upheld throughout the electoral campaign. Once their basic right to free elections was enforced, the miners quickly repudiated the corrupt and criminal leadership of the union at the national level.

In their limited way South Chicago people have continued to take part in the political processes which produce change in national institutions. Thus two leaders from the community attended the 1972 Democratic National Convention as delegates on both sides of the divided Chicago delegation. The role which these South Chicago leaders played at the convention was in no way unique since many other delegates also found themselves aligned on one side or another of this serious factional dispute. On the other hand, when they returned to

South Chicago these leaders' political careers once again became subject to the continuous course of political negotiation which ultimately determines how their factions realign themselves.

Similarly, in 1973, South Chicago steel unionists became involved in an intense political campaign to choose a new director of the steelworkers' union in the Chicago-Gary metropolitan area. This struggle for leadership of the largest district in the national union once again brought up a range of issues concerning the desire of rank-and-file steelworkers to make their union more democratic and more representative, in its leadership, of the changing age and racial composition in the area's mills and factories. Since the Chicago-Gary steelworkers' district has long been one of the most influential power blocs in the national union, this election was carefully watched by national level leaders throughout the labor movement. Therefore, despite the general provincialism and cultural isolation of this large blue collar community, in their ward and union political institutions the residents do find opportunities to bring local issues to bear on the affairs of more remote national political institutions.

Ward Politics
and National Cleavage

South Chicago residents were represented at the 1972 Democratic National Convention by two delegates, Carmen Chico and Edward Vrdolyak, local leaders whose membership in political primary groups clearly reflects the cleavage in the community between newcomers and older South European ethnic groups. Tenth Ward alderman and Democratic committeeman Edward Vrdolyak was visibly upset upon his return to Chicago from Miami. The regular Chicago Democratic delegation was unexpectedly defeated by its liberal and minority group opponents on the floor of the convention, all in full view of a national television audience. Nevertheless, Edward Vrdolyak still represented the aggregation of dominant political groups in South Chicago politics, and as various members of his family and his precinct organization stated, "We are the ones who win the elections here and we are going to be around for a long time no matter what happens to Mayor Daley or to the National Committee. These people are going to have to deal with us if they expect to get anywhere in South Chicago." Carmen Chico, on the other hand, remained at the convention and actively participated in the deliberations of the Chicago delegation, the Chicano caucus, and the women's caucus. A member of South Chicago's large Chico family, she was the first woman from the Mexican neighborhoods to achieve prominence in the politics of metropolitan Chicago, an achievement largely made possible in the years preceding the convention when Mexican precinct and unionist leaders solidified their ranks and made their first forays into local electoral politics. As Carmen Chico described it,

The Convention was one of the most exciting times of my life. We hardly slept because we were always going from one meeting to another. I got to know people, especially in women's politics and in the Chicano movement from all over the city and the country. We're still working even now that the elections is over. We couldn't do that much for McGovern, but we worked hard in Daniel Walker's campaign for Governor, and he won.

In comparing the role of such local leaders in national politics, it is too easy to accept the view that the 1972 Democratic Convention represented the victory of "new voices" in the national party and the defeat of the older, generally more conservative leadership symbolized by men such as Mayor Daley and George Meany. First, the results of the 1972 presidential election demonstrated that the convention victory threatened to make the Democrats a minority party in national politics. Second, any analysis of political processes which rests on ideas of heroes and villains is bound to be inadequate in providing an understanding of the actual processes which shape political institutions. For example, in many reform political circles local leaders such as Edward Vrdolyak are generally despised. They are labeled "ward bosses" who thrive on racial hostilities and the petty favors of a patrimonial style of politics which should have no place in modern government. In contrast, articulate representatives of black and Latin groups are highly sought after to join coalitions with reform groups in an effort to wrest power from the "corrupt and bigoted" machine leaders. In fact, analysis of who benefits from such coalitions should make one suspicious of moralistic appeals for political loyalty crossing class lines.

Returning to South Chicago in 1973 to observe the important union election that year, I found that many of the reform Democrats who had been active with South Chicago leaders during the preceding years were preparing to assume jobs and power in the recently elected reform gubernatorial administration of the state. For their part, however, none of the working-class leaders who had worked over the years in reform campaigns were preparing to "move to Springfield." Such inequities are often rationalized with the observation that such blue collar leaders do not have enough cosmopolitan contacts. They also lack educational and professional qualifications required for higher level political posts. According to this reasoning the South Chicago political activists ought to continue to focus on the politics of their local communities. They should attempt to win power and institute reform in their own neighborhoods and their local political institutions. Implicit in this reasoning is the recognition that on the basis of their class and ethnic backgrounds, the blue collar leaders who become active with middle-class reform politicians actually have greater social and cultural affinities with the more provincial southern European ethnic and neighborhood factions of the area. Ironically, it is the political power of this segment of urban society which reform politicians often attempt to usurp or otherwise destroy.

Working-class politics does not frequently produce leaders who are well liked in the communities at a comfortable remove from the mills and factories. This is largely a class bias which does not justify the destruction of blue collar political institutions in favor of more impersonal administrative agencies such as housing authorities and welfare bureaucracies. It is true, but somewhat trivial, to note that success in ward politics does not always bring out the best human qualities. More important is the fact that the most idealistic or the more deserving local factions rarely succeed to power until they have proved their allegiance to the parochial values of neighborhood solidarity. These are values which invariably compromise idealism of all types. Even when black and Latin groups eventually succeed to power in such communities, their leaders are usually not the same heroes as those of the preceding era, who made up in idealism what they lacked in organization and local influence. But whoever their leaders may be, their succession to power in such communities rests on the processes which make it possible for working-class citizens of different ethnic and racial backgrounds to live with each other and to achieve honor and security for their local cultural groups. It is with leaders from this community background that those who wish to gain the allegiance of blue collar America must bargain as equals.

Bound to uphold the values of neighborhood social organization, the leaders of party organizations in blue collar communities often reinforce the residents' cautious attitudes toward new ideas and new residents. This does not mean, however, that oligarchical rule, personalistic politics, and the exclusion of new residents is a necessary condition of blue collar communities. On the contrary, the processes which bring ethnic and neighborhood groups together in local political institutions also account for patterns of class mobility in such communities. New groups and new leaders do succeed to status and power; new coalitions are formed and new leaders are selected who in various ways may be better than their predecessors. The extent to which this occurs rests quite heavily on the outcome of political competition in organizations which most clearly represent the class interest rather than the community status of the residents.

Union politics at the local, the metropolitan, and the national levels presents the greatest potential for change in blue collar communities. Here I refer in particular to the type of political organization which allows new groups to begin to establish their leadership without destroying other local institutions in which the residents build the respectability and the security of their families and their cultural groups. It is also in industrial union politics that one finds the most clearly defined conflict between conservative and progressive factions within working-class society. A final, brief case of steelworkers' politics in metropolitan Chicago highlights the promise and the difficulty in seeking change through industrial unionism.

Steel Unionism and
Institutional Change

Through the fall and winter of 1972–73, large groups of unionists from South Chicago and all the other steel-producing communities of the region waged a political campaign to determine who would run the affairs of the Chicago-Gary (Calumet) District (31) of the United Steelworkers of America. The election was extremely important for a number of reasons. This largest district of the steelworkers' union has traditionally played a major role in determining which leadership factions govern the International Union apparatus in Pittsburgh and Washington, D.C., but before 1973 the Chicago–Gary District of the union had not had a contested election for its leadership since 1947.[4] Issues of rank-and-file influence in union affairs, particularly the power of the young, the new minorities, and workers in smaller, more marginal local unions, were becoming increasingly pressing. Over decades of highly personal rule, the district leadership had taken care to sponsor individual ethnic leaders for union staff positions, but it also had consistently crushed the formation of opposition caucuses within the district. Finally, in its involvement with civic political leaders the district leadership had compiled a dubious record. It had given massive financial and political support to progressive, labor-oriented candidates such as United States Senator Paul Douglas of Illinois. But in more local politics the district leadership tended to support some of the region's most reactionary and corrupt public officials. This was especially true in Lake County, Indiana, where the union's direct intervention in local politics has greater impact than it does in the more complex and autonomous Chicago political system. For these reasons the 1973 district election tended to set a generation of steel unionists, men who had maintained their power in the district since the 1930s, against a large coalition of generally younger and more progressive local unionists throughout the vast Calumet steel-producing region. A veteran steelworker and unionist from Gary explained the situation thus:

This election is going to be a real squeaker because Joe Germano is coming to the end of his career. We call him "Big Tuna." He's been the Director in the Calumet District ever since the union was organized. Now he is retiring and he wants the job filled by Sam Evett. Evett has been the Assistant Director since Joe appointed him in 1937. The only time they had an opposition was in 1947. After that the union upped the number of local union nominations you need to get to be on the ballot so they've been able to keep anybody from going against them. Germano has about sixty staff guys who owe him their jobs, and he has put people in his family in places where they can do him the most good. It's been almost impossible for a rank and filer or even a staff man to get anywhere against that organization.

Germano's been a kingmaker in the union for many years because this district has more votes in it than any other in the country. The Pittsburgh area is cut into smaller Districts, but Joe has always managed to keep them from breaking up the Calumet District. Your average district has maybe 30 or 40 thousand voting members but this one has over 130,000. Joe organized a lot of the support to put Able in office when he ran against McDonald in 1965, so you can bet that nobody who opposes him in this area is going to get any help at all from Pittsburgh.

Ed Sadlowski is running against Germano's man. The Pollack surprised everyone by putting together good strength in getting on the ballot. Sadlowski is young but he's worked in the mills, he was president at the South Works, and he's done real well as a staff organizer in South Chicago. A month ago nobody gave him a chance of winning but he's a hustler. There's a real good bunch of younger local officials and rank-and-file people working the streets with him.

Especially in the big mills around Indiana Harbor, South Chicago, and Chicago Heights, Sadlowski is going to do real well. People are pissed as hell about inflation, jobs getting eliminated or combined, and delays in getting their grievances processed. There's a lot of talk about getting some tougher leadership.

In the smaller plants its uphill for Sadlowski. There are over five

hundred shops. This means you've got to run all over hell and gone to
these small "bucket shops." The small fabrication factories and
specialty shops are like machine precincts. Lots of the workers are new,
and in a lot of 'em the local union officials are afraid to take a leak
without running to their staff man. The staff man runs the local for
them and gets them to bring out the vote he wants. If Sadlowski can cut
into this vote he could win. Like I say, this election is going to be real
tough.

Union elections such as this one represent a uniquely working-class
political phenomenon. These campaigns are usually planned and
executed strictly by the unionists and steelworkers themselves. Although
outsiders may play some role in finance and propaganda, their
participation in the mobilization of campaign workers or in the
planning of campaign strategy is normally quite limited. Generally only
the union leaders and active workers themselves can possibly ask their
friends and fellow workers to make the sacrifices of lost pay and
physical hardship required to mount large union campaigns. For
example, steelworkers' International and district elections occur in
February, in the dead of winter, and the men and women who become
involved in these campaigns must be prepared to spend long hours in
the grimmest freezing weather outside the mill gates. Rarely does one
find non-steelworkers who will adjust their time schedules to the
arduous requirements of such campaigns. Campaigning begins at
5:30 A.M. as the unionists congregate at tavern headquarters and coffee
shops throughout the district. Once assembled they go off to various
factories where they will talk to other workers entering the plant on the
day shift, or leaving it after the night turn. After a morning of
exhausting campaigning many of those who campaigned in the early
hours will enter their own plants for work on the three-to-eleven shift.

This is a political campaign situation which brings steelworkers
together from every possible ethnic, racial, and neighborhood background. In such contests the incumbent faction usually has an
advantage in that through the union staff officials, and local union
officers who owe their allegiance to staff officials, the incumbents have
greater access to rank-and-file workers in the plants. For their part, the
challengers must attempt to locate and recruit rank-and-file leaders
who will join them on the basis of appeals which combine elements of
status and class interest. Among the most important of these appeals
are those based on the issue of rank-and-file leadership versus loyalty to
the administrative leadership of the union. Another important set of
appeals are those to negotiated groups of ethnic and unionist leaders

from various community backgrounds in the industrial area. In the case of District 31, the issue of rank-and-file power versus loyalty to the union bureaucracy was clearly drawn among the younger unionists and steelworkers. A good example of the balancing of class issues with appeals to specific ethnic groups is the manner in which a Polish candidate approached the need to recruit black steelworkers in his campaign.

The Old Guard
versus the Young Turks

Much of the impetus for change in the American labor movement emanates from the generation of younger industrial labor leaders, as was represented in the coalition of rank-and-file unionists who supported Edward Sadlowski in the Chicago-Gary 1973 election. Representative of a new generation of experienced labor leaders from traditional working-class communities, the leadership of the Sadlowski faction averaged in their early forties. Their opponents were approximately ten to fifteen years older. The younger group tended to stress issues which would appeal to steelworkers, who wish the union to invest more authority at the local level. Thus the right of rank-and-file workers to vote directly on contracts negotiated between union staff and national corporations was one of the primary issues of the campaign. Whatever the direct content of their election campaigns, however, the younger unionists often appealed directly to cultural differences between younger and older workers. A good example of this appeal was found in the area's newest steel mill located on the periphery of Gary, in Indiana.

The Bethlehem Steel plant at Burns Harbor, Indiana, is one of the few major basic steel mills which have been constructed in the Calumet area since the 1960s. As such its labor force and the manner in which its workers participate in the politics of their union are indicative of changes and continuities in working-class communal organization. The workers at the Burns Harbor plant voted overwhelmingly for the insurgent Sadlowski faction in the District 31 election. A twenty-eight-year-old crane operator and union activist from this plant anticipated his mill's vote shortly before the election.

The thing about our mill that knocks me out is that we have rollers and guys in high seniority jobs like that who are only thirty. The average age in the plant is less than thirty. We got in on things right at the beginning after the plant was built. A lot of people in the mill come

from Gary and places around Gary where their dads are steelworkers.
Some of the younger guys in our plant have as good a job as their
fathers ever had.

The big reason why it looks like our mill is going for Sadlowski is that
we're tired of hassling with the union staff and the management about
discipline problems. We're making good money and all that, but we
always have people being sent home for smoking dope and coming in
late and things like that. We've been waiting for someone a little
younger to come along and talk about getting some basic change the
way the union is run. I don't think there is any real feeling that the
discipline thing is going to change much with new leadership, but the
guys don't feel the Germano people really know anything about us or
our grievances. Up to now the union has been separate from us; not too
many of our people feel the union will really back them up.

When we had our mass meeting the people went big for Sadlowski over
Evett because they appeared together and Sadlowski did a real good job
of talking our language. He was gutsy and he showed he knows where
our heads are at. Since then the word has gone out in the shops that
Sadlowski is our man.

Among the young workers at the Burns Harbor plant one finds the
same racial and ethnic negotiations as those which are the substance of
primary group formation in the older steel communities. Here,
however, there is generally less tension generated over ethnic and racial
cleavage. As the workers marry and establish families they tend to
move into more or less segregated blue collar neighborhoods in the
Gary area, but they have also begun to establish quite remarkable
traditions of interracial primary groups in the mill and in their local
union. Their leadership has fostered the organization of informal
meeting places where black and white workers gather for relaxation
and entertainment during their leisure hours. Thus the strongest
emphasis in their participation in union affairs is not on ethnic politics
but on their desire to win a more potent voice in establishing union
policy and in selecting the union's future leaders. Although they are
recruited on the basis of appeals to their shared identity as young
steelworkers, these appeals also articulate their desire to take their
place in making the future of the labor movement and the working
class it represents.

A similar combination of appeals based on status and class interest is
evident in the negotiations which allowed a candidate from a Polish
South Chicago background to recruit black unionists throughout the
metropolitan area. Here the challenge is not to recruit black unionists
and workers to be followers in a campaign dominated by whites but to

negotiate coalitions in which there is cooperation among workers who deal with each other as equals.

Black Unionists and Community

The most severe problem a Polish candidate might expect to have in Chicago is the recruitment of black support. As a black unionist in the Sadlowski faction admitted:

On the West Side of Chicago the situation between blacks and Pollacks is kinda bad. In fact in a lot of shops all over the district the "ski" ain't going to win many votes for us. There's plenty of blacks who'd vote against him just cause of the name.

During the nominations there were shops where the other people put out the word that Evett was black. They'd say "vote for the brother" to the blacks at the meeting. Then we put both pictures on one of our leaflets so everybody could see they're both white.

It's really hard to say what's going to happen. The black member isn't different from anybody else. He'll come to the hall to vote because someone he likes tells him this is the program, or he'll listen to the talk, read the stuff people give him, and try to decide who's saying the best things about what he thinks the union should be doing.

As these remarks suggest, experienced unionists actually found it difficult to assess potential trends in the black vote in this election. Neither side had any reliable data on racial and ethnic voting patterns in the hundreds of plants involved, and given the ethnic and racial diversity of the rank and file, no candidate could depend primarily on appeals to ethnic or racial solidarity. For example, although a large proportion of the union members on the west side of Chicago are of Polish ethnicity and could be expected to vote in disproportionate numbers for the Polish candidate, many of them are older men with extensive obligations to the incumbent unionist faction. The same situation applies to black steelworkers in District 31. There were some mills and factories in which black workers could be expected to vote heavily for one of the candidates. In the more common situation, however, they, like other workers, had to be appealed to in terms of their class interest rather than to their sense of racial solidarity. Of course this does not mean that racial and ethnic organization was not extremely critical in such campaigns. In organizing crews of campaign workers, both sides were anxious to demonstrate that they had the support of influential ethnic and racial leaders from all segments of the union polity.

In recruiting black campaign workers, the incumbent faction could depend upon the services of a small number of black staff officials and a larger number of local union officials who depended heavily on staff support. These unionists could be expected to campaign primarily, although by no means exclusively, among the black rank and file. For this reason, the tactics of the challenging faction are more instructive because they could not rely upon material inducements or administrative pressure to organize black support. The challengers had to call upon the support of interracial unionist primary groups which had been negotiated in local union politics over the preceding decade.

As detailed in an earlier chapter, it is increasingly common in Chicago's steel industry to find black unionist leaders succeeding to power in local unions in which the majority of the workers are still of European and Latin ethnicity. In even more instances in District 31, black unionists are winning local elections in plants where blacks are numerically the dominant groups but in which various white ethnic groups and Mexicans must also be recruited on campaign slates. For this reason few black unionists, or any others for that matter, could simply "go through the motions" of supporting one of the candidates. Their individual and collective political fates could ride on their participation in this campaign. Equally important at times was the fact that groups of black unionists regarded one or another of the competing factions as including their "close buddies" in the union. This intermingling of motivations is evident in the way a prominent black unionist from South Chicago summarized this situation.

Most of us here in South Chicago are going with our Pollack friend. We've all been working together for years at South Works and a lot of the other mills around here. Eddy and all of us know each other since we was punk kids. We know this man and his family and he knows us the same way. He's done a great job as staff man; gotten some of the best contracts around and worked real hard to cut down on the time to get grievances processed.

This campaign is really a chance for all of us South Chicago guys to do something big in the union. If we put Sadlowski in as director it's going to mean more chances for blacks to go up for union office everywhere in the district because it's really going to open things up after so long.

One of our real problems is that we're South Chicago people. We can rap with the brothers in Gary, you know, and tell 'em why we think Sadlowski is the best man for the job. But those people have their community thing out there just like we have ours here. Just cause we're the same color doesn't mean we carry much weight out there. This is really a beginning for us to get it together all over the district.

The intimacy of relations between blacks and whites in industrial union politics should correct the stereotypical view of pervasive white working-class racism and black militancy. Indeed there are few institutions outside the working class where such large numbers of men and women of different races regularly form close associations. It is particularly in the large mills with their heterogeneous labor forces that ability and character may come to override distinctions based on racial and ethnic identity. As indicated in this steelworker's comments, however, these unionist primary groups are formed through competition and cooperation in specific blue collar communities. They do not easily encompass new groups in other communities without further years of competition and negotiations among such community groups. Unfortunately, oligarchical rule at higher levels of union politics has tended to impede the full development of such interracial coalitions. On the other hand, the union election campaign waged in the Chicago and Gary metropolitan area in 1973 is only one of many signs that the old order of industrial union politics is gradually changing. It is being replaced by a more fluid and perhaps more democratic pattern of political competition and primary group negotiation among younger blue collar leaders throughout this and other industrial regions of the country.

The Meaning
of Blue Collar Politics:
No Victorious Messengers

After a campaign in which unionists and rank-and-file steelworkers themselves distributed over a million and a half pieces of campaign literature, held mass rallies and campaign functions in every area of the district, and organized hundreds of steelworkers in campaign organizations from South Chicago to Joliet and from Gary to Cicero, neither side could claim a clear victory when the votes were counted. Three days before the election Joe Germano himself claimed, "We are going to show those people. We are going to put Sam in by a big margin." On the other side the younger unionists believed that they had organized and campaigned well enough to upset the traditional order of authority in the district. Both estimates were wrong.

Out of more than 45,000 votes cast, the results showed that the incumbent faction had won by slightly over 2,000 votes. The young unionists won their home area in South Chicago and the neighboring Indiana Harbor area by a two-to-one margin. In general they won the election in almost all the large mills of the district, but they saw their lead whittled away in the smaller shops where they had often been unable to campaign, or where their campaign workers were barred from entry on election day. On their side, although they seemed to have won the election, the incumbent Germano-Evett group saw their unquestioned rule in this powerful union district come to an end. The results of the election were immediately challenged, eventually to become a case before the United States Department of Labor and federal court, another sign that the era of unregulated elections and personal rule in the unions is approaching an end.

The ambiguity of the election results in District 31 might seem to contradict the earlier statement, "Union politics at the local, the metropolitan, and the national level presents the greatest potential for change in blue collar communities." Yet any student of working-class communities and blue collar politics soon learns that the official outcomes of political movements and election campaigns rarely deliver on the promise of far-reaching change without additional years of continuing political negotiation and exhausting competition. As seen through the limited experience of South Chicago residents, none of the political events or electoral contests analyzed in this volume ever singly brought lasting change in the more fundamental patterns of negotiation and competition among community groups. The Memorial Day Massacre, the Tenth Ward Spanish Speaking Democrats, the election of the first black president at South Works, the rise of Edward Vrdolyak to power in South Chicago, and the District 31 election, are all brief glimpses of the specific events which have aroused the passionate partisanship of South Chicago people. That they have so often experienced disappointment or tragedy is further reason for admiring the tenacity with which working-class people focus their aspirations and their grievances on political movements.

If the victorious messenger rarely comes riding to announce that their goals have been attained, every political event nevertheless furthers the development of their communal and civic attachments. In becoming involved in political contests generations of South Chicago people have continually modified their definitions of who "belongs" in the community. And through the negotiation of new primary groups in local politics South Chicago people also create a blue collar culture which all local groups, even those who are initially the most feared, eventually come to share.

Appendix

Methodological Notes on Studying South Chicago

In gathering the material for this study I attempted to use whatever data and methods of analysis seemed appropriate or feasible. Among these methods were making field notes on my observations and discussions with community residents; collecting archival materials; analyzing precinct voting tallies and census tract data; interviewing community and neighborhood leaders; attending the yearly round of social and political events for all ethnic and neighborhood groups; compiling family histories; being employed for six months in one of the area's steel mills; and actively participating in most of the political campaigns described here. Like most community studies, however, this one came to depend primarily on my first-hand involvement with the people and the situations described. The process in which the student gradually becomes a participant in the milieu studied constitutes much of the substance of "field methods" in the social sciences. Issues such as "establishing rapport with respondents," "discovering" one's specific research focus, becoming aware of one's biases, and insuring the privacy of one's informants are some of the well-known methological problems of this research style. For the purpose of this appendix all these issues may be subsumed in a discussion of the unique problems encountered in conducting this study.

In retrospect, my most difficult task was the necessity of learning at first hand about a wide variety of neighborhoods, ethnic groups, organizations, friendship groups, work groups, and families. Closely related to the problem of becoming accepted in such a diverse range of social settings is the fact that membership in one set of community groups often precludes membership in others. This is particularly true in situations where one is studying political competition and negotiation. Here the researcher faces the choice of maintaining a superficial acquaintance with all the antagonists or of taking sides in partisan competition in order to understand what occurs behind the scenes. Also, in daily face-to-face political competition, where commitment is highly valued, the researcher is under constant pressure to "put it on the line" even though this may mean losing some friends and making some enemies. Since partisanship did not become an option or an obvious problem until the study was well under way, I should outline the earlier phases of research which led me to form later commitments.

Choosing the Subject
and Finding the People

When I returned to Chicago from a research sojourn in Yugoslavia in the fall of 1967, a number of participants in the Center for Social Organization Studies at the University of Chicago, and Morris Janowitz in particular, expressed interest in sponsoring a study of Chicago's South Slavic ethnic groups. Since I had conducted some research on local community organization in Yugoslav communities jointly with Professors Terry Clark and Peter Jambrek, I too was quite interested in seeing for myself what cultural and social adaptations the Yugoslav immigrants generally made in their American settlement. Perhaps, I naively flattered myself, such a project could become a more current and more technically sophisticated companion to W. I. Thomas's *The Polish Peasant in Europe and America*. The "Chicago School" sociologists are read quite seriously by students at the University of Chicago both for their strengths and weaknesses. I believed that modern studies of ethnic social organization must correct the tendency of earlier Chicago writing to "neglect the political processes per se as if it were a derivative aspect of society." These somewhat grandiose intentions aside, I had little awareness that I was beginning a study which would occupy the bulk of my intellectual and political efforts from 1967 to 1973.

Census tract data and the *Chicago Community Fact Book* quickly revealed that the main areas of South Slavic settlement were in South Chicago and in the Pulaski-Milwaukee section of the city's northwest side. Thus during the winter of 1967 I spent time interviewing Croatian and Serbian immigrant intellectuals and clerics. I began frequenting the immigrant coffee shops, soccer clubs, newspaper offices, and taverns on both sides of Chicago. In these forays into the Old World culture of Slavic immigrants I gradually began to gravitate toward the steel mill neighborhoods of South Chicago. This was partially a choice based on social scientific grounds, and partially due to the fact that I became friendly with the owners and patrons of a Serbian restaurant in the neighborhood I later learned was called Slag Valley.

In the initial stage of a community study the researcher frequently hesitates to make commitments. The choice of a specific set of research sites and questions, the selection of a place to live, a group of people to become friendly with, and a way of explaining one's purposes to residents, all seem like irreversible decisions. During this rather normal period of "hanging back" and surveying the diversity of people and situations, one is likely to feel extremely alien and isolated. Perhaps for this reason many fieldwork projects begin with the author seeking out a place to become known, one which advances familiarity with the people but does not necessitate lasting commitment. Thus in *Street Corner Society*, William F. Whyte explains how he became friendly with the family of an Italian restaurateur who provided him with a congenial base from which to plan his further participation in the community's life. Following this precedent I found a Serbian immigrant restaurant run by an enormous peasant woman and her very slight husband. Radmilla and Mike appreciated my halting attempts to converse with them in Serbo-Croatian, and they introduced me to the establishment's regulars. The majority of the patrons were Serbian immigrant men in their mid-thirties to early forties. Almost all were steelworkers. On Friday and Saturday nights they filled the restaurant to eat, drink, and dance to the popular music of contemporary Serbia.

One Friday night I entered in the middle of a brawl, which I learned was the continuation of an argument started in the steel mill three blocks away. While the electric guitar and accordion ensemble played on, three or four men were shouting in Serbo-Croatian and pushing each other. At this point Radmilla, who weighed at least 250 pounds, stepped into the crowd to separate the antagonists. As she did this, a man named Stanko seized a bar stool but she pushed him away easily. Infuriated, he threw the stool at her husband, Mike, who had had just enough to drink that he did not duck in time and was struck on the head and shoulders. In the ensuing melee I tended to the fallen Mike while Radmilla cleared the tavern and restored calm. After that evening I became a welcome friend in their tavern and I felt I had found a place where I did belong in the community. It soon became apparent, however, that I was viewing the ethnic group and the community from one of its most peripheral social circles.

Although it was a congenial spot to stop on my visits to South Chicago, most of the patrons at the Neretva Lounge were among the most recent arrivals to the city from Serbia. As such they were generally men without families, or whose families had remained in Yugoslavia. Along with an assortment of non-Serbian alcoholics and a few transient Mexicans the group was quite distant from the more established networks of South Chicago Serbian ethnicity. Socially they were even farther from the networks of people who involved themselves in the life of the larger community. The people at the Neretva were somewhat involved with other Serbian groups in establishing a new Serbian church. Since they had broken away from the church established by the pioneer generation of Serbian settlers, there was a great deal of tension in the relationships between these factions. The native-born Serbians and Croatians referred to the immigrants as DP's while their own ethnic identity and social institutions seemed to me to be largely the product of their experience in South Chicago and other industrial communities of this society. To learn more about the differences between native-born and immigrant South Slavs, I began spending more time among native-born Serbian and Croatian residents. Thus at the end of 1967 I began looking for a place to settle in the community.

Settling in the Community
and Making Friends

As I began hunting for an apartment, it became clear why I had chosen to study this community rather than other South Slavic neighborhoods elsewhere in the metropolitan area. South Chicago fascinated me. I had never seen such heavy industry at close range, and I was awed by the immensity of the steel mills and the complexity of the water and rail arteries which crisscrossed the area's neighborhoods. In the people's faces and in their neighborhoods I saw more of the spectrum of cultural groups which had settled and built the community. Thus I was beginning to see that my study would have to concern itself as much with the larger community as it would with the cultural and social adaptations of Serbian and Croatian settlers. In the impressive series of community studies compiled by Chicago sociologists there were none which explicitly focused on this type of community. Therefore, I came to feel that in addition to studying the cultural and social adaptations of South Slavic people, my work should also include material on this important industrial community, one which was itself a "natural area" in the true sense of the term.

This was also the period of increasingly bitter sentiment against the war in Indochina. Campus political groups were continually debating the issue of how to involve "the working class" in antiwar activities, or if such a task could be accomplished at all. Surprisingly few of my university friends had any knowledge even of the working-class communities nearest to the University of Chicago. Mention of the fact that I was spending time in the steel mill neighborhoods of South Chicago often brought the response, "Oh, you mean all those neighborhoods around Gary?" Chicago's mill neighborhoods begin on 79th Street, just nineteen blocks from the university, but they are often perceived as being closer to Gary, more than thirty miles to the south. Indeed the blue collar neighborhoods which begin in South Chicago bear great similarity to those continuing past Gary to South Bend, Indiana. I thus resolved that whatever else it accomplished my study should attempt to show what life is like in such places. It should show what political questions actually do challenge the residents, and among these would likely be the issue of working-class race relations.

In March 1968 my wife and I moved into a tenement flat in Irondale, one of the oldest neighborhoods of first settlement in the community. Irondale was a logical choice for a number of reasons. First, it had been one of the most popular neighborhoods for South Slavic immigrant settlement earlier in the century. It still retained a significant population of older settlers plus an increasing number of younger "DP" families. Second, it had been the site of the severe racial rioting which I read about in Frank London Brown's novel *Trumbull Park*. The late black author had vividly described the awful experience of trying to survive (with his family) in the neighborhood's housing project. Fourteen years had passed since these riots, but they were well remembered in Chicago. I suspected, rightly as it turned out, that we would be living among many of the people who had done the rioting. We would have a chance to see the issues from their perspective and learn how the intervening years had softened their violently defensive behavior. What I did not fully understand, however, was that Irondale was also becoming a Mexican neighborhood. In various ways the Mexicans were acting as a transition group to the eventual settlement of more black families in the neighborhood.

When our first child was born, after a year in Irondale, we began spending a great deal of time with our Mexican neighbors because they were more likely to have young children than our somewhat older South Slavic and Italian neighbors. From them, and especially from the Mexican youth groups which hung out on our corner, I learned that there was continual conflict with the Mexicans from the Millgate and Bessemer Park neighborhoods on the other side of the community. Similar to the opposition which existed between native-born and immigrant South Slavic groups, this opposition between the Mexican neighborhoods conformed quite closely to the pattern of "ordered segmentation" which Gerald Suttles analyzed in *The Social Order of the Slum*. The first level of opposition or conflict between ethnic groups in the community did not involve different cultural groups but occurred among equivalent territorial groups of the same ethnicity.

The next level of opposition tended to unify diverse groups from Irondale against those in geographically separated neighborhoods such as the East Side. On the other hand, all the residents whom I spoke to referred to the entire area as South Chicago, and they considered themselves residents of that community.

This perception seemed somewhat paradoxical. On the one hand so many people I met were generally involved in provincial feuding within their ethnic groups, and on the other they were in various ways quite clearly becoming involved in the life of the larger community. To investigate this problem it again seemed important to become familiar with the way the larger industrial and political institutions of the community operated. In particular it would be necessary to understand how experiences in the steel mills, the labor unions, and the political institutions of the community in various ways modified the residents' notions of which groups and individuals are worthy of their trust. In answering these questions I believed I would also begin to understand the processes whereby so many cultural groups had learned not only to coexist with each other but to adjust their basic patterns of ethnic social organization to compete in the class and status systems of the community and the major society. From the start of my work I had been meeting and interviewing people whom I identified as leaders of various cultural and political institutions in the community. It appeared that I would need to follow their activities at a much closer range.

Soon after moving into the community I had begun a systematic effort to attend any and all public meetings in the community, to identify local leaders, and to arrange to meet with them for an introduction or a formal interview. Before long I learned to resist the "compulsion to confess" which often troubles field researchers. Most people I met in the course of my daily life were interested in why I had settled in the community. In answering this question I explained that I was teaching at the nearby University of Indiana, Hammond extension, while my wife was a student at the University of Illinois Circle Campus in the central city. The Irondale location was a halfway point for both of us. This was true, and although it omitted my main motives for settling in South Chicago it made routine social intercourse much easier. If to every tavern clique and candy store acquaintance I had divulged my intentions to study the community, I would have probably elicited some parody of life in sociological jargon. But when I introduced myself to specific residents of the community, or whenever I interviewed someone, I attempted to explain the goals of my study as simply and consistently as I could, and the interview would generally proceed without misunderstanding of my goals.

Gradually, through these introductions and interviews I began to become friendly with a rather large number of political activists and neighborhood leaders. After introducing myself to a local labor leader, for example, I would then find myself meeting that person during my regular round of visits to public places and community events. These encounters would lead to new introductions and greater familiarity. By the end of my first year in South Chicago I counted well over fifty persons who had expressed interest in my study and were in various ways providing me with information about the underlying meaning of the political and social events I observed. Among the circles in which I was becoming more or less accepted were a group of Italian and Serbian steelworkers from Irondale who ran the local union at one of the area's large mills, a group of younger political activists from the East Side who met regularly to discuss community events and to plan political activities, two groups of ward political activists of mixed ethnicity, and friendship groups which met regularly in about fifteen taverns where I made rounds. In addition to participating in the informal life of these groups I attended as many functions of the Serbian and Croatian ethnic groups as possible. Also, through the normal course of life among my Mexican neighbors I had many opportunities to observe the culture and social organization of Mexican neighborhood ethnic groups. Fieldwork was becoming more than a full time occupation, and I often found myself dictating slurred field notes at 4:00 A.M. after a full day of meetings and social drinking in the area's taverns and political clubs. Despite the full schedule I had developed, I began to feel that the more I learned about the community through my friends and informants, the more necessary it was for me to commit myself to a greater degree to South Chicago's life style. I felt like a knowledgeable outsider who was missing some of the most important experiences of life in the community. At this time, in the middle of my second year of fieldwork in South Chicago, a friend whose opinion I highly valued, the Serbian president of a local steel union, confronted me with a serious challenge. "How can you really understand what goes on here," he asked, "if you've never spent any time inside a steel mill." I replied that it had been my desire to work in a mill, that I agreed it was necessary, but when I had applied to work in one of the area's large mills a few months earlier I had been turned down because I had "too much education to push a broom in a laborer's job." Amused, my unionist friend asked me if I would like a job in the mill he represented. He assured me that he would arrange things so that my job would allow me to "get a real education inside the mill." Before I was given the job my friend called me one night to ask, "Bill, you're not one of these S.D.S. guys are you? You know there's a lot of talk these days about radicals coming into the mills to stir up trouble." I assured him that such was not my intention and within another week I was hired as a sub-foreman in the steel mill described in this volume.

Mill Work:
Increasing Commitment

I approached my job in the mill with some embarrassment. As a sub-foreman I was nonetheless a representative of management when most of my sympathies and many of my friendships were with rank-and-file workers. Outside the mills, in social circles frequented by steelworkers and their families, one rarely met any foremen or managerial officials, and indeed management was often spoken of with some disdain. Also, as a foreman I was not allowed to perform manual work since the union viewed that as an encroachment on workers' jobs in the plant. My job was to oversee and coordinate the work of about thirty men who were chippers, laborers, machine operators, cranemen, and loaders. As the men taught me how to accomplish my work with a minimum of conflict and disruption of their normal institutional arrangements with each other and with management, I began to see that my friend had situated me in a difficult job but one which was about the best position a sociologist could have had.

In performing my duties as sub-foreman I had to understand how the work on my end of the mill fit into the overall division of labor in the entire plant. As a managerial employee I could circulate relatively freely throughout the mill to learn how steel was produced and to converse informally with workers in hundreds of different occupations. Since mine was the lowest status managerial position possible, I represented little threat to anyone. Most of my rank-and-file peers were making more money than I was, and, as they delighted in pointing out, their jobs did not include the headache of being responsible to higher level managerial officials. In reflecting on the differences between my low level managerial position and the more narrowly circumscribed activities of the rank-and-file workers with whom I spent the bulk of my time, I began to understand from a personal viewpoint more of the meaning of unionism and labor bargaining for the average steelworker. The other foremen with whom I worked were much more concerned about pleasing their superiors than were the rank-and-file workers. The latter were guaranteed advancement through the seniority system as long as they learned their jobs and performed them reliably. In case of trouble the workers could turn to their grievancemen and the union officials they had elected to intercede on their behalf in their dealings with management. The foremen had none of this protection. Although they claimed they did not need it, and indeed the vast majority of their superiors were considerate, experienced men, their occupational culture was full of stories of ambitious young foremen who had crossed high level officials at the wrong time and had been set back in their careers. None of our superiors in the rolling mill were vindictive types, but I was warned that Mr. W——, a high level managerial official who circulated throughout the entire plant, should be carefully avoided when he came into our mill.

Shortly thereafter, during a week when my turn was working nights, my general foreman warned me that the feared W—— had been seen leaving the adjacent mill heading in the direction of my work area. I was advised to make sure my men were all working properly and then to go off on an errand elsewhere in the mill. Here I should note that company officials were not aware of my intention to write about mill work. I rationalized this situation by attempting to do my job so that my personal motives for being in the mill would not compromise the performance of my work. On this occasion, however, I did not heed the older foreman's well-intentioned advice. Instead I loitered in my work area to see for myself what an encounter with W—— would be like. When he entered my area of the mill, he walked directly up to me. Without introducing himself, he barked a question which produced the following dialogue:

W——.   What's that steel being loaded into those cars?
Kornblum. Oh, that's a mixed order of spring steel and 30 foot rounds that we're trying to load before the switch comes in.
W——.   I can see what it is. Who is it for? Where's it going?
Kornblum. Well, let's see, I think it's for . . .
W——.   God dammit. Do you know who that steel is for or don't you?
Kornblum. I'm not sure.

W———.   You damn well better get off your dead cock and find out
          what's being done around here or you're not going to last.
          This is a steel mill and not a nursery school. We've got too
          too many jagg offs like you who sit around with their
          thumbs up their assholes and don't know what's going on.

The official strode away leaving me trembling with anger and humiliation. I had worked in many blue collar jobs before entering the steel mill, and as a laborer on an East River construction dock in Manhattan I had seen corruption and violence which made the normal routine of mill work seem tame. Since I was doing a relatively good job as a new foreman in a mill beset with serious racial and ethnic cleavages, I did not believe I should be treated in this way by someone who had never seen me before. It is true that I should have known the answer to his question and he was justified in "chewing me out." But except in jest the foremen on the shop floor rarely spoke to their own men in such terms. The dictates of common sense and the watchful influence of union representatives usually prevented such confrontations between foremen and workers. In general such personal experiences as this made me a good deal more sensitive to the style and content of interactions in the mill and deepened my desire to understand the meaning of unionism in the context of my study. Thus I pursued this goal while I worked in the mill and later when I assisted my unionist friends in their political campaigns.

Many sociologists have regarded "informal organization" as an inevitable characteristic of industrial bureaucracies, but one which in the interest of rationality and productivity must be manipulated through the techniques of "industrial relations." Given the orientation of my research I could not view the issue in this way. The study of informal relations among the workers became another aspect of my inquiry into how steel production creates an occupational community inside the mill. I thus attempted to discover the conditions under which revelations of character on the job could be as important as ethnic and racial categories in guiding the workers' behavior. My run-in with W——— for example, immediately became the subject of gossip and bantering in work groups throughout the mill. "How could a kid with your education act like such a dummy?" asked the chief loader. This question launched a long philosophical discussion in the loaders' shanty. Most of the loaders worried that the incident would hurt my chances for advancement in the company. Others suggested that it should make me question the desirability of holding a job with management. Finally, a young Mexican loader, who was also a friend from the neighborhood, settled the argument in a statement which has remained in the front of my mind ever since. "What you guys don't understand," he stated, "is that Kornblum isn't stuck here like most of us stiffs. In his life he can do just about anything he really wants to do." Although perhaps somewhat obvious, this insight made me much more sensitive to the workers' attempts to express their own individuality throughout their careers in the steel mill. I also understood another side of this remark from my own difficulties in attempting to carry on my other fieldwork while remaining in the mill.

One morning after I had been working in the mill for almost six months I boarded a bus with a large group of Tenth Ward Spanish Speaking Democrats to attend the Chicago Democratic Day at the Illinois State Fair in Springfield. Since I had worked the previous night turn I immediately fell asleep. When I awoke about an hour later everyone on the bus was laughing at me. One of my neighbors had told those who did not know me that I was a worker at the Ford assembly plant down the road from our steel mill. He explained that I had fallen asleep and missed my stop. Some of South Chicago's Mexican activists still jokingly refer to me as "the guy from the Ford plant." This Springfield outing ended back in South Chicago about fifteen minutes before my shift began again in the mill. After eight hours of seeking places to steal a few minutes' sleep, I realized that I was reaching a point of diminishing returns in my participation inside the mill. Political events were rapidly accelerating in the outside community, and I could not become as involved in them as I wished because of the severe physical and temporal demands of mill work.

From the beginning of the research I had followed political campaigns and the careers of local politicians quite closely. At first I had attended meetings of campaign workers on both sides of the factional disputes in the community, thereby developing a large number of informants who supplied me with details of events I had witnessed. Generally it was necessary to compare carefully the accounts of a number of informants in order to compensate for individual biases and personal perceptions. At the same time I was beginning to feel that I had accumulated personal debts to many local groups, especially to my unionist friends and to many of my Slavic and Mexican neighbors. Working in the mill had brought me much more general acceptance in the community, but acceptance also subjected me to the same pressures to commit myself in partisan campaigns that others felt.

Partisanship and
Personal Growth

The pressure to become committed to other people is a general characteristic of community life in South Chicago, but during the time I lived in the community this pressure was probably as great as it had ever been. This was a time when the community was involved in sorting out the leadership of its most central institutions. For this reason all my friends and informants found themselves in one way or another drawn into competition between aggregations of community groups. It seemed that only the most financially secure or socially marginal people could afford not to take sides. This same spirit of partisanship also affected me. I began to feel that I could not remain aloof from political commitment when all the people I cared for had so much more at stake than I did. Aside from the personal aspect of this decision, there are very real limitations to what one can learn about political processes through informants. If one wishes actually to watch decisions being made in a competitive political system, it is often necessary to become part of the decison-making body itself. I did this by taking highly partisan, although "behind the scenes" roles in most of the political campaigns reported in this study.

The liabilities of this strategy are numerous and deserve some attention. First, it is obvious that the more committed one is to a particular faction, the less one can learn, at first hand, about others. This may not be quite so true in higher levels of political competition where political expertise is more rationally calculated and more often bought and sold, but it is certainly the case in community politics. Even though the competition is highly institutionalized, when neighbors and workmates compete against each other, careful attention is payed to one's affiliations, and trust is easily jeopardized. In consequence of this, whenever I committed myself to a given faction I attempted to function as much as possible in capacities which would require little public exposure. In order to keep up with events in opposing factions I attempted to explain my affiliations as frankly as possible to friends on opposite sides, in much the same terms as any other resident of the community would. In this way it was possible to act as a partisan and still communicate with friends in opposing factions who acted as my informants. Here the amount of time spent in fieldwork was extremely important. I did not become actively committed until the third year of my research. By that time I had friends throughout the community who could understand, if not always agree with my partisanship.

Another problem in taking on partisan roles as a researcher is that it almost inevitably causes bias in favor of those to whom one is committed. In my case, again, the answer to this problem was to maintain close informants on opposing sides, and to try, in the analysis of events, to be on guard against my own partialities so that I might correct them or use them knowingly. It is also true that by taking on activist roles the researcher's own actions may alter the situation. Aside from the problems of analysis which this presents, it may also draw one into further commitment. For example, in becoming involved with South Chicago political leaders, and especially with unionist politicians, I began to feel responsible for the future. Once having taken an active part in political competition, I no longer felt that my relationship with the community would end when the study was completed.

My family and I moved from South Chicago to Seattle in 1970, and most of the study was written in the calmer, more reflective climate of the Pacific Northwest. Nevertheless, I returned periodically to South Chicago and surrounding steel mill communities to continue my involvement in local political competition. Thus during the winter of 1972-73 I worked as a writer and office worker for Ed Sadlowski and other friends who were in the steelworkers' Calumet District election. As I have indicated at the conclusion of this volume, this election was only one step on the long and exhausting process to bring about change in a major political institution. Although the election itself is over, I expect to remain deeply involved with my steelworker friends in the Calumet area for many years to come.

In writing this study there were many possible overall orientations to choose from. Especially during my first year in South Chicago I met many people whose attitudes concerning racial matters conformed to the stereotypical version of white working-class bigotry. Throughout the years I spent in the community I also met workers and families who had been victimized in various ways by their class position. On the other hand, the more time I spent in the community, the more I gained insights about my own character. Through working in the steel mill, and generally allowing myself to become caught up in partisan political struggles, I encountered the people of South Chicago on a more equal footing than I might have otherwise. This gave them a chance to assess my own capabilities just as I was judging theirs. If people who had little of the middle-class advantages that I possess could easily judge my behavior for its strengths and weaknesses, how could I fail to write about the aspects of working-class society which made their insights possible? Also, despite the antagonistic feelings which so many South Chicago residents harbored over ethnic and racial issues, I discovered in that antagonism itself the processes which unify. Given the great ignorance about working-class life which exists elsewhere in society, the choice of these underlying themes seemed necessary in order to do justice to the institutions South Chicago residents have created over the generations.

Notes

1. The Ecology of Neighborhood Settlement and Ethnic Change

1. In the "Classic" period of Chicago social sciences, South Chicago was considered a "natural area" par excellence. Sociologists such as Robert Park, Ernest Burgess, and R. D. McKenzie refer to it as typical of the industrial enclave in the city. Much of their knowledge of the community was derived from the writing of early pioneers in the field of social work, including Edith Abbott, *The Tenements of Chicago, 1908-1935* (Chicago: University of Chicago Press, 1936); Emily G. Balch, *Our Slavic Fellow Citizens* (New York: Charities Publication Committee, 1910); John Morris Gillette, *Culture Agencies of a Typical Manufacturing Group: South Chicago* (Chicago: University of Chicago Press, 1901); and Helen Elizabeth MacGill, "Land Values as an Ecological Factor in the Community of South Chicago," master's thesis, Department of Sociology, University of Chicago, 1927.

2. Evelyn Mae Kitagawa, *Local Community Fact Book, 1960* (Chicago: Chicago Community Inventory, University of Chicago, 1963); Albert Dale Hunter, "Local Urban Communities: Persistence and Change," Ph.D. dissertation, Department of Sociology, University of Chicago, 1970.

3. Oscar Handlin, *The Uprooted* (Boston: Little, Brown, 1951); Robert E. Park and William Miller, *Old World Traits Transplanted* (Chicago: Society for Social Research, University of Chicago, 1925).

4. Gerald D. Suttles, *The Social Order of the Slum* (Chicago: University of Chicago Press, 1968), pp. 8-12.

5. St. Clair Drake and Horace R. Cayton, *Black Metropolis* (New York: Harcourt, Brace & World, 1945), 1: 17-34.

6. Emile Durkheim, *The Division of Labor in Society* (Glencoe: Free Press, 1933), Preface to the second edition.

7. Edward Shils, "Primordial, Personal, Sacred and Civil Ties," reprinted in *Center and Periphery: Essays in Macrosociology* (Chicago: University of Chicago Press, forthcoming); and "The Study of the Primary Group," in Daniel Lerner and Harold D. Lasswell, eds., *The Policy Sciences* (Palo Alto: Stanford University Press, 1951).

2. Mill Work and Primary Groups

1. Everett C. Hughes, "The Knitting of Racial Groups in Industry," *American Sociological Review* 7 (October 1946), 514; Alvin W. Gouldner, *Patterns of Industrial Bureaucracy* (Glencoe, Ill.: Free Press, 1954).

2. John Morris Gillette, *Culture Agencies of a Typical Manufacturing Group*, p. 35.

3. See Robert Blauner, *Alienation and Freedom: The Factory Worker and His Industry* (Chicago: University of Chicago Press, 1964).

4. Donald Roy, "Quota Restriction and Goldbricking in a Machine Shop," *American Journal of Sociology* 57 (March 1952): 427–42.

5. On the history of racial discrimination in the International Harvester Company, see Robert Ozanne, *A Century of Labor Management Relations at McCormick and International Harvester* (Madison: University of Wisconsin Press, 1967).

6. Elton Mayo and George F. Lombard, *Teamwork and Labor Turnover in the Aircraft Industry of Southern California*, Harvard Business Research Studies, no. 32 (Cambridge, Mass., 1944); Delbert C. Miller and William H. Form, *Industrial Sociology* (New York: Harper & Row, 1964), pp. 223–87.

3. Primary Group Formation in Mill Neighborhoods

1. Unlike most of the industrial communities studied earlier in this century, South Chicago is a community within the larger city. It therefore does not maintain the full range of social classes, nor can it be studied without continual reference to the location of its neighborhoods with respect to other areas of the city. For examples of studies of more "self-contained" industrial communities, see Elin Anderson, *We Americans* (Cambridge: Harvard University Press, 1937); Hylan Lewis, *Blackways of Kent* (Chapel Hill: University of North Carolina Press, 1955); Robert S. Lynd and Helen M. Lynd, *Middletown in Transition* (New York: Harcourt, Brace, 1937); Charles R. Walker, *Steeltown* (New York: Harper & Row, 1950); and W. Lloyd Warner et al., *The Social Life of a Modern Community*, Yankee City Series, vols. 1–4 (New Haven: Yale University Press, 1959).

2. Louis Wirth, *The Ghetto* (Chicago: University of Chicago Press, 1956), p. ix.

3. Nathan Kantrowitz, "The Polish Vote in Chicago: 1912," seminar paper, Department of History, University of Chicago, 1968. Of course, the fact that a particular ethnic group shares its neighborhoods with other groups does not mean that, with respect to the population of the larger city, the group is not highly segregated.

4. On the Trumbull Park episode, see Frank London Brown, *Trumbull Park* (Chicago: Regnery, 1959).

5. Suttles, *The Social Order of the Slum*, "Primary Groups and Personal Identities," pp. 175–94.

6. Sherri Cavan, *Liquor License* (Chicago: Aldine Publishing Co., 1966), p. 36.

7. Michael Young and Peter Willmott, *Family and Kinship in East London* (New York: Free Press of Glencoe, 1957).

8. George Homans, *The Human Group* (New York: Harcourt, Brace, 1950), pp. 415-40.

9. Hughes, "The Knitting of Racial Groups in Industry," p. 514; Orvis Collins, "Ethnic Behavior in Industry: Sponsorship and Rejection in a New England Factory," *American Journal of Sociology* 51 (January 1946): 514-26.

4. Local Unions and Their Neighborhood Histories

1. Gillette, *Culture Agencies of a Typical Manufacturing Group*, p. 17.

2. Marshall Olds, *Analysis of the Interchurch World Movement Report on the Steel Strike* (New York: G. P. Putnam, 1923).

3. Ibid., p. 81. Judge Gary certainly could have been expected to supply an estimate of the number of workers on twelve-hour days which was favorable to U.S. Steel's position on the issue.

4. Ibid., pp. 97-98.

5. Quoted in Interchurch World Movement, *Public Opinion and the Steel Strike* (New York: Harcourt, Brace, 1921), pp. 58-59.

6. David Sappos, "The Mind of Immigrant Communities in the Pittsburgh District," *Public Opinion and the Steel Strike*, pp. 224-42.

7. Ozanne, *A Century of Labor Management Relations at McCormick and International Harvester*, p. 132.

8. The type of information presented in table 7 was closely guarded during the organizing drives and was frequently destroyed after elections. I was fortunate to find not only the lists, but a breakdown in those lists by plant department and job description.

9. U. S. Congress, Senate Committee on Education and Labor, "Violations of Free Speech and Rights of Labor" (Washington, D.C.: U. S. Government Printing Office, 1939), parts 14-15A, pp. 367-84.

10. Tom Girdler, *Bootstraps* (New York: Charles Scribner's Sons, 1943), p. 231.

11. U. S. Congress, "Violations of Free Speech and Rights of Labor," p. 372.

12. From memos in files of Sub-District 3, United Steelworkers of America, AFL-CIO.

13. On the very significant role played by black organizers both before and after the massacre, see St. Clair Drake and Horace Cayton, *Black Metropolis*, pp. 320-25.

14. U. S. Congress, "Violations of Free Speech and Rights of Labor," p. 381.

15. Personal interview with survivors of the Memorial Day Massacre at Republic Steel, August 1970.

16. David Brody, *Steelworkers in America: The Nonunion Era* (Cambridge: Harvard University Press, 1960), pp. 223-24.

17. Robert Brooks, *As Steel Goes* (New Haven: Yale University Press, 1940), pp. 138-52. This section is also based on my own interviews with George Patterson, now a retired staff official of the USWA.

18. The analysis in this section owes much to the ideas and experience of Edward Sadlowski, Staff Official, United Steelworkers of America, Sub-District 3, AFL-CIO.

5. The Dynamics of Union Succession

1. For one of the best, although now dated, criticisms of the American labor movement, see C. W. Mills, *The New Men of Power* (New York: Harcourt, Brace, 1948); a more recent critique of organized labor from a socialist perspective is Andre Gorz, *Strategy for Labor* (Boston: Beacon Press, 1967). The best-known study of the conditions for two-party democracy in a labor union is Seymour Martin Lipset, Martin Trow, and James S. Coleman, *Union Democracy* (Glencoe, Ill.: Free Press, 1965). Representative of the "industrial relations" school of labor movement criticism is Leonard Sayles and George Strauss, *The Local Union* (New York: Harcourt, Brace & World, 1967).

2. Scott Alan Greer, *Last Man In: Racial Access to Union Power* (Glencoe, Ill.: Free Press, 1959); Noreen Cornfield, "Local Industrial Unions, Political Competition, and Negro Representation," Ph.D. dissertation, University of Chicago, 1970.

3. The use of concepts relating to territorial segmentation in this study owes much to Gerald Suttles's important study, *The Social Order of the Slum*.

4. William Kornblum, "Ethnicity, Work, and Politics in South Chicago," Ph.D. dissertation, University of Chicago, 1972, pp. 55–72.

5. Blauner, *Alienation and Freedom*.

6. This view of black union participation modifies the most frequently cited studies on the subject: William Kornhauser, "The Negro Union Official: A Study of Sponsorship and Control," *American Journal of Sociology* 57 (March 1952): 443–52; and Collins, "Ethnic Behavior in Industry: Sponsorship and Rejection in a New England Factory," pp. 293–98.

7. These projections are based on estimates carried out by USWA staff members during the previous local union election. The members stood at the doors of the polling place with hand counters and tallied voters of different backgrounds.

8. Frank Tannenbaum, *A Philosophy of Labor* (New York: Knopf, 1951), p. 10.

6. The Political Ecology of an Industrial Ward

1. Harold Gosnell, *Machine Politics, Chicago Model* (Chicago: University of Chicago Press, 1939); Edward C. Banfield and James Q. Wilson, *City Politics* (Cambridge, Mass.: Harvard University Press and M.I.T. Press, 1963).

2. This is not limited to working-class communities, but may apply to the mobilization of middle-class participants in local politics also. See James Q. Wilson, *The Amateur Democrat* (Chicago: University of Chicago Press, 1962), pp. 21–27.

3. This chapter is partially intended to update the standard reference on precinct workers in the urban machine, Sonya Forthall, *Cogwheels of Democracy: A Study of the Precinct Captain* (New York: William Frederick Press, 1946).

4. This modifies the suggestion in Wilson, *The Amateur Democrat*, that local political activists who fit the description of the "amateur" are most likely to

be recruited by anti-machine movements in club politics.

5. Lawrence H. Fuchs, ed., *American Ethnic Politics* (New York: Harper Torchbooks, 1968); Robert A. Dahl, *Who Governs?* (New Haven: Yale University Press, 1961).

6. Letters to the Editor, *Daily Calumet*, vol. 89, no. 174 (1969).

7. Mexican Succession in Ward Politics

1. Robert A. Dahl, *Who Governs?* pp. 34–36. Dahl outlines a familiar stage model of the assimilation of ethnic groups in community political institutions. This model leaves out analysis of the internal politics of ethnic groups which makes assimilation possible.

2. An alternative is for such groups to turn to another party, as did the Italians in many cities where the Irish controlled local ward politics, see Dahl, *Who Governs?* for further analysis of this phenomenon. In the more traditional urban one-party system this alternative, while available, is not always very attractive.

3. Gosnell entitled a chapter of his *Machine Politics* "You Can't Beat a Ward Boss."

4. As predicted, the next two years of Mexican politics in the Seventh and Tenth Wards saw wives of Mexican political leaders take the initiative in putting themselves up as political candidates in a number of races.

5. Within two years this coalition had dissolved. The liberal attorney went on to challenge the Daley Democratic Organization at every turn, while the Tenth Ward unionists and precinct activists were given little opportunity to take leadership roles in the coalition.

6. *Who Governs?* pp. 34–36.

8. Slavic Succession in Ward Politics

1. Most analysis of ethnic politics in the United States has dealt with situations in which ethnicity is used for instrumental purposes in organizing a political following among groups who clearly control a given political territory. Perhaps an equally common situation, one which this analysis considers, is the case of ethnic groups which at no time have the numerical strength to command leadership positions in territorial political organizations.

2. For one of the most colorful portrayals of the "golden age" of Chicago machine politics, see Lloyd Wendt and Herman Kogan, *Bosses in Lusty Chicago* (Bloomington: Indiana University Press, 1967).

3. Fuchs, ed., *American Ethnic Politics*, especially "Bosses, Machines, and Ethnic Groups," the chapter by Elmer E. Cornwell, Jr., pp. 194–216.

4. Lack of available meeting places is often a problem in middle-class communities where many rooms are available but none can be easily appropriated by an insurgent political group for use as an organizing base and a center of informal social relations.

5. Irving Spergel, *Racketville, Slumtown, and Haulburg: An Exploratory Study of Delinquent Subcultures* (Chicago: University of Chicago Press, 1964).

9. Working-Class Society and the Nation

1. Daniel Bell, *The Coming of Post-Industrial Society* (New York: Basic Books, 1973), pp. 163–64.

2. Clifford Geertz, "The Integrative Revolution: Primordial Sentiments and Civil Politics in the New States," in *Old Societies and New States* (Glencoe, Ill.: Free Press, 1963), pp. 105–58; see also Michael Hechter, *Internal Colonialism* (London: Routledge, 1974).

3. Nathan Glazer and Daniel P. Moynihan, *Beyond the Melting Pot*, 2d ed. (Cambridge, Mass.: M.I.T. Press, 1970), p. 60.

4. John Herling, *Right to Challange: People and Power in the Steelworkers Union* (New York: Harper & Row, 1972), pp. 38–39 and passim.

Selected Bibliography

Abbott, Edith. *The Tenements of Chicago, 1908-1935*. Chicago: University of Chicago Press, 1936.

Anderson, Elin. *We Americans*. Cambridge: Harvard University Press, 1937.

Arensberg, Conrad M., and Kimball, Solon T. *Culture and Community*. New York: Harcourt, Brace & World, 1965.

Balch, Emily G. *Our Slavic Fellow Citizens*. New York: Charities Publication Committee, 1910.

Banfield, Edward C., and Wilson, James Q. *City Politics*. Cambridge: Harvard University Press and M.I.T. Press, 1963.

Bendix, Reinhard, and Roth, Guenther. *Scholarship and Partisanship: Essays on Max Weber*. Berkeley: University of California Press, 1971.

Blauner, Robert. *Alienation and Freedom: The Factory Worker and His Industry*. Chicago: University of Chicago Press, 1964.

Bonney, Norman. "Unwelcome Strangers." Ph.D. dissertation, University of Chicago, 1972.

Brody, David. *Labor in Crisis: The Steel Strike of 1919*. Philadelphia: Lippincott, 1965.

Brooks, Robert. *As Steel Goes*. New Haven: Yale University Press, 1940.

Cavan, Sherri. *Liquor License*. Chicago: Aldine Publishing Co., 1966.

Collins, Orvis. "Ethnic Behavior in Industry: Sponsorship and Rejection in a New England Factory." *American Journal of Sociology* 51 (January 1946): 293-98.

Cornfield, Noreen. "Local Industrial Unions, Political Competition, and Negro Representation." Ph.D. dissertation, University of Chicago, 1970.

Dahl, Robert A. *Who Governs?* New Haven: Yale University Press, 1961.

Drake, St. Clair, and Cayton, Horace R. *Black Metropolis*. New York: Harcourt, Brace & World, 1945.

Durkheim, Emile. *The Division of Labor in Society*. New York: Free Press of Glencoe, 1964.

Forthall, Sonya. *Cogwheels of Democracy: A Study of the Precinct Captain*. New York: William Frederick Press, 1946.

Friedmann, George. *The Anatomy of Work*. London: Heinemann, 1961.

Fuchs, Lawrence H., ed. *American Ethnic Politics*. New York: Harper Torchbooks, 1968.

Gans, Herbert. *The Urban Villagers*. New York: Free Press of Glencoe, 1962.

Gillette, John Morris. *Culture Agencies of a Typical Manufacturing Group: South Chicago*. Chicago: University of Chicago Press, 1901.

Girdler, Tom. *Bootstraps*. New York: Charles Scribner's Sons, 1943.

Gortz, André. *Strategy for Labor*. Boston: Beacon Press, 1967.

Gosnell, Harold. *Machine Politics, Chicago Model*. Chicago: University of Chicago Press, 1939.

Gouldner, Alvin W. *Patterns of Industrial Bureaucracy*. Glencoe, Ill.: Free Press, 1954.

Greer, Scott Alan. *Last Man In: Racial Access to Union Power*. Glencoe, Ill.: Free Press, 1959.

Gross, Edward. *Work and Society*. New York: Crowell, 1958.

Handlin, Oscar. *The Uprooted*. Boston: Little, Brown, 1951.

Hechter, Michael. *Internal Colonialism*. London: Routledge, 1974.

Herling, John. *Right to Challenge: People and Power in the Steelworkers Union*. New York: Harper & Row, 1972.

Hughes, Everett C. "The Knitting of Racial Groups in Industry." *American Sociological Review* 11 (October 1946): 514.

Hunter, Albert Dale. "Local Urban Communities: Persistence and Change." Ph.D. dissertation, University of Chicago, 1970.

The Interchurch World Movement. *Public Opinion and the Steel Strike*. New York: Harcourt, Brace, 1921.

Janowitz, Morris. *W. I. Thomas: On Social Organization and Social Personality*. Chicago: University of Chicago Press, 1966.

―――. *The Community Press in an Urban Setting*. Chicago: University of Chicago Press, 1967.

Kantrowitz, Nathan. "The Polish Vote in Chicago: 1912." Seminar Paper, University of Chicago, 1968.

Kitagawa, Evelyn Mae, and Taeuber, Karl E., eds. *Local Community Fact Book, Chicago Metropolitan Area, 1960*. Prepared by the Chicago Community Inventory, University of Chicago, 1963.

Kremen, Bennet. "No Pride in This Dust." *Dissent* (Special Issue, Winter 1972), pp. 270–78.

Lewis, Hylan. *Blackways of Kent*. Chapel Hill: University of North Carolina Press, 1955.

Lynd, Robert S., and Lynd, Helen M. *Middletown in Transition*. New York: Harcourt, Brace, 1947.

MacGill, Helen Elizabeth. "Land Values as an Ecological Factor in the Community of South Chicago." Master's thesis, University of Chicago, 1927.

Mack, Raymond W. "Ecological Patterns in an Industrial Shop." *Social Forces* 2 (May 1954): 351–56.

Miller, Delbert C., and Form, William H. *Industrial Sociology*. New York: Harper and Row, 1964.

Mills, C. Wright. *The New Men of Power*. New York: Harcourt, Brace, 1968.

Ozanne, Robert. *A Century of Labor Management Relations at McCormick and International Harvester*. Madison: University of Wisconsin Press, 1967.

Park, Robert E., and Miller, William. *Old World Traits Transplanted*. Chicago: Society for Social Research, University of Chicago, 1925.

Polsby, Nelson W. *Community Power and Political Theory*. New Haven: Yale University Press, 1963.

Roth, Guenther. *See* Bendix, Reinhard.

Sayles, Leonard, and Strauss, George. *The Local Union*. New York: Harcourt, Brace & World, 1967.

Shils, Edward. "Primordial, Personal, Sacred and Civil Ties." Reprinted in *Center and Periphery: Essays in Macrosociology*. Chicago: University of Chicago, forthcoming.

Suttles, Gerald D. *The Social Order of the Slum*. Chicago: University of Chicago Press, 1968.

Walker, Charles R. *Steeltown*. New York: Harper and Row, 1950.

Warner, W. Lloyd, et al. *The Social Life of a Modern Community*. New Haven: Yale University Press, 1959.

Wendt, Lloyd, and Kegan, Herman. *Bosses in Lusty Chicago*. Bloomington: Indiana University Press, 1967.

Whyte, William F. *Street Corner Society*. Chicago: University of Chicago Press, 1961.

Wilson, James Q. *The Amateur Democrat*. Chicago: University of Chicago Press, 1962.

Wirth, Louis. *The Ghetto*. Chicago: University of Chicago Press, 1928. Phoenix Books, 1956.

Young, Michael, and Willmott, Peter. *Family and Kinship in East London*. New York: Free Press of Glencoe, 1957.

Index

Abbott, Edith, 16
Adolescents: corner groups of, 21, 74, 114, 117-18, 162, 195-96; fighting among, 30-31, 72, 117-18, 120, 162
AFL, 3, 106, 107
Age, 15, 119, 125-26, 165-67, 223. *See also* Generational differences; Seniority
Alcoholics, 80
Aldermanic election, 179-81
Alienation, concept of, viii-ix
Amalgamated Iron and Steel Workers, 107
Americanism, 110, 111, 150
Americanization programs, 94, 96-98, 99
Aspirations of workers, 3, 19, 209-10
Associated Employees, 107

Bessemer Park, 14, 26, 27, 106, 200
Bethlehem Steel Plant, 223-24
Blacks: competition among, 48, 126-28; gang membership among, 48; obstacles to unity of, 40, 52, 81, 117, 119; relations with foremen, 48-51, 58; relations with Mexicans, 73, 179; relations with Poles, 224-26; residence of, 2, 3, 4, 13, 14, 30-31, 40, 71, 72-73, 81, 82, 128-29, 207-8, 214-15; resistance to settlement of, 1, 3, 4, 13, 30-31, 37, 72-74, 81, 82, 179, 190, 202-3, 207-8, 213-15, 233; rural-urban cleavage, 48; and seniority, 40, 55, 56, 64; tavern patronage of, 81-82; union membership of, 100-101; as union leaders, 31, 37, 116, 125-29, 131, 132, 226; in union politics, 13, 31, 37, 58-59, 116, 125-29, 225-27; in ward politics, 3-4, 13, 31, 176, 178-79, 219, 225-27
Bonuses, incentive, 46, 47, 51, 61-62
Bott, Elizabeth, 34
Bottle gangs, 80
Branko's tavern, 84-85
Brown, Frank London, 233

Buchannan, John, 151-52, 189, 190
Burgess, Ernest, 34
Burns Harbor plant, 223-24
Bush, the, 10, 14, 27, 31, 79, 106
Businessmen, 14-15, 25, 28

Calumet District steelworkers' election (1973), 217, 220-28, 241
Calumet River, 9-10
Campaigns: union, 93, 113-14, 116, 119, 220-28, 241; ward, 147, 150-53, 156, 167-81, 190-91. *See also* Mobilization, political
Caucuses, black, 125-26
Cavan, Sherri, 75
Chavez, Cesar, 166
Cheltenham, 14
Chicago, earlier studies of, 33-35
Chicago-Gary District steelworkers' election (1973), 217, 220-28, 241
"Chicago School" of sociology, viii, 33, 230
Chicano movement, 180, 181-82. *See also* Mexicans
Chico, Carmen, 217-18
Chico, John, 164, 166; background, 188; candidacy for Constitutional Convention, 169, 170-72, 175-77
Children, ambitions for, 209-10, 213
Chippers, 43, 51; job duties of, 46, 47, 51; racial and ethnic distribution of, 39, 51; relations with foremen, 51-52
Churches, 10, 69, 194; as basis of primary groups, 25, 69, 74, 85; competition between, 153-54; ethnic composition of, 14, 23-25, 26, 28, 195; and ethnic culture, 211-12; and ward politics, 185, 192-93
CIO: competiton with company unions, 98-99, 108; and progressives, 110; relation to independent unions, 93, 98-101,

253

Blue Collar Community

William Kornblum

South Chicago is a large steel mill community with a predominantly working-class population. Like steel towns throughout the United States, South Chicago is made up of the ethnic and racial groups which have settled in industrial towns over the last century. *Blue Collar Community* explores the complex social organization of this community—one completely dominated by heavy manufacturing.

William Kornblum and his wife moved into an apartment in South Chicago in 1968 and stayed for two and a half years. Kornblum spent some time working in a mill, helped with several political campaigns, and made friends in the neighborhood taverns. By participating in local activities, he was able to examine at close range the impacts of residential segregation, ethnic identification, age groupings, job status, and patterns of leisure style upon the social cohesion of the community.

"Kornblum presents a concise overview," writes Morris Janowitz in the Foreword, "of the elaborate social organization of a locality which has been dominated by heavy manufacturing for nearly a century. His underlying question is a version of the classic one in political sociology: Why was there and is there no powerful working-class political movement which could be called socialist in the United States?"

The author reviews the similarities and differences between past and present trends in ethnic and racial succession. He finds that

(Continued on back flap)